Assessment for Learning in Primary Language Learning and Teaching

EARLY LANGUAGE LEARNING IN SCHOOL CONTEXTS

Series Editor: **Janet Enever**, *Umeå University, Sweden*

The early learning of languages in instructed contexts has become an increasingly common global phenomenon during the past 30 years, yet there remains much work to be done to establish the field as a distinctive area for interdisciplinary investigation. This international research series covers children learning second, foreign and additional languages in educational contexts between the ages of approximately 3 and 12 years. The series will take a global perspective and encourage the sharing of theoretical discussion and empirical evidence on transnational issues. It will provide a platform to address questions raised by teachers, teacher educators, and policy makers who are seeking understanding of theoretical issues and empirical evidence with which to underpin policy development, implementation and classroom procedures for this young age group. Themes of particular interest for the series include: teacher models and teacher development, models of early language learning, policy implementation, motivation, approaches to teaching and learning, language progress and outcomes, assessment, intercultural learning, sustainability in provision, comparative and transnational perspectives, cross-phase transfer issues, curriculum integration – additional suggestions for themes are also most welcome.

All books in this series are externally peer-reviewed.

Full details of all the books in this series and of all our other publications can be found on http://www.multilingual-matters.com, or by writing to Multilingual Matters, St Nicholas House, 31-34 High Street, Bristol BS1 2AW, UK.

EARLY LANGUAGE LEARNING IN SCHOOL CONTEXTS: 5

Assessment for Learning in Primary Language Learning and Teaching

Maria Britton

MULTILINGUAL MATTERS
Bristol • Blue Ridge Summit

https://doi.org/10.21832/BRITTO0640
Library of Congress Cataloging in Publication Data
A catalog record for this book is available from the Library of Congress.
Names: Britton, Maria, 1983- author.
Title: Assessment for Learning in Primary Language Learning and Teaching/
   Maria Britton.
Description: Bristol, UK; Blue Ridge Summit, PA: Multilingual Matters, 2021. |
   Series: Early Language Learning in School Contexts: 5 | Includes bibliographical
   references and index. | Summary: "This volume provides a detailed account
   of the practical use of Assessment for Learning (AfL) in primary language
   classrooms. It gives an in-depth account of the ways in which eight experienced
   primary language teachers incorporated this type of assessment into their
   practice and discusses the possible impact of AfL on primary language
   learning"—Provided by publisher.
Identifiers: LCCN 2020052588 (print) | LCCN 2020052589 (ebook) |
   ISBN 9781800410633 (paperback) | ISBN 9781800410640 (hardback) |
   ISBN 9781800410657 (pdf) | ISBN 9781800410664 (epub) | ISBN 9781800410671
   (kindle edition) Subjects: LCSH: Language arts (Primary)—Evaluation.
Classification: LCC LB1528 .B69 2021 (print) | LCC LB1528 (ebook) |
   DDC 372.6—dc23 LC record available at https://lccn.loc.gov/2020052588
LC ebook record available at https://lccn.loc.gov/2020052589

British Library Cataloguing in Publication Data
A catalogue entry for this book is available from the British Library.

ISBN-13: 978-1-80041-064-0 (hbk)
ISBN-13: 978-1-80041-063-3 (pbk)

Multilingual Matters
UK: St Nicholas House, 31-34 High Street, Bristol BS1 2AW, UK.
USA: NBN, Blue Ridge Summit, PA, USA.

Website: www.multilingual-matters.com
Twitter: Multi_Ling_Mat
Facebook: https://www.facebook.com/multilingualmatters
Blog: www.channelviewpublications.wordpress.com

The policy of Multilingual Matters/Channel View Publications is to use papers
that are natural, renewable and recyclable products, made from wood grown in
sustainable forests. In the manufacturing process of our books, and to further
support our policy, preference is given to printers that have FSC and PEFC Chain
of Custody certification. The FSC and/or PEFC logos will appear on those books
where full certification has been granted to the printer concerned.

Typeset by Deanta Global Publishing Services, Chennai, India
Printed and bound in the UK by the CPI Books Group Ltd.
Printed and bound in the US by NBN.

Contents

Part 3 Impact of AfL on Learning

Illustrations

Tables

Abbreviations

Abbreviations related to assessment for learning

AfL	Assessment for learning
CC	Colour coding (an AfL technique)
FA	Formative assessment
FTF	Find the fib (an AfL technique)
ICS	I can statements (an AfL technique)
IMWE	Indicate mistakes without explanation (an AfL technique)
ITT	Increased thinking time
LO	Learning objective
LPs	Learning partners (an AfL technique)
MM	Mind maps (an AfL technique)
NST	Next steps (an AfL technique)
PPRR	Perfect purple and red to remember (an AfL technique)
SC	Success criteria (an AfL technique)
SCH	Star charts (an AfL technique)
SF	Smiley faces (an AfL technique)
SST	Sheriff's star (an AfL technique)
STM	Sharing two models (an AfL technique)
THUD	Thumbs up or down (an AfL technique)
TL	Traffic lights (an AfL technique)
TSAW	Two stars and a wish (an AfL technique)
WALT	What are we learning today?–type questions (an AfL technique)

Key Abbreviations

AfL	Assessment for learning
AO	Age of onset
AoL	Assessment of learning
BAF	Barcelona Age Factor project
CA	Conversation analysis
CAE	Cambridge Assessment English (Starters, Movers, Flyers)

CBA	Classroom-based assessment
CEFR	Common European Framework of Reference
CP	Critical period
DQ	Delayed questionnaire
EAL	English as an additional language
EFL	English as a foreign language
ELL	Early language learning
ELLiE	Early Language Learning in Europe
ELP	European language portfolio
ESL	English as a second language
EYFS	Early years foundation stage
FA	Formative assessment
FG	Focus group
FL	Foreign language
FLL	Foreign language learning
IH	Interaction hypothesis
IND	Individual work
INT	Interview
IWB	Interactive whiteboard
L1	First language
L2	Second language
L3	Third language
L–C	Learner–class (type of interaction)
LL	Groups
L–L	Learner–learner (type of interaction)
LRE	Language-related episode
MFL	Modern foreign language
NC	National curriculum
NNS	Non-native speaker
NS	Native speaker
PD	Professional development
SNS	Social networking sites
T	Teacher
T–C	Teacher–class (type of interaction)
T–1L	Teacher–learner (type of interaction)
T–xLL	Teacher–group of x learners (type of interaction)
TEFL	Teaching English as a foreign language
VYL	Very young learner
YLL	Young language learner
ZPD	Zone of proximal development

Acknowledgements

This book would not have been possible were it not for the editor Professor Janet Enever's unwavering enthusiasm. Her words of encouragement and thoughtful comments have been invaluable.

I would like to thank Professor Shelagh Rixon and Professor Gudrun Ericson for the very useful feedback on the earlier drafts of this manuscript which they kindly offered.

Finally, I would like to pay tribute to the support and patience of my husband, Neil.

Thank you.

1 Introduction to the Book

Introduction

This book is about how assessment for learning (AfL), innovative in mainstream education in the UK and the USA in the early part of the 21st century, is finding its way into the specific curricular context of primary language education. It reflects findings from my own research in Poland where English is taught as a foreign language. Throughout this volume, I also give indications of how AfL might be relevant in the many contexts globally from which the intended readership is drawn.

AfL is an approach that can make a significant contribution to the improvement of the quality of primary language learning and teaching. The claims that learning and achievement could be facilitated by formative assessment (FA) (Black & Wiliam, 1998) have attracted considerable research attention. Despite the criticism (Bennett, 2011; Dunn & Mulvenon, 2009) that questioned the validity of Black and Wiliam (1998) comparing the 250 diverse studies in their meta-analysis or the methodological rigour of some of those studies, their 1998 article inspired a significant amount of research. The outcomes of that research, while complex, suggest that AfL and FA may facilitate the learning process (e.g. Earl, 2012; Ruiz-Primo & Furtak, 2006; Sly, 1999).

However, despite a growing research interest in assessment practices in primary language teaching contexts (Prošić-Santovac & Rixon, 2019; Tsagari, 2016) and simultaneously growing interest in FA in language education (Butler & Lee, 2010; Lee & Coniam, 2013; Öz, 2014; Porter, 2019), very little empirical evidence has been reported on the use of AfL with primary-aged learners. Calls for further research of AfL and its potential to benefit learning have also been made (Bennett, 2011; Dunn & Mulvenon, 2009; Nikolov, 2016). This volume addresses that gap by providing a detailed account of the practical use of AfL in primary language classrooms. Furthermore, the discussion of those findings highlights the relationships between using AfL and teaching and learning in primary language classes.

What is Assessment for Learning?

Formative evaluation was initially discussed by Scriven (1967), who applied it to educational programmes. The idea was further developed by Bloom (1984), who argued that a tutor can improve a tutee's learning by providing feedback (information that an error has occurred) and correctives (interventions which help repair the error). This early principle of providing feedback on the ongoing learning in order to facilitate it seems consistent with the present definitions of FA and AfL, as discussed in Chapter 2.

AfL strategies and techniques

In order to facilitate learning through assessment, teachers are advised to: ensure that learners understand learning objectives (LOs) and criteria for success; elicit evidence of student understanding during lessons; provide feedback which can help to progress learning; help activate learners as learning resources for themselves and for each other (Black & Wiliam, 2009). These key strategies can be implemented through a variety of practical techniques. In order to inform children of the aims of each lesson and the expected outcomes, teachers can introduce, for example, success criteria (SC); LOs; what are we learning today?–type questions (WALT); or I can statements (ICS). Teachers can also use various techniques to provide learners with feedback. This can be done through monitoring while learners are still working on a task, or soon after a task has been completed. The aim of the feedback is to highlight the extent to which children have met the expectations set for them and to indicate next steps in learning. Teachers can use techniques such as colour coding (CC); indicating mistakes without explanations (IMWE); smiley faces (SF); traffic lights (TL); next steps (NST); or two stars and a wish (TSAW), to name just a few examples. These AfL techniques are discussed in detail in Part 2 of this volume.

As outlined above, the purpose of AfL is to support learners in improving their learning outcomes by helping them to reflect on the extent to which they already meet LOs and on how best to move their learning forward. This conceptualisation of AfL seems to be related to other pedagogic initiatives such as cognitive acceleration programmes (Black & Wiliam, 2009), Learning How to Learn (Black *et al.*, 2006) or Growth Mindset (Dweck, 2006).

Contextual consideration

The practical implementation of AfL using key strategies and techniques will vary across educational contexts. It may be shaped by factors such as local assessment traditions and expectations, teacher cognition and knowledge, class size or learner age.

In contexts where it is well established, as is the case in the UK's mainstream primary education, AfL seems to permeate everyday teaching and may be incorporated under a wider philosophy, such as Growth Mindset (Dweck, 2006). In other teaching cultures, especially those traditionally dominated by competitive, test- and exam-based assessment practices, it is more challenging to embed AfL. In such contexts, teachers may rely on implementing AfL techniques (see Part 2 for examples) into their established practice, rather than changing the teaching culture in order to embed 'genuine AfL' (Swaffield, 2011) into it through more democratic or participatory approaches.

In contexts where participatory approaches to teaching and assessment are the norm, sharing the objectives of a lesson and/or SC with learners could be implemented with relative ease. For example, to clarify what outcomes are expected, a teacher might say that by the end of a lesson they would expect each learner to be able to talk about five things which they had done the day before. In this example, the teacher would be focusing the lesson on introducing an element of grammar linked to talking about the past. By representing the pedagogical aim in a way that is personalised and measurable, teachers can make LOs accessible even to young children. Not every objective lends itself well to making it measurable. In such cases, teachers can accompany an LO with SC. For example, when the LO is to describe a person or a character from a story, children can be given a list of components that a good quality text should contain. These could comprise items such as: (1) include looks, likes and habits; (2) use a minimum of seven describing phrases; (3) include at least one question. Such SC would support learners in completing the task by prompting them to describe physical appearance, preferences and typical activities; to use adjectives and adverbs; and to vary sentence structure by introducing at least one question.

Why is AfL Important in Primary Foreign Languages?

A note on clarification of the terms which I use to refer to various age groups is introduced here, given their varied meanings in different school systems. UNESCO's (2011) International Standard Classification of Education (ISCED) uses the term *primary* to refer to children who start compulsory education around the age of 6 up to the end of primary schooling, approximately the age of 12. In language education, the term *young learners* (YLs) has been used since the 1980s. Initially, it referred to adolescents. However, in recent years it seems to have evolved and now also encapsulates younger children as 'the age at which children begin to learn additional languages in school contexts has fallen rapidly, with national policy currently stabilising somewhere between the ages of 6–9 years in government-funded schools in many parts of the world' (Enever & Driscoll, 2019: 3). To illustrate the confusion surrounding the terminology associated with the learners' age, Ellis (2014) lists a plethora of terms used to refer to various subgroups, arguing that more consistency is needed in the field. In this volume, I follow the terminology adopted by Enever and Discoll (2019), which is consistent with the UNESCO (2011) classification. Consequently, I use the term *primary* to refer to children aged approximately 6–12 years old.

While many teachers believe that primary-aged children should be assessed and that outcomes of assessment in primary languages should predominantly serve to inform future teaching (formative function), the practices they report seem to rely largely on mini summative tests (Rea-Dickins & Rixon, 1999). These focus predominantly on lexical and grammatical aspects of language proficiency and tend not to be incorporated into the teaching and learning activities. This volume demonstrates clearly that AfL is much better suited to fulfilling the formative function of assessment.

Studies conducted in various teaching contexts globally have identified the key characteristics of effective and valid assessment of primary languages. Most significantly, assessment processes should incorporate setting clear goals, monitoring progress towards those goals, frequent questioning and providing quality feedback (Edelenbos & Vinjé, 2000); assessment methods should account for the way in which children learn languages (McKay, 2006); and assessment tasks should be contextualised through teaching activities, designed in a child-friendly format and implemented over a period of time, not as a one-off event (Hasselgreen, 2000). Strategies and techniques inherent to AfL can offer a practical solution to address such recommendations.

Overview of the Book

The purpose of this book is threefold: to provide much needed insights into the practical use of AfL in primary language teaching and learning by reporting in detail the ways in which eight experienced primary language teachers implemented this type of assessment into their practice; to discuss the relationship between AfL and language learning in childhood; and finally, to highlight paths for future action with the focus on implementing and researching AfL in primary language contexts. To best serve these purposes, this volume is divided into three parts. Following this introductory chapter, in Part 1, I set the scene by clarifying the theoretical framework of AfL (Chapter 2) and reviewing the current body of knowledge about assessment and learning in primary languages (Chapter 3). The review is completed with a discussion of studies that focus on the relationship between learning and assessment in childhood from either the cognitive constructivist (Chapter 4) or the sociocultural perspectives (Chapter 5).

Part 2 includes Chapters 6–9, which focus on different aspects of the practical implementation of AfL. Throughout Part 2, I also reflect on the possible impact that the practical implementation reported in each chapter could have on learning. I ground the discussion in the findings from my own research into the use of AfL with learners aged 7–11. The significant data set which I collected by observing lessons, analysing school documents and interviewing teachers resulted in several useful outcomes. First, it allowed for creating an inventory of AfL techniques used in primary language lessons, complete with a detailed account of the ways in which they were used (Chapters 6 and 7). Secondly, a comparative analysis of the use of AfL in the two age groups (7–9 and 10–11) highlighted some interesting age-specific considerations relevant to the implementation of AfL (Chapter 8). Thirdly, analysing the frequency and diversity of use across teachers resulted in identifying factors which may facilitate or impede the use of AfL (Chapter 9). Part 2 concludes by proposing a model of AfL implementation in primary language education, identifying four distinct types of classroom practice (Chapter 9).

Part 3 concludes this volume. In Chapters 10 and 11, I consider different aspects of the impact that implementing AfL could have on teaching and learning additional languages in a primary school context. Chapter 10 focuses on the interactions that occur during the use of AfL, highlighting some possible links between AfL and improved achievement. In Chapter 11, I synthesise the findings about the relationship between AfL and the teaching and learning processes that occur in lessons. The discussion focuses around the concept of the assessment spiral. I propose that this is an accurate and helpful way of capturing the process of AfL in primary language learning and that it can be used as a springboard for further research into the impact of AfL on improving achievement. Finally, in Chapter 12, I consider useful directions for future action with regard to implementing and researching AfL and age-appropriate assessment methods in contexts where children are learning languages.

Part 1

Defining Assessment for Learning in Primary Contexts

2 What is AfL in Primary Language Teaching Contexts?

> I would say that AfL is a kind of philosophy that involves measuring your students'
> progress minute-by-minute of the lesson on the ongoing basis and checking that
> they have the understanding of something and it also involves them knowing what
> to do in order to achieve goals
> (T2/FG)

Introduction

In this chapter, I discuss the theoretical framework of assessment for learning (AfL). The picture that emerges from a review of the literature demonstrates that there is a need for clarifying the terminology used, especially the definitions of *formative assessment* (FA) and *assessment for learning*. The confusion around the terminology is so considerable that, as Bennett (2011: 7) claims, a well-known assessment expert 'Richard Stiggins has stopped using the term "formative assessment", presumably because that phraseology had lost its meaning'. Consequently, we cannot start discussing the use or the impact of AfL without first turning our attention to its theoretical framework and the associated use of terminology.

As Bennett (2011) rightly notices, although FA is popular among various groups of professionals, including researchers, teachers and test publishers, these groups seem to use the term to refer to different concepts or practices. While test publishers, and perhaps some teachers, consider FA to be an instrument that can be used for diagnostic purposes, researchers and educators tend to conceive of it as a process (Popham, 2008) which offers a chance to evaluate learners' understanding (Shepard, 2008). The situation is further complicated by the fact that some consider FA and AfL to mean the same, while others draw distinctions between the two terms.

In order to clarify the conceptualisation of AfL adopted in the present volume, I discuss several popular definitions of AfL and FA. A careful review of these definitions suggests that AfL and FA are complex concepts. The discussion highlights seven key components that should be considered when defining them: functions, instruments, aspects, processes, beneficiaries, participants and timing of assessment. However, before we turn our attention to discussing the theoretical framework of AfL, the chapter commences with a brief review of the key terminology related to AfL: psychometric and pedagogical paradigms, assessment and learning outcomes.

The Concepts Involved in Assessment for Learning

Psychometric and pedagogical paradigms

The psychometric paradigm is the older perspective on assessment within which assessment is predominantly concerned with measurement. In the psychometric paradigm, both reliability and validity are important features of assessment methods. Validity is linked to whether an assessment task measures what it is supposed to measure. If an assessment task is reliable, then students with a similar level of skills and knowledge should obtain similar results. Typical assessment practices under the psychometric paradigm include predominantly testing.

However, as Teasdale and Leung (2000: 163) argue, 'psychometric approaches may not provide an adequate response to pedagogic and policy developments'. In order to fulfil the formative, pedagogic and/or learning functions of assessment, we need a shift towards the 'pedagogical paradigm' (Torrance, 1995: 55). The more modern, pedagogical paradigm focuses on collecting information through assessment which can be used to make teaching and learning processes more effective. Harlen and James (1997) argue that usefulness and validity are most important for formative assessment and that in order to ensure those, reliability may be compromised. AfL clearly falls within the pedagogical paradigm. Therefore, it follows that judgements made through AfL should be accurate (valid) and beneficial to teaching and learning (useful).

Assessment

Definitions of assessment tend to be developed alongside changes in the conceptualisations of learning. In language education, the mid-1990s witnessed a shift from psychometric testing towards more communicative and context-sensitive approaches, which included developments in performance-based (Upshur & Turner, 1995) and interactional assessment (Bachman, 2007). Notably, there was a transition from understanding assessment as mainly about measuring students' performance towards recognising the influence of assessment on teaching and learning (Carless *et al.*, 2006) and towards perceiving assessment 'as a tool for supporting student learning' (Öz, 2014: 775). From the 1990s, assessment procedures increasingly came to account for the characteristics of learners and tasks (O'Sullivan & Green, 2011); the contexts and the consequences of assessment (Stoynoff, 2012). Importantly, the need to integrate assessment with the teaching and learning process was also recognised (Stoynoff, 2012).

Although the formative function of assessment had been discussed previously to that time (Bloom, 1984; Scriven, 1967), it was not until the mid-1990s that the term AfL was coined to emphasise the contribution that assessment is expected to make to learning (Gipps, 1994).

Nowadays, in foreign or second language education, assessment is often conceptualised as a complex process in which teachers and learners make evidence-based judgements about learning and use them to inform decisions about further steps (Drummond, 2003). Depending on the purpose for such decisions (e.g. reporting to stakeholders, addressing gaps in learning), assessment practices vary in function and the use of method. For example, Rea-Dickins (2001) observed bureaucratic, pedagogic and learning functions of assessment. Others draw a distinction between formative and summative functions of assessment (Bennett, 2011; Stoynoff, 2012). Table 2.1 outlines these different functions.

Table 2.1 Functions of assessment

Function of assessment	Description
Bureaucratic	Concerns reporting to various stakeholders (Rea-Dickins, 2001)
Pedagogic	Used to inform decisions about teaching and learning (Rea-Dickins, 2001)
Learning	Focuses on learning through assessment and on the learner's role in the assessment process (Rea-Dickins, 2001)
Formative	Uses assessment evidence to benefit the learning process (Wiliam, 2011)
Summative	Focuses on measuring learners' progress (Stoynoff, 2012)

It is important to note that the functions themselves are not equivalent to methods of implementation. For example, the outcomes of summative tests could, theoretically, be used for formative purposes. However, Klenowski (2011) warned against the frequent implementation of summative tests to replace embedded classroom practices, arguing that such implementation could not be considered AfL. Support for such a view is shared by Harlen (2005) who argued that as a result of teachers misinterpreting ongoing summative assessment as formative assessment, there is a lack of genuine formative assessment; a type of assessment which is especially important for learning with understanding – deep learning. A similar view on (mis)interpreting AfL and a call for a more genuine AfL was shared by Swaffield (2011). As different assessment methods may lend themselves better to different functions of assessment, practitioners should be advised to plan their implementation of such methods with consideration for the primary and secondary purpose of assessment (Bennett, 2011).

As recently as 2016, Nikolov (2016) pointed out that the terms testing and assessment are sometimes used interchangeably in the literature. This can be problematic because as Prošić-Santovac and Rixon (2019: 1) rightly note, assessment includes 'activities that are more varied than tests and examinations'. Testing is effectively just one way in which the summative function of assessment can be realised. This is an important consideration to bear in mind as the two terms are not always consistently used in the literature.

Learning outcomes

The notion of learning outcomes is important to consider when discussing assessment. Those educational contexts in which learners' progress is measured against predefined outcomes are referred to as criterion referenced. Arguably, many language teaching contexts are criterion-referenced systems as they use frameworks such as the Common European Framework of Reference (CEFR) (Council of Europe, 2001) with its subsequent updates and extensions (Council of Europe, 2020) or its adaptations for younger age groups (see also Hasselgreen, 2005; Hasselgreen & Caudwell, 2016). The predefined end-of-year outcomes which are included in the teaching programme may be translated into a series of lesson-by-lesson learning objectives (LOs). A list of examples of such incremental LOs which correspond to CEFR descriptors has recently been published by the Council of Europe for learners aged 7–10 (Goodier, 2018a) and 11–15 (Goodier, 2018b). The authors collated themes developed in various language portfolios for young learners to provide useful practical guidance for translating CEFR descriptors into LOs for children and adolescents.

Research suggests that learners may take different trajectories to achieve predefined outcomes (Mihaljević Djigunović, 2015). This demonstrates that there is a need for teachers and learners to reflect on and adapt the learning process while it is happening. As a result, teachers might need to offer different types of scaffolding to various learners to help them meet the LO for each lesson, or the LOs might be adapted for different learners or groups of learners. This is a challenge for teachers who should design such teaching and learning conditions in which children receive ongoing guidance for their individualised next steps in learning. As, by definition, AfL aims to support learning, it would be interesting to understand whether AfL might play a role in guiding learners on their individual learning paths in order to help them achieve the expected outcomes.

Fitness for Purpose

Assessing entails making evidence-based judgements about learning (Drummond, 2003). According to the purpose of such decisions, teachers can choose different assessment methods. James (2013) recognises the importance of the relationship between the purpose and the methods of assessment and argues that *fitness for purpose* should guide all assessment practices. This requires that appropriate methods are carefully selected to accurately serve the intended purpose of assessment.

Formative and Summative Functions

A distinction is often drawn between formative and summative functions of assessment. Bennett (2011) argues convincingly that the primary function of AfL is formative and that it also has a secondary, summative function. He juxtaposes it with assessment of learning (AoL) whose primary function is summative and secondarily, formative. Practically, this means that AfL primarily aims to collect information that will inform the next steps in learning (the formative function). However, when using AfL techniques, teachers will effectively collect some information about what has already been learnt (the summative function). Bennett (2011) uses the term *type of assessment* to refer to summative and formative assessment. In this volume, I adopt the term *function* to refer to those terms, as does Wiliam (2011). It is important to note that Bennett (2011) and Wiliam (2011) agree that when defining assessment, we should consider its function together with its purpose, that is to say what the assessment information is used for. Wiliam (2011) also suggests that the term AfL focuses on the purpose of assessment (i.e. evidence is used to support learning, namely the *for-learning* purpose), while the term formative assessment refers to the function of assessment.

The importance of considering the function and the purpose when defining assessment has direct consequences for its practical implementation. For example, if AfL is used to inform future decisions about learning (the formative function) but the collected evidence is not actually used to facilitate learning, should such use of assessment be considered AfL? Black and Wiliam (1998: 140) argue that 'assessment becomes formative assessment when the evidence is actually used to adapt the teaching to meet student needs'. However, it could also be argued that if evidence collected through AfL is not used to facilitate learning, despite the intention to do so, then there is a problem with the process involved in enacting AfL. This highlights the dichotomous nature of assessment, which consists of instruments and processes, each of which must be accurate (Bennett, 2011) in order to ensure validity. For example, a good assessment instrument will not provide valid evidence of learning if it is not used correctly. Similarly, a well-designed process will not yield valid assessment data if the instruments used in that process are flawed. Therefore, it is important to consider the instruments and the processes of assessment when defining and researching it. I discuss these in the following sections.

The Instruments of AfL

As indicated earlier, it is important to consider the instruments as well as the processes involved in collecting assessment evidence and making judgements. We will now turn our attention to a conceptualisation of AfL that provides guidance on what instruments to use in order to practically implement it.

> **Definition proposed by the Third International Conference on AfL:**
> Assessment for Learning is part of everyday practice by students, teachers and peers that seeks, reflects upon and responds to information from dialogue, demonstration and observation in ways that enhance ongoing learning (Klenowski, 2009: 2).

The above-quoted definition confirms that the main purpose of AfL is to facilitate learning. Additionally, Klenowski (2009) suggests three types of techniques ('dialogue, demonstration and observation') which can be used to enact the for-learning purpose of assessment. In her elaborations on the foregoing definition, Klenowski (2009) clarifies that no special AfL instruments are needed. Instead, activities which teachers do with learners during lessons can be used as a vehicle for AfL.

> Special assessment tasks and tests can be used formatively but are not essential; there is a risk of them becoming frequent mini-summative assessments. Everyday learning tasks and activities, as well as routine observation and dialogue are equally, if not more, appropriate for the formative purpose. (Klenowski, 2009: 2)

Two important points highlighted by this quote are useful for our discussion. The first one is that AfL does not require any additional tasks or tests but is an integral part of teaching and learning and can be enacted through the usual lesson activities. The second point is that designing separate instruments for AfL may pose a risk of mistaking mini-summative assessments for AfL. This warning is consistent with the critique of AfL implementation in some contexts in the UK (Harlen, 2005; Swaffield, 2011).

If AfL is best implemented by integrating it into teaching and learning, then any teacher perusing this chapter might ask themselves at least one of the following questions. The first question is *Do I already use AfL, perhaps without consciously knowing that I do?* To answer it, a teacher should consider whether they collect information about the learning that is happening in their classes in a systematic way and whether they consequently adapt their teaching to address the misconceptions that may occur and/or whether they provide opportunities for learners to further extend their understanding and skills. Most teachers probably do that to some degree. But do they (you) also encourage the learners themselves to reflect on learning in a similar way and take some ownership of their learning?

The second question one might ask is *How would I have to adapt my teaching in order to use AfL (more) effectively?* To answer that, a teacher should reflect on whether they could become more effective or systematic in how they: (1) make judgements about learning; (2) support individuals; and (3) develop learners' ownership of and responsibility for their own learning. If, having reflected on these two questions, a teacher feels that assessment is detached from what they normally do with their learners, I invite them to read Chapters 6 and 7 of this volume. These chapters provide practical insights into the ways in which AfL could be integrated into language teaching. Furthermore, they outline how AfL can be implemented in lessons to engage primary-aged learners in assessment in a way that is age appropriate and can help children become more autonomous learners.

Aspects of AfL

As has already been indicated, there are many definitions of AfL and the field is in need of developing agreed-on definitions of AfL and FA (Bennett, 2011). Some attempts to provide such definitions have been made (Black & Wiliam, 2009; Klenowski, 2009; Wiliam, 2011). One of the most useful attempts aimed to discuss a theoretical framework of FA and to relate it to other well-established pedagogical theories such as self-regulation and accelerated learning (Black & Wiliam, 2009). Although Black and Wiliam (2009) only use the term FA, they discuss a theoretical framework which, as I examine below, evidently refers to practice that aims to facilitate learning, that is to say, it serves the for-learning purpose.

The theoretical framework discussed by Black and Wiliam (2009) was initially proposed by Wiliam and Thompson (2007). Black and Wiliam (2009) are referenced here, as they provide a more comprehensive discussion of that framework. The authors take into account the strategies used by teachers, learners and their peers at each of the three stages of learning proposed by Ramaprasad (1983). These include: establishing where learners are in their learning; where they are going; and how best to get there. Black and Wiliam (2009) summarise the resulting strategies under five aspects of AfL.

Within Aspect 1, teachers employ strategies to clarify 'learning intentions and criteria for success' (Black & Wiliam, 2009: 8) and the learners' role is to understand what the teacher is communicating. Black and Wiliam (2009) also suggest that the role of peers is to share and help others understand success criteria (SC) and LOs. LOs and SC are discussed in greater detail in Chapter 1. Because Aspect 1 entails sharing LOs and SC, how it is enacted will be linked to the way in which:

(1) LOs are set: Are they based on the curriculum or generated by learners who follow their own interests?
(2) Success measured: What is evaluated – the effort, the processes which the learners go through or their final performance?

This may differ across educational contexts. Therefore, there is value in investigating whether all strategies incorporated in Aspect 1 can be identified in language lessons at the primary school level.

Aspects 2 and 3 concentrate on how teachers can elicit evidence of the extent to which learners meet the LOs and SC (Aspect 2) and how teachers can use evidence-based judgements to facilitate learning (Aspect 3). Within the final two aspects, Black and Wiliam (2009) discuss the role that peers can play in monitoring and evaluating learning (Aspect 4) and they indicate that learners can self-monitor and self-assess (Aspect 5). Importantly, in considering the latter two aspects, we should account for learners' metacognitive development (Wiliam, 2011). This is discussed in Chapter 4.

It is important to note that the framework proposed by Black and Wiliam (2009) is not specific to any context. Therefore, it would be interesting to investigate whether the five aspects of AfL proposed by Black and Wiliam (2009) are reflected in data from a primary language context.

The Process of AfL

In the UK, the work of the Assessment Reform Group (ARG) has been significant in promoting the implementation of AfL in schools. Therefore, it seems useful to consider how ARG defines the concept.

Definition proposed by the Assessment Reform Group (2002: 2–3) in the UK:
    Assessment for Learning is the process of seeking and interpreting evidence for use by learners and their teachers to decide where the learners are in their learning, where they need to go and how best to get there.

First, the above definition highlights the importance of collecting evidence which can inform the judgements made in the process of assessment. Secondly, it emphasises that the purpose of such decisions is to establish how best to facilitate the ongoing learning. Based on the foregoing definition, the steps involved in the AfL process, as defined by ARG (2002), appear to be

(1) Collect evidence ('to decide where learners are in their learning').
(2) Set clear objectives, presumably using insights gained from the sum-
     mative information ('where they need to go').
(3) Provide support in reaching the objectives ('how to best get there').

Although it helped to clarify what the purpose of AfL is and what processes are involved in implementing it, neither the ARG definition nor
the 10 principles which were published with it (ARG, 2002: 2–3) offered
clear advice for teachers regarding practical use. Consequently, the ways
in which teachers collected evidence and set objectives depended on their
interpretations and/or the educational contexts in which they worked.
Not surprisingly, this led to rather diverse practices. On one hand,
using AfL to set attainment targets posed a risk that objectives were not
informed by assessment evidence, namely they were not the next steps
which would be most appropriate for the learners but instead, they were
the next steps as prescribed by the curriculum. On the other hand, an
overreliance on the first step of the AfL process led to practice that could
be more accurately described as a series of mini-summative assessments
(Harlen & James, 1997) and therefore could not be easily classified as
AfL. These issues in implementing AfL led to researchers calling for
genuine AfL (Swaffield, 2011) and for ensuring a better understanding of
AfL by teachers (Harlen, 2005). The issue of instrumentation was later
addressed in the definition proposed by the Third International Conference on AfL in 2009, which is discussed earlier in this chapter.

Participants and Timing

The ARG (2002) definition (see above) indicates that learners as well
as their teachers are important participants in the AfL process. This is
also reflected in the definition proposed by Thompson and Wiliam (2007).

Definition proposed by Thompson and Wiliam (2007: 6):
Students and teachers, using evidence of learning to adapt teaching
and learning, to meet immediate learning needs, minute-to-minute and
day-by-day.

Not only does the above definition draw our attention to the need for
learners' participation in AfL but also, more importantly, it proposes
that in order to serve the for-learning purpose, assessment should
happen alongside teaching and learning. This could be during lessons
('minute-to-minute') and across lessons ('day-by-day'). Importantly, by
indicating that the for-learning purpose of assessment could be enacted
during and across lessons, this definition suggests that the beneficiaries

of AfL are the participants of these lessons. As the primary aim for teachers is to teach and for learners is to learn, it could be argued that the primary beneficiaries of an assessment process which aims to serve the for-learning purpose are learners. Furthermore, Thompson and Wiliam's (2007) definition recognises the need for learner agency in AfL. It proposes that learners can collect evidence of their own learning and adapt their behaviour to facilitate further learning. This is linked to self-regulation, which encompasses metacognition and motivation (Boekaerts & Cascallar, 2006) and develops throughout childhood (see also Chapter 4).

Some researchers even argue the need for immediate use of assessment evidence in order to facilitate learning effectively in various school subjects (e.g. Cowie & Bell, 1999; Shepard *et al.*, 2005). This is not to suggest that learning happens only during lessons when teachers are present and that this is when assessment should occur. On the contrary, research suggests that factors outside the classroom can also contribute to learning (Enever, 2011). So, the requirement for immediate feedback could simply apply to only those situations when a teacher is present. This interpretation has implications for practice. Specifically, in a class where there is one teacher and a group of students, it might be challenging to provide immediate feedback to all individuals. That is, if we assume that only a teacher could be a feedback provider. However, as discussed by Black and Wiliam (2009), learners and peers also provide feedback on learning. Insights into feedback provision through AfL gained from my own research are reported in Chapter 7.

The notion of achieving learning outcomes requires some elaboration. In criterion-referenced contexts, the expected outcomes of learning are prescribed in the form of attainment targets. However, learners could presumably take different trajectories to achieve those outcomes. Hence, ongoing learning is a non-linear process, specific outcomes of which may not be possible to (pre-)determine. Therefore, teachers need tools to observe learning, evaluate students' performance and make accurate evidence-based judgements about the ongoing progress and about the learning needs of individual learners. As suggested by the definitions of AfL discussed so far, AfL could help teachers support learners in following their individual trajectories in order to achieve their predefined attainment targets (see also Chapter 10).

Who Benefits?

The sensitivity towards the timing and the beneficiaries of AfL, highlighted in the previous section, is also reflected in the conceptualisation proposed by Swaffield (2011). She argues that if the impact of AfL on learning is deferred in time, or if it focuses on other participants of the lesson (e.g. it builds the teacher's experience of teaching a particular topic), the for-learning purpose of assessment is realised to a lesser degree. Black and Wiliam (2009) agree that the formative function of assessment can be realised to a greater or a lesser extent.

> **Definition of formative practice proposed by Black and Wiliam (2009: 10):**
>
> Practice in a classroom is formative *to the extent* that evidence about student achievement is elicited, interpreted, and used by teachers, learners, or their peers, to make decisions about the next steps in instruction that are likely to be better, or better founded, than the decisions they would have taken in the absence of the evidence that was elicited. (my emphasis)

Black and Wiliam (2009) suggest that the impact of formative practice is on instruction, which the authors use to denote teaching and learning. This suggests that by implementing formative practice, teachers can have an impact on their teaching as well as their learners' learning. This distinction is important because it illustrates that it is possible that the teacher uses collected evidence formatively to adjust how they teach a given topic in the future, but does not necessarily adapt their practice in the lesson during which the evidence was collected. In such a case, the evidence would be formative for teaching but may not serve the for-learning purpose during that lesson and for those learners. However, such distinction would be problematic because it assumes that teaching and learning can truly be separated. It would not be authentic to do so because teaching and learning happen alongside each other over a period of time and are intertwined. For example, if the same teacher adapts their approach to better suit the needs of the same group of learners in the following lessons, surely their learning will also benefit. Therefore, it seems more authentic from a pragmatic perspective to use the terms FA and AfL interchangeably. Complicating the discussion by differentiating between the two terms might distract from what is truly at the heart of AfL: the for-learning purpose of assessment.

The Adopted Conceptualisation of AfL

In the discussion throughout this chapter, I have highlighted features that are key to defining AfL. Most significantly, AfL serves the for-learning purpose, which means that it aims to facilitate learning. Moreover, the process of AfL does not require any special instruments but can be integrated into what teachers, learners and peers routinely do during lessons. This means that lesson activities can be used to collect assessment data, for example, through 'dialogue, demonstration and observation'

(Klenowski, 2009: 2) in order 'to adapt the teaching to meet student needs' (Black & Wiliam, 1998: 140) and enact the five aspects proposed by Black and Wiliam (2009).

In the following sections, I will compare the above conceptualisation to the understanding of AfL that a group of primary language teachers shared with me.

An Empirical Investigation into Teachers' Understanding of AfL

So far, in this chapter, I have highlighted the lack of a generally accepted theoretical framework and terminology for AfL and clarified the definition adopted in this volume. Because various definitions of AfL exist, teachers can understand the concept in different ways. Therefore, investigating teachers' understanding of AfL is a prerequisite for conducting research into its implementation in primary language teaching. Thus, the central question to be answered is: Having used it in teaching English to young learners (aged 7–11), how do teachers understand AfL?

In my study, data were collected from eight teachers through individual, semi-structured interviews and verified through one focus group with all the participants. All participating teachers were native or native-like speakers of English, had university degrees as well as additional qualifications to teach young learners. They had between 5 and 18 years of teaching experience. Each of them had used AfL with children aged 7–11 for at least one academic year before the study commenced.

The interview protocol included 13 open-ended questions. These were piloted with two teachers, who were later not included in the main sample. Interviews were used to collect information about teachers' understanding of AfL in primary language teaching, and their accounts of the practical implementation and the impact of AfL. This choice was similar to other studies that investigated teachers' beliefs about self and peer assessment (Dixon *et al.*, 2011) or teachers' interpretations of the effectiveness of assessment (Butler & Lee, 2010).

Focus groups were used in my study to: (1) verify the draft findings from individual interviews (Somekh & Lewin, 2005); (2) gain more nuanced understanding of teachers' reports about AfL; and (3) obtain collective (not individual) understanding of AfL through the discussions within the group (Morgan, 1988). The focus group prompts were informed by the preliminary findings from the analysis of teacher interviews.

The data set included eight audio-recorded and subsequently transcribed, individual interviews and one focus group with eight teachers (see Appendix 1 for the transcribing convention). The validity and reliability of the interpretations resulting from the qualitative analysis of the transcripts were warranted by ensuring agreement across the coders (the researcher and the inter-rater) and by verifying the findings from teacher interviews with the respondents through the focus group.

What do primary language teachers consider as AfL?

Nikolov (2016) calls for research into teachers' emic perspectives on assessment in primary language contexts. The need to investigate teachers' thoughts and beliefs was initially highlighted in the mid-1970s. This marked a shift in thinking about teaching as behaviour to conceptualising it as thoughtful behaviour (Borg, 2003) which has been shown to play an important role in ensuring the effective implementation of pedagogical innovations (Rixon, 2017). Consequently, teachers are conceived of as those who enact agency and make decisions about what happens in the classroom. Adopting this sensitivity and responding to Nikolov's (2016) call, this chapter reports on an investigation into teachers' understanding of AfL. The findings help to provide a more detailed picture of AfL in primary language education, one which could not be achieved solely by observing how AfL is implemented.

It is important to remember that the findings discussed here are based on data collected from eight teachers, all of whom worked at the same school. Therefore, I do not make claims about the generalisability of these findings. Nonetheless, they are very useful because they provide the context for the remaining chapters, which focus on the implementation and impact that AfL could have on teaching primary languages. Additionally, teachers' understanding of AfL is compared with the definitions of AfL available in the literature. The outcomes of that analysis provide interesting insights into the context-specific nature of AfL. Moreover, they indicate areas which would warrant future enquiry.

Integrating AfL into teaching and learning

> *it's sort of like you were trying to put the assessment and the teaching together* (T2/INT)

As illustrated by T2's quote, the findings of my own study indicate that teachers considered AfL to be a way of integrating assessment into teaching and learning. This was one of the strongest themes identified in the data. Such conceptualisation is consistent with the proposition that AfL does not require any special instruments but that '(e)veryday learning tasks and activities, as well as routine observation and dialogue are equally, if not more, appropriate for the formative purpose' (Klenowski, 2009: 2). Figure 2.1 demonstrates the five ways in which the participating teachers reported integrating AfL into their lessons. Each section is supported by several examples of quotes sourced from the data.

As is evident from Figure 2.1, the participating teachers identified five different ways in which AfL can be integrated into teaching and learning.

However, before turning our attention to discussing them in detail, it is interesting to share some of the quotes in which teachers explained that AfL is compatible with primary language teaching.

> *to a certain extent it [AfL] is the means to an end just a part of what you're doing anyway with them just teaching them in slightly different way and it is helpful* (T6/INT)

> *with the primaries this is all seamless and normal* (T2/INT)

The quotes from T6 and T2 illustrate what teachers thought about the feasibility of using AfL when teaching primary languages. Evidently, both of them indicate that incorporating AfL within typical lesson activities is not only possible but also, and perhaps more importantly, that it is 'helpful' (T6), 'seamless and normal' (T2).

This finding is context specific because it demonstrates that AfL can be compatible with the type of teaching that was used by the teachers in this context. They reported using communicative methodology and basing their lessons around a published coursebook. However, the quality of the teaching or the methodological choices made by teachers was not evaluated as part of my research. Therefore, this finding remains open to the possibility that in other teaching cultures, it may be more challenging to integrate AfL into teaching.

Importantly, the finding that primary language teachers considered AfL to be an integral part of what happens in lessons illustrates a similarity between the understanding of AfL reported by them and the definitions proposed by Klenowski (2009). In the focus group discussion, the participating teachers agreed that 'the whole thing is about that (1) getting them to understand what to do and then to figure out how well they have done it and it doesn't matter which techniques you use' (T3/FG). The teachers indicated that the ways in which this can be achieved are by: (1) making the learners aware of what they are learning; (2) focusing the learners' attention on achieving the LOs; (3) providing meaningful feedback on performance; (4) activating and motivating learners; and (5) continuously building AfL opportunities into lessons. The five ways (Figure 2.1) in which teachers reported integrating AfL into their lessons provide interesting insights into the practical implementation.

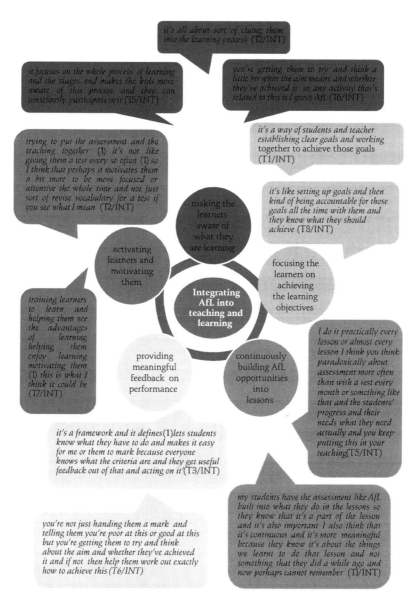

Figure 2.1 Integrating AfL into primary language lessons

Making learners aware of what they are learning

The participating teachers' reports (Figure 2.1) suggest that AfL can be integrated into lessons by raising young learners' awareness of the LOs. This resonates with Aspect 1 of AfL as proposed by Black and Wiliam (2009), which suggests that the teacher's role is to clarify LOs and SC; the learners' role – to understand those; and peers' role – to help each other understand the LOs and SC. However, it is interesting to note that the teachers did not comment on the role of peers in enacting Aspect 1. The findings presented in Figure 2.1 suggest that in language lessons at the primary level, only teachers and their students can work to share LOs and SC. This finding could be related to the context in which these teachers worked where primary-aged learners with low levels of proficiency in an L2 were taught only through that L2 (English). It is conceivable that in such a context, peers could not play an active role in Aspect 1 if LOs and SC were communicated through English and/or referred to the new vocabulary, grammar or other concepts which would be taught. The reason for that finding could be simply that learners did not have enough knowledge of the L2 to actively enact Aspect 1 as peers. While they knew enough of the L2 to try to understand what they are going to learn about (LOs) and how (SC), they might not have been able to support others in understanding the LOs and SC. This finding suggests that teachers believed that their role was to clarify LOs and SC, while students' roles were predominantly to understand the LOs and SC but not necessarily to help others understand. This finding could be interpreted as a context-specific characteristic of AfL which is linked to the characteristics of learners. However, more research is needed to validate such an interpretation.

The interpretation proposed above resonates with Jones and Wiliam's (2008) discussion of using AfL in modern foreign language (MFL) teaching in the UK. The authors suggest that 'judicious use of English [which in that context is the L1] provides an opportunity for students to become more active learners (...) and to reap the benefits of formative assessment' (Jones & Wiliam, 2008: 4). The authors recognise that operating solely in an L2 in a context in which the learners do not speak the L2 fluently may pose some challenges to effectively implementing the formative function of assessment. However, in contexts where there is no lingua franca among the teacher and the students, such a solution is not possible. This was the case in the classrooms included in my own study. Therefore, the findings discussed in this chapter provide an interesting new insight which extends the advice on implementing AfL in MFL (Jones & Wiliam, 2008). It demonstrates which aspects of AfL can be implemented through an L2 even in contexts where the learners are at the initial stages of the language. This is an important finding that has pedagogical implications for teachers in various language teaching contexts, including primary languages, English as a second language (ESL), MFL, community, minority and heritage languages or English as an additional language (EAL) contexts (Murphy, 2014).

The foregoing discussion highlights that two out of three strategies involved in Aspect 1 (Black & Wiliam, 2009) were evident in the participating teachers' understanding of AfL. Aspect 1 is a vital element of the AfL framework proposed by Black and Wiliam (2009). However, it seems to be the most complex of all five aspects. This is because it incorporates three strategies, one for each type of participant in the teaching and learn-ing process. The remaining four aspects incorporate one strategy each. Within Aspect 1, the teacher's role is to clarify LOs and SC; peers should understand and share them with others; and each learner's role is to understand the expectations expressed with LOs and SC. The outcomes of my research indicate that primary language teachers reported that AfL involves teachers sharing LOs and SC and learners working to under-stand those. However, it also indicates one discrepancy: the lack of an active role for peers in sharing LOs and SC. This finding may be related to the learners' low levels of the L2; primary-aged learners might have found it challenging to share expectations expressed through LOs and SC in the L2 due to their low level of that L2. Effectively, when reporting on their understanding of AfL, primary language teachers did not consider that strategy of Aspect 1 an integral part of the concept.

This poses an important question about the definition of AfL: Can the conceptualisation reported by teachers be considered as AfL if it does not incorporate all components included in Aspect 1? It is essential to note that the participants themselves believed that they were discussing AfL. Consequently, it might be more accurate to consider whether all the strategies discussed by Black and Wiliam (2009) are essential in defining and implementing AfL or whether some might be optional, depending on the educational context. The understanding of AfL as reported by primary language teachers seems to indicate that within Aspect 1 not all strategies are equally important. In contexts where the means of teach-ing is a foreign language, primary-aged children may find it challenging to incorporate the peer-sharing strategy that is proposed within Aspect 1 (Black & Wiliam, 2009). Despite that, it is possible to use AfL in such a context.

This interpretation is consistent with claims that all assessment prac-tice should be guided by its purpose. Specifically, within Aspect 1 the purpose is to ensure that expectations are effectively shared; this requires that LOs and SC are clearly communicated to learners and consequently understood by all of them. This purpose can be satisfied if such com-munication comes solely from the teacher. Consequently, it seems of secondary importance whether peers also play an active part in sharing expectations. As long as each learner correctly understands the expecta-tions communicated through LOs and SC, it does not appear critical that all strategies included in Aspect 1 are enacted. Various strategies might suit different educational contexts due to factors such as learners' age, language level, assessment culture and/or teachers' knowledge and expe-rience of using AfL.

Focusing the learners' attention on achieving the learning objectives

Another strong theme that teachers reported as a way of integrat-ing AfL into teaching and learning was to help primary-aged language

learners focus their efforts on achieving the LOs. Teachers would monitor how learners were progressing towards their aims and they would
intervene if additional scaffolding was needed. This interpretation is
supported by a discussion during the focus group, quoted in Extract 1.

EXTRACT 1
(From the focus group discussion)

[1]   **T2:** *with time input from teacher should be smaller=*
[2]   **T5:** *=mhm=* **[nods]**
[3]   **T2:** *=because they know their success criteria how to do it or they should be*
[4]   *aware of what is expected (1) but I think at that point monitoring becomes*
[5]   *more effective to make sure that they're actually doing it properly (1) they*
[6]   *might think they know what they are doing but they may have the basics*
[7]   *established but actually without the monitoring in place they could then go off*
[8]   *down different roads and do different things and you know*
[9]   **T4:** *I think this is a very good point*
[10]   **T1:** *yes more time to monitor better*

The exchange between the four teachers in Extract 1 indicates that
when learners were aware of LOs and SC, they were able to work
with a greater degree of independence. The teachers agreed that this
created conditions in which the role of the teacher was to monitor the
ongoing work to ensure that learners focused their efforts on meeting the LOs. Teachers were able to do this by providing additional
scaffolding through demonstration or dialogue. In order to be able
to identify what support learners needed, the teachers had to use
their diagnostic competence (Edelenbos & Kubanek-German, 2004).
The impact that such interventions could have on language learning
would constitute an interesting focus for future research. The findings
discussed in the current section demonstrate how Aspect 2 (Black &
Wiliam, 2009) was understood by primary language teachers. The outcomes highlight another similarity between the teachers' understanding of AfL and the definitions available in the literature, namely that
AfL can be used to 'elicit evidence of student understanding' (Black
& Wiliam, 2009: 8).

Providing meaningful feedback on performance

The third theme which emerged from the teachers' reports on how
they integrated AfL into teaching and learning was that AfL was used
to provide meaningful feedback on performance. As is evident in T3
and T6's quotes (Figure 2.1), feedback should be linked to the LOs
and SC. In Chapter 1, I outlined how LOs and SC can be used to guide
learners towards meeting the pedagogical aims of lessons. The findings

presented in this chapter suggest that LOs and SC can be used to focus teachers' feedback. The teachers commented that learners were able to better understand feedback if it was connected to the LOs and SC. This finding resonates with the outcomes of a large-scale study conducted in the Netherlands (Edelenbos & Vinje, 2000). The authors conducted a comparative analysis of the results of English as a foreign language (EFL) tests administered at the end of primary school with children aged 12. The differences in the results obtained by the two cohorts included in the study were attributed to the teaching methodology and the time of exposure to the L2. The study concluded that 'setting clear goals, sequencing materials, frequent questions to monitor progress in the learning process, opportunity to learn, testing and quality feedback are all important characteristics from which early foreign language learning can benefit tremendously' (Edelenbos & Vinje, 2000: 160). These resemble the components of AfL discussed in the present chapter.

The findings of my research also indicate that it is not enough to just provide feedback. As T3 (Figure 2.1) indicates, it is crucial that the feedback is used and that learners act on it, thereby fulfilling the for-learning purpose of AfL. The issue of L2 learners understanding and acting on feedback to improve their learning was researched by Nicol and Macfarlane-Dick (2006). Although their study was conducted with university students, it provides a useful finding for primary language teaching. The authors argued that there is a relationship between feedback and the self-regulation of learning. The ability to self-regulate requires the use of metacognitive and motivational strategies (Boekaerts & Cascallar, 2006). However, control of such strategies develops through childhood. As a result, younger children may not have such strategies at their disposal (Flavell *et al.*, 1993). Research suggests that children could be taught how to use metacognitive strategies (e.g. Butler & Lee, 2006, 2010; Gu *et al.*, 2005). Therefore, it seems important to consider AfL strategies together with age-related factors such as the development of metacognition and self-regulation.

The present section illustrates how teachers understand Aspect 3 (Black & Wiliam, 2009). It highlights yet another similarity between their understanding of AfL and the definitions available in the literature.

Learner agency

According to the framework discussed by Black and Wiliam (2009: 8), learners have an important role to play in their own and their peers' learning by acting as 'instructional resources for one another' (Aspect 4) and becoming 'the owners of their own learning' (Aspect 5, Black & Wiliam, 2009: 8). References to both aspects were evident in the findings from a primary language teaching context.

With regard to Aspect 4, teachers commented:

> *I think the biggest benefit for my groups has been the peer learning working together and not being competitive in their English but being supportive of each other's learning* (T1/INT)

> *I used this with primaries mainly to involve more pair work and it sort of helps them get what pair work is about* (T7/INT)

T1 explains that because teachers used various games and races, children could sometimes become competitive during lessons, even when they were not participating in a game. (S)he explained that by using AfL to structure pair work, (s)he was able to encourage students to work out solutions and find answers together, supporting each other rather than competing. A similar observation was expressed by T7. These quotes suggest that AfL might be a way of encouraging learner agency in the learning process by facilitating conditions for developing collaborative skills. This is an important finding because it highlights that interactions with peers are an integral element of the language learning process in childhood.

Considered from the sociocultural perspective, the above finding indicates that while collaborating in dyads, or perhaps also small groups, learners might be able to participate in at least one of the two processes which have been shown to support language learning. First, the learners could fulfil the role of *a more capable peer* for one another. This could be with reference to very small components of tasks, for example, knowing a certain word in English. A more capable peer provides scaffolding needed to complete a task which is within the learner's *zone of proximal development* (ZPD) (Vygotsky, 1987) but which the learner could not do without support. With practice, the learner becomes more proficient at completing that type of task independently; demonstrating learning. Second, while working in dyads, learners could negotiate for meaning and enter interaction types with a high level of mutuality (Storch, 2002). Research in this area has demonstrated that these types of conversations can contribute to language learning (e.g. Oliver, 1998, 2000; Swain, 2000). Therefore, it seems that investigating the types of interactions that occur during primary language lessons could provide insights into whether either of the two processes actually takes place and whether there are relationships between AfL and these processes (see also Chapter 11).

With regard to Aspect 5, teachers reported that:

> *it was amazing how quickly kids got used to taking some responsibility and when you think about young learners they still don't have that concept of taking responsibility for their learning until you start using AfL* (T4/INT)

> *you're getting them to try and think about the aim and whether they've achieved it and if not then help them work out exactly how to achieve this* (T6/INT)

The above quotes demonstrate that these teachers believe that primary-aged learners were able to monitor and evaluate their own learning. Self-evaluation in primary language teaching was researched by Butler and Lee (2006, 2010). They investigated the validity of on-task and off-task self-assessment of 9 to 12-year-olds. The results indicate that self-evaluation not related to a specific task (off-task self-assessment) was less accurate than self-evaluation conducted directly after a task (on-task self-assessment). When AfL is integrated into the process of teaching and learning, it involves predominantly on-task self-assessment, which promises to provide conditions for more accurate self-evaluations. Butler and Lee (2006) also found that younger learners (9 to 10-year-olds) were not able to self-assess as accurately as their older counterparts (11 to 12-year-olds). As indicated earlier, the relationship between age and learners' ability to self-assess might be related to their metacognitive development (see also Chapter 4). Finally, Butler and Lee (2006) reported that in both age groups, learners developed self-assessment skills over time. Children's ability to develop accuracy in self-assessment over time was later confirmed by Butler and Lee (2010) who reported an intervention study with 254 students aged 11–12. These research findings highlight the need for the systematic use of self-evaluation, which would enable children to develop self-assessment skills. Similar sensitivity to the regular implementation of AfL was reflected in the quotes from T1 and T5 in Figure 2.1.

I am certain that many teachers and researchers reading this section will recognise the need and value in incorporating peer support, self-monitoring and meaningful teacher evaluation into their language classes. However, they might also think that it is a challenging task and that they would appreciate practical guidance on how to achieve it. The primary language teachers in my own study shared their accounts of how they were able to continuously implement AfL into lessons through various techniques (see also Chapters 6 and 7).

Purposes for using AfL

As discussed earlier, fitness for purpose should be the main principle for selecting assessment methods. In this section, I report data which indicate that fitness for purpose guides the implementation of AfL in primary language classes.

Teachers reported that they used AfL to serve the following purposes:

(a) to set expectations (sharing aims, criteria for success and instructions):

> *success criteria which I use for speaking and writing tasks and generally any kind of instructions that require two or more sentences* (T5/INT)

> *I wanted to use it more so I started using especially success criteria for listening tasks with how they have to approach it (1) how they have to do it* (T1/INT)

(b) to monitor progress and learners' confidence about their learning:

> *I also use thumbs (1) thumbs up for good things and feeling confident and moving thumbs around for different levels of confidence* (T1/INT)

> *AfL is what helps them monitor themselves a little too* (T4/FG)

(c) to evaluate achievement (including feedback provision):

> *I used some of the techniques for marking writing such as two stars and a wish and perfect purple and green for growth* (T3/INT)

In the focus group discussion, teachers also seemed to agree that the purpose for which they use various AfL techniques guides their choice regarding the implementation of AfL. This finding is well illustrated by Extract 2.

EXTRACT 2
(From the focus group discussion)

[1] **T3:** the whole thing is about that getting them to understand what to do and then
[2] to figure out how well they have done it and it doesn't matter which techniques
[3] you use, right?
[4] **T5:** I see what you're saying but I also think that they need to know what they
[5] need to improve you know (1) like they need to know why they are getting an
[6] amber light, yes?
[7] **T3:** yeah ok (1) yes (1) yes (1) that too
[8] **T1:** it does perhaps depend on the groups or how you present it but I think my
[9] students would get a bit bored if it was just success criteria and traffic light I feel
[10] like they are more with me if I vary it a bit I mean I keep the same focus as you
[11] said it is about sharing the purpose of this lesson and then if they achieved the
[12] goal and maybe getting them to think how they can get better but I feel that it
[13] needs variety
[14] **T8:** I'll support that actually both of you I think (1) some variety is needed but in fact
[15] it's the purposes that make it all meaningful and worthwhile
[16] **T2:** so I would say that AfL is a kind of philosophy that involves measuring your
[17] students' progress minute-by-minute of the lesson on the ongoing basis and checking
[18] that they have the understanding of something and it also involves them knowing
[19] what to do in order to achieve goals
[20] **T5:** yeah I guess

Importantly, the discussion in Extract 2 indicates the teachers recognise that various techniques could be devised to ensure variety and learner engagement. However, they evidently indicate that using AfL techniques is not synonymous with using AfL. Rather, they seem to conceive of AfL as a 'philosophy' (T2/FG). According to those teachers, the overarching aim for using AfL is to develop a participatory approach to language learning in primary classrooms by providing ongoing opportunities for learners to take an active role in improving their knowledge, skills and understanding. Such conceptualisation of AfL indicates that this approach to assessment is related to other pedagogic initiatives such as cognitive acceleration programmes (Black & Wiliam, 2009), Learning How to Learn (Black et al., 2006) or Growth Mindset (Dweck, 2006).

The indication that the implementation of AfL is guided by the purpose of assessment is helpful because it provides insights into the way in which teachers make decisions about implementation of AfL. This will be useful in interpreting findings about the practical use of AfL (Part 2).

AfL techniques

As discussed in the previous section, the purposes for using AfL can be categorised into three groups: (1) to share expectations (LOs, SC and instructions); (2) to monitor progress; and (3) to evaluate achievement. The main tool which primary language teachers used to integrate the key AfL strategies into lessons were AfL techniques. T6 explained that 'there are a lot of techniques to check understanding (1) success criteria (1) yes it's good and helps to clue them in a bit into what they learn' (T6/INT).

In my own research, I observed teachers implement a variety of AfL techniques to meet each of the above purposes during primary language lessons. When teachers used AfL techniques to share LOs, they focused on clarifying expectations of outcomes and/or on explicitly raising students' awareness of what they were learning. Monitoring was done by referring to the expectations set earlier in the lesson or by providing feedback on short fragments of the learners' performance. The evaluation of achievement included self-reflection or peer and/or teacher feedback. The AfL techniques that were deployed for teacher feedback were also used for peer feedback while those that were used for self-assessment were different from the first group. An inventory of all AfL techniques which were observed to serve each of those purposes is presented in Table 2.2. Detailed descriptions and examples of the use of those AfL techniques are reported in Chapters 6 and 7.

As can be observed from the data presented in Table 2.2, some techniques were used to serve more than one purpose. For example, SC were used for all three purposes. Careful scrutiny of the field notes from lesson observations helped to explain this finding; depending on the lesson stage, the same AfL technique could be used for different purposes. Specifically, when used at the beginning of a lesson, SC helped to clarify the standard of performance expected from the students. When used while learners were working towards their LOs, SC served as a reference for teachers and learners to help them monitor children's progress. Finally, the same SC could be used to provide feedback on performance and next steps in learning, if used in the final stages of lessons. This indicates that there is a relationship between the timing of the lesson and the purposes for using AfL techniques.

As could be expected, those AfL techniques that were used to ensure that the students understood the expectations of good performance, the LOs and their teacher's instructions were observed at the initial stages of lessons or tasks. As students continued working, their attention was drawn to monitoring their ongoing performance with techniques used for providing feedback from the teacher or peer and for self-reflection. Further feedback was provided after the task was completed. The techniques used at that stage served the purpose of checking if students knew what

Table 2.2 Purposes for using AfL in primary language teaching

Purposes for using AFL	Examples of AfL techniques used for each purpose	Notes on use
To share learning objectives and expectations	Success criteria (SC) Sharing two models (STM) Increased thinking time (ITT) WALT-type questions (WALT) Mind maps (MM) Thumbs up or down (THUD) Learning partners (LP)	These AfL techniques tend to be used at the beginning of tasks or lessons. They aim predominantly to ensure that learners understand the expectations of good performance, the learning objectives and their teacher's instructions, and to gauge the extent to which learners already meet the LOs.
To monitor progress	Indicating mistakes without explanations (IME) Success criteria Thumbs up or down Learning partners	These techniques, which are used for teacher or peer feedback on ongoing performance mostly while the learners are working towards the LOs, can provide useful information about the ongoing learning and what support is needed in order for each of the learners to meet the LO.
To evaluate achievement	Two stars and a wish (TSAW) Traffic lights (TL) Colour coding (CC) Perfect purple/red to remember (PPRR) 'I can' statements (ICS) Success criteria Next steps (NS) Smiley faces (SF) Star charts (SCH) Indicating mistakes without explanations (IMWE) Find the fib (FTF) Learning partners (LP) Sheriff's star (SST) Mind maps	These techniques help teachers gauge if students know what they have learnt, and what the areas for improvement are. They tend to be used towards the end of a lesson or a task.

they had learnt, and for identifying areas for improvement for individual learners.

As can be observed in Table 2.2, most of the techniques used to monitor progress were also used to set expectations. Chapter 6 provides a detailed account of how AfL techniques were implemented for the purposes of sharing objectives and expectations and monitoring progress. Another group of techniques were used to evaluate achievement. The details of the implementation of those techniques are reported in Chapter 7.

How do primary language teachers describe the process of AfL?

The findings discussed so far correspond to all three stages in the AfL process as defined by the ARG (2002) and are summarised in Table 2.3. The evidence summarised in Table 2.3 suggests that the process of using AfL proposed in the literature can be implemented in primary language teaching.

Table 2.3 The process involved in implementing AfL in primary language teaching

AfL process defined by ARG (2002)	AfL process reported by the participating teachers
Collect evidence	Monitor progress towards LOs
Set clear objectives	Sharing LOs and SC
Provide support in reaching the objectives	Giving feedback and fostering learner agency in self and peer evaluation

With regard to the timing of AfL, the findings of my research indicate that teachers understood AfL as something that can be used predominantly during lessons. For example:

> *depending on the lesson plan we use the techniques at different parts throughout the lesson* (T7/INT)

However, three out of eight teachers also reported some use of AfL outside the classroom, for example, for homework.

> *sometimes I ask them to write the success criteria if it's for homework in their notebook* (T5/INT)

This finding resonates with the definition proposed by Thompson and Wiliam (2007: 6) who state that AfL can be used during lessons 'minute-to-minute' as well across lessons 'day-by-day'. This interpretation suggests that the timing of AfL is another area of similarity between the theoretical framework available in the literature and the participating teachers' understanding of AfL.

Summary of the Chapter

In this chapter, I have discussed definitions of AfL and formative practice available in the literature. The discussion highlighted that a commonly accepted definition of AfL does not exist. Therefore, it was vital to investigate the participating teachers' understanding of AfL in order to contextualise the findings about practical implementation. This emic perspective has been adopted in my own study.

The discussion in the first part of the chapter clarified that definitions of AfL included processes, aspects, participants, timing, beneficiaries and instruments. The conceptualisation of AfL adopted in the present volume highlights that AfL does not require any special instruments and that typical lesson activities and observations can be used to support learning (to enact the for-learning purpose of assessment) during and across lessons.

In the second part of the chapter, I discussed the findings of my study investigating primary language teachers' understanding of AfL. These strongly propose that teachers understand AfL as a type of ongoing assessment which is integrated into the teaching and learning that take place in the classroom. This conceptualisation resonates with the theoretical framework outlined in the first part of the chapter. Additionally, the findings provide useful insights into teachers' beliefs about the practical implementation of AfL. The discussion highlighted some context-specific features of AfL related to learners' low levels of proficiency in the L2 and to their age.

The findings also highlight that the participating teachers considered the purpose of assessment as the driving force behind decisions on how to use AfL in lessons. The three main purposes identified by the teachers were: sharing objectives and criteria for success; monitoring progress; and evaluating performance.

3 What Research Tells Us about the Use of AfL in Primary Language Teaching

Introduction

This chapter builds on the discussion in Chapter 2 and aims to review what is already known about the use of assessment for learning (AfL) in primary language teaching. By focusing on the reports of the practical implementation of AfL available in the research literature, I aim to achieve two goals. Firstly, I identify gaps in the current body of knowledge about the practical use of AfL in primary language classes. Secondly, I reflect on the suitability of AfL as an assessment method in primary language teaching contexts. By focusing the discussion around these two aims, I demonstrate how the study reported here contributes to this worthwhile research focus, providing new and useful insights to practitioners and researchers.

Assessment in Primary Language Contexts

In this section, AfL is placed in the bigger picture of various assessment practices used with primary-aged language learners. The review of the literature has indicated that published research on assessment in primary language contexts focused on the following:

- The assessment of language proficiency at the end of the primary phase (Edelenbos & Vinje, 2000; Johnstone, 2000).
- The use of the Common European Framework of Reference (CEFR) (Council of Europe, 2001, 2020) to aid portfolio assessment (Hasselgreen, 2005) or in large-scale standardised tests (Bailey, 2005).
- Classroom-based assessment (CBA) (Hill & McNamara, 2012), including teachers' competence to conduct it (Edelenbos & Kubanek-German, 2004; Hawe & Dixon, 2014; Tsagari, 2016) and teachers' practice (Butler, 2009; Hild & Nikolov, 2010).
- The formative function of assessment (Gattullo, 2000; Hasselgreen, 2000).
- Self-assessment (Butler & Lee, 2006, 2010; Little, 2009).

Some of the studies quoted in this section focused on the summative function of assessment. It is believed that reviewing such studies alongside those which investigated the formative function of assessment will offer the opportunity to identify the insights that they provide into language learning and progression in childhood, vital for in-depth understanding of how assessment can support learning. The studies that investigated formative assessment will provide insights with direct relevance to the first aim of this chapter.

Assessment at the end of primary education

Research into summative assessment at the end of primary education suggests that assessment results are linked to classroom teaching. In particular, it has been argued that 'setting clear goals, sequencing materials, frequent questions to monitor progress in the learning process, opportunity to learn, testing and quality feedback are all important characteristics from which early foreign language learning can benefit tremendously' (Edelenbos & Vinje, 2000: 160). These findings suggest that some of the processes inherent in AfL (clarifying learning goals, guiding learning through success criteria and questioning or providing formative feedback) can benefit foreign language learning (FLL) in childhood.

Another important factor which can facilitate language learning is the time of exposure to a second language (L2) (Edelenbos & Vinje, 2000). Such a finding corroborates the indication that a longer time of exposure may be beneficial to primary-aged language learners, who tend to learn implicitly (e.g. Muñoz, 2006, discussed in Chapter 4). Both studies (Edelenbos & Vinje, 2000; Muñoz, 2006) are especially informative as they provide longitudinal perspectives and because they were conducted with large cohorts of learners (1000 12-year-olds and 2000 8 to 11-year-olds, respectively).

Another study that investigated foreign language (FL) assessment at the end of primary school (Johnstone, 2000: 140) suggested that there is a need for 'more consensus on the aims and intended outcomes' of primary language programmes and for research which would help to establish what should constitute various levels of proficiency. Such calls for clarifying the construct of assessment in language education, which were echoed by Butler (2009), Mihaljević Djigunović (2011) and Cojocnean (2012), were partially addressed by studies which explored the use of the CEFR at primary school level.

Construct of assessment

In Europe, the attempts to develop a construct of assessment have included investigations into possible adaptations of the CEFR for use in primary contexts. While arguably a lot more research in this area is needed, the studies published in recent years have indicated that:

(1) CEFR descriptors at the two lowest levels (A1 and A2) have been adapted for use in portfolio assessment in a number of European countries (Goodier, 2018a, 2018b; Little, 2009), for example, England and Wales (Cameron, 2003), France (Debyser & Tagliante, 2001) and Ireland (Little, 2005).

(2) CEFR descriptors up to B2+ were developed for reading and writing tasks at secondary school level, and were later adapted for primary school learners, in a unique study in Norway (Hasselgreen, 2005).

(3) Effective language assessment in primary contexts should provide positive feedback, highlighting to learners what they have already achieved and that task design should captivate learners' attention and allow for some support to be provided to them (Hasselgreen, 2005; Hasselgreen & Caudwell, 2016).

(4) When marking the writing of 13 to 16-year-olds against the CEFR descriptors, raters supplemented the CEFR criteria with additional criteria not included in the CEFR scales (Huhta *et al.*, 2014), pointing to the subjective human factor playing a role in making judgements about learning.

(5) A number of summative tests which claim to assess language proficiency at different levels of the CEFR have been developed commercially for use with primary-aged language learners by various examination providers, for example, Cambridge Assessment English, Pearson Global Scale of English for Young Learners, Trinity or City and Guilds English for Speakers of Other Languages (ESOL).

(6) The CEFR descriptors do not allow for capturing the slow incremental progress made by primary-aged language learners (Enever, 2011).

(7) Tasks included in tests used to assess primary language learning demonstrate a mismatch between stated teaching aims and the knowledge, skills and understanding actually assessed (Rea-Dickins & Rixon, 1999).

The above findings suggest that CEFR descriptors, which were developed for adult learners, can be adapted to primary contexts to serve as predefined learning outcomes. Recently, Goodier (2018a, 2018b) provided a useful set of practical examples of how CEFR descriptors have been translated into specific learning objectives for learners aged 7–10 and 11–15 in various European language portfolios. Additionally, Nikolov and Mihaljević Djigunović (2011: 109) warn that '(l)ow proficiency levels need to be defined and described along a continuum in small steps so that children's relatively slow development can be documented'. As is argued in Chapters 4 and 5, such steps should also take into account children's first language (L1) literacy levels as well as their cognitive, social and emotional development. This would help to align assessment practice with the foci of teaching programmes, as called for by Inbar-Lourie and

Shohamy (2009) and Cojocnean (2012). This seems especially important because assessment tasks used with primary-aged learners 'do not always reflect the range of activities within the primary FL classroom; neither are they necessarily able to capture the different aspects of language use that are taught at primary level' (Rea-Dickins & Rixon, 1999: 97).

A lack of clarity on what should be assessed in primary language programmes was also reported in Japan, South Korea and Taiwan (Butler, 2009). Although those countries' governments provided summative tests to be used to evaluate learning at the primary level, the details of the tests were not released to the public. As a result, it was impossible to analyse the criteria on which the assessment tools were based.

The need to develop a clear construct of language assessment in primary contexts is of importance for AfL because having clearly defined learning outcomes would help to make judgements about learning. Such judgements could be used to provide students with individualised formative feedback and guidance on the next steps to take in order to achieve the expected learning outcomes.

Diagnostic competence

In order to be able to make accurate judgements about learners' progress, teachers must develop their diagnostic competence (Huhta et al., 2014). It has been reported that primary language teachers are rarely experts in language assessment (Hasselgreen, 2005; Johnstone, 2000; Rea-Dickins & Gardner, 2000). Additionally, it has been recognised that there is a need to develop teachers' diagnostic competence (Edelenbos & Kubanek-German, 2004) and to upskill teachers in order to help them conduct effective CBA (Butler, 2009). Recent studies which focused on the professional development (PD) of teachers (Prošić-Santovac et al., 2019; Shin & Crandall, 2019) confirmed the need for teacher training in order to support the effective implementation of AfL.

Classroom-based assessment

As indicated by studies reviewed so far, in primary contexts there is a close relationship between assessment and teaching and learning. A particular type of assessment which is integrated into the classroom practice is referred to as classroom-based assessment. It is defined as 'any reflection by teachers (and/or learners) on the qualities of a learner's (or group of learners') work and the use of that information by teachers (and/or learners) for teaching, learning (feedback), reporting, management or socialization purposes' (Hill & McNamara, 2012: 396). This definition of CBA brings together the two functions of assessment: summative (evaluating what children have already learnt) and formative (advancing learning). Therefore, it will be interesting to review what the research

Table 3.1 Research on teachers' practice and competency in classroom-based assessment in primary language contexts

Focus of the study	Sample	Context	References
Processes of classroom-based assessment	3 teachers and their students aged 11–13	Primary (Year 6) and secondary (Year 7) schools, Victoria, Australia	Hill and McNamara (2012)
Nature of classroom assessment	9 inner-city schools	England	Rea-Dickins and Gardner (2000)
Use of classroom-based assessment	8 teachers, teaching 10–12 year olds	Primary schools, Greece and Cyprus	Tsagari (2016)
Teachers reports on use of classroom-based assessment	4 primary school teachers of English	Primary schools, Romania	Cojocnean (2012)
Assessment practices	114 primary school teachers	Primary schools, Serbia	Prošić-Santovac et al. (2019)
Teacher's diagnostic competence	49 lessons from 10 schools and the teachers who delivered the lessons	Primary schools, Germany and the Netherlands	Edelenbos and Kubanek-German (2004)
Assessment in in-service PD for teachers	20 teachers of learners aged 7–12	Private language school, Peru	Shin and Crandall (2019)

into CBA in primary language contexts reveals about formative assessment. A list of studies which explored this area is provided in Table 3.1.

The studies quoted in Table 3.1 have revealed that:

- A relatively small amount of time tends to be devoted to formative assessment in lessons (Edelenbos & Kubanek-German, 2004; Tsagari, 2016).
- Although teachers recognised that assessment should be part of every lesson, the majority did not follow that in practice (Prošić-Santovac et al., 2019).
- CBA can occur during *assessment opportunities* in lessons (Hill & McNamara, 2012). Assessment opportunities are defined as 'any actions, interactions or artefacts (planned or unplanned, deliberate or unconscious, explicit or embedded) which have the potential to provide information on the qualities of a learner's (or group of learners') performance' (Hill & McNamara, 2012: 398).
- In some primary contexts, teachers consider oral assessment with the focus on communication not only suitable but also desirable (Cojocnean, 2012), while in others they tend to evaluate language skills, grammar and pronunciation in isolation, neglecting communicative competence (Prošić-Santovac et al., 2019).

- Teachers use data from classroom interactions to make judgements about learning (Rea-Dickins & Gardner, 2000).
- Investigations into CBA should account for what teachers do, what information they collect to inform assessment and teachers' and learners' theories and beliefs about learning and assessment (Hill & McNamara, 2012).
- CBA tends to be regarded as a low-stakes assessment (Rea-Dickins & Gardner, 2000).

The outcomes of this body of research confirm the importance of teacher agency in assessment, as discussed in the previous sections. My own research that lies at the heart of much of the discussion in this volume has been sensitive to this outcome by contextualising the analysis of the use of AfL with learners aged 7–11 (Part 2) through their teachers' understanding of AfL (Chapter 2).

Furthermore, research has revealed that CBA serves predominantly the summative function. It would be interesting to explore what actually happens when the formative function of assessment is implemented in the classroom. The next section explores that focus, aiming to review what is known about the practical use of AfL and factors which can facilitate or inhibit implementation.

Assessment for Learning in the Primary Language Classroom

The available published research on AfL in primary language contexts has focused on exploring self-assessment (Butler & Lee, 2006, 2010) and teachers' practice in the classroom (Gattullo, 2000; Porter, 2019) and evaluating the strengths and weaknesses in FL performance (Hasselgreen, 2000). An overview of the studies is provided in Table 3.2.

Table 3.2 Empirical studies into AfL in primary language teaching

Focus of the study	Sample	Location of primary schools	References
Use of AfL	4 teachers and 70 learners aged 8–10	Italy	Gattullo (2000)
Integrating AfL into FL (French) instruction	45 learners aged 9–11	England	Porter (2019)
On-task and off-task self-assessment	70 learners aged 9–10 and 81 learners aged 11–12	Seoul, South Korea	Butler and Lee (2006)
Effectiveness of self-assessment	254 learners aged 11–12 in 2 schools	Seoul, South Korea	Butler and Lee (2010)
Measuring strengths and weaknesses in FL performance	1000 learners aged 11–12 in 34 schools	Norway	Hasselgreen (2000)

Source: Adapted from Britton (2015) and updated.

As is evident from Table 3.2, a very limited number of studies examined the use of AfL in primary language contexts. Therefore, this literature review was extended to incorporate similar instructed educational contexts. Two categories which are key to defining the primary language teaching context were used: students' age and FL as the subject of tuition. This resulted in identifying two relevant contexts: (1) primary school English as an additional language (EAL) or modern foreign languages (MFL) teaching; and (2) the teaching of English as a foreign language (TEFL).

Classroom implementation of AfL in those two contexts has been investigated predominantly through small-scale studies which focused on the use of AfL alongside other assessment practices (Ahlquist, 2019; Rea-Dickins, 2001; Rea-Dickins & Gardner, 2000); feedback on writing (Lee, 2007; Lee & Coniam, 2013); classroom interactions (Leung & Mohan, 2004; Rea-Dickins, 2006); self-assessment (Dann, 2002); and students' evaluative competence (Hawe & Dixon, 2014). An inventory of those studies is presented in Appendix 2.

Implementation of AfL

Outcomes of the body of research quoted above suggest that AfL can be and is used in primary language classrooms (Gattullo, 2000; Porter, 2019; Tsagari, 2016). However, it has also been highlighted that summative assessment and testing still dominate primary language teaching (Cojocnean, 2012; Edelenbos & Kubanek-German, 2004; Prošić-Santovac *et al.*, 2019; Rixon, 2013; Tsagari, 2016).

The picture that emerges suggests that there are a number of challenges to the effective implementation of AfL. First, in some countries the inhibiting factors comprise externally mandated policies or exams (Butler, 2009; Carless, 2005; Cheng *et al.*, 2004; Gattullo, 2000; Lee, 2007; Lee & Coniam, 2013). But even in those contexts where the use of AfL has been encouraged though policy, classroom practice does not seem to follow consistently (Lefever, 2019). Outside of language education, Rixon (2017) discusses the introduction of AfL into mainstream schools in England as an example of the successful implementation of policy into practice. She explains that the main reason for its success was the 'great responsibility that senior school staff there currently have taken on for observation and coaching of colleagues' (Rixon, 2017: 90). If a similar situation was to occur in language education, it would necessitate buy-in, expertise and commitment from senior leaders across various primary language teaching contexts globally.

Perhaps the challenges to implementation could also be explained with findings of studies which suggest that while primary language teachers tend to be motivated to use AfL in their lessons (Butler & Lee, 2010; Gattullo, 2000; Hill & McNamara, 2012), little practical advice is available to them to inform implementation (Ellis & Rixon, 2019). Such practical guidance seems important because it has been reported that teachers need training and experience of using AfL in order to incorporate it into their practice (Lee & Coniam, 2013; Little *et al.*, 2017; Prošić-Santovac *et al.*, 2019; Shin & Crandall, 2019). In contexts where there was not enough practical guidance on the implementation of AfL, teachers were observed to misinterpret the appropriate assessment mode, for example as a series of mini-summative tests (Swaffield, 2011). As a result, calls have been made for practitioners to lead in the development of domain-specific models of AfL implementation through their reflective practice and PD opportunities (Ellis & Rixon, 2019; Jones, 2014; Rea-Dickins & Gardner, 2000; Rixon, 2017). My own research aimed to address this gap by reporting on how AfL was practically implemented in lessons with primary-aged learners, thereby providing valuable and timely new insights (see Part 2).

Relationships between pedagogy and AfL

It is now generally recognised that assessment practices should be aligned with teaching methods appropriate for learners' ages (Gattullo, 2000; Hasselgreen, 2000; McKay, 2006; Lefever, 2019). Therefore, it seems especially important to analyse whether AfL techniques can be integrated within the pedagogical approaches used in primary language teaching (see Chapter 8). This would be best achieved if multiple reports of practical implementation were published by researchers and practitioners. In this section, I present the picture which emerges from the available research, while recognising that much more empirical evidence is needed in order to develop practical models of implementation.

The outcomes of a large-scale study with 1000 learners in Norway (Hasselgreen, 2000) suggest that for assessment to be appropriate for use with primary-aged language learners, it should be conducted in a series of shorter tasks over a period of time (two weeks in the Norwegian study), rather than as a one-off task or test. Furthermore, based on the findings which indicated that the participants were highly engaged in the activities requiring them to find a missing elephant, Hasselgreen (2000) convincingly argued that assessment materials should be contextualised and engaging for children. Hasselgreen (2000) also observed that learners were motivated to participate in the self-assessment component, reflecting a growing sensitivity in the field for learner agency in the classroom and the assessment process (Ellis & Rixon, 2019).

Research suggests that the process of implementing AfL involves an explicit planning stage before implementation, as well as the monitoring and dissemination of results (Rea-Dickins, 2001). The outcomes of the monitoring of collected data feed into the planning process, creating *an assessment cycle* (Rea-Dickins, 2001). In other contexts, however, teachers were also observed to use it in an incidental manner, in addition to the preplanned use (Ahlquist, 2019). As it appears possible for the incidental use of AfL to provide data necessary to plan further steps in learning, it seems that such use could also successfully serve the formative function of assessment. Both types of use were shown to be compatible with primary language teaching (Ahlquist, 2019; Rea-Dickins, 2001).

Self and peer assessment

Another theme which is evident in research on the practical implementation of AfL is the use of self-assessment with children. The outcomes of that body of research suggest that over time and with training, learners aged 11–12 are able to develop accuracy in self-assessment (Butler & Lee, 2010). A different study (Butler & Lee, 2006) demonstrated that learner judgements made directly after completing a task (on-task assessment) were more accurate than those unrelated to a specific task (off-task). This suggests that teachers should aim to incorporate self-assessment within or directly after tasks in order to aid accuracy of learners' self-evaluations. This corroborates the reports from mainstream primary classrooms, which suggest that AfL should and can be integrated into teaching and learning (Dann, 2002; Ellis & Rixon, 2019).

The outcomes of Butler and Lee's (2006) study also indicated that older learners (11 to 12-year-olds) were able to self-assess more accurately than their younger counterparts (9–10). This finding is consistent with the development of metacognitive abilities in childhood, as discussed in Chapter 4.

The effective use of self-assessment techniques can help primary-aged learners evaluate the extent to which they meet predefined learning objectives. Little (2009) argues convincingly that greater use of self-assessment as part of portfolio assessment could benefit language learning. He discusses classroom examples to illustrate how CEFR descriptors could be used in primary school contexts to guide self-assessment.

The use of AfL and language skills

Another important strand of research has suggested that oral interactions (Leung & Mohan, 2004; Rea-Dickins, 2006) and feedback on writing (Lee & Coniam, 2013) can provide practical opportunities for implementing AfL in language classrooms.

Research which focused on analysing interactions between teachers and learners has indicated that the formative and summative functions of assessment not only co-occur during assessment episodes, but more importantly can complement one another (Rea-Dickins, 2006). That study suggested that language learning could happen through assessment during interactions. This corroborates outcomes of research which proposed that teachers can support learning by eliciting reasons for answers given by children as young as 8–9 years of age (Leung & Mohan, 2004). Classroom research has also indicated that learner–learner interactions provide opportunities for learner agency in feedback provision and that this could support learning (Leung & Mohan, 2004). Consequently, it would seem of value to investigate teacher–learner and learner–learner interactions which occur during assessment to identify whether and how learning can take effect through those interactions. Therefore, in my own research I have analysed interactions which occurred while AfL techniques were being used.

Initial evidence points to the opportunities for using feedback on writing to implement the formative function of assessment in a language classroom (Lee & Coniam, 2013). However, studies have also indicated that requirements to prepare learners for external examination could lead to the summative function of assessment taking precedence (Carless, 2005; Lee, 2007). Lee and Coniam (2013) suggest that learners in their study might have ignored formative feedback when presented with summative assessment results. Their interpretation is consistent with Butler (1988) who reported that learners were able to focus on moving learning forward more effectively when provided with comments alone, but were more likely to ignore the formative feedback when it was accompanied by summative grades.

Similar to the research on interactions, investigations into the use of AfL with writing tasks point to the importance of developing learner evaluative competence and suggest that this could be done through providing formative feedback (Hawe & Dixon, 2014). This suggests that consistency in the use of AfL over time might be needed before the impact of AfL on learning can be observed. To explore this area further, longitudinal studies are needed.

Summary of the Chapter

In this chapter, I have reviewed studies which explored assessment in primary language contexts. As the number of studies into AfL conducted in such contexts is limited, the review also included relevant studies from EAL and MFL contexts with primary-aged learners as well as from adolescent FL contexts.

The outcomes of the review highlight several features which assessment suitable for use with primary-aged children should contain. First, it should be incorporated into classroom processes through setting clear goals, monitoring progress towards those goals, frequent questioning and providing quality feedback. Secondly, assessment tasks should be contextualised through teaching activities and should happen in every lesson, which teachers seem to find challenging to implement. Thirdly, attainment at the primary school level can best be captured as a series of small incremental steps. Finally, in order to implement assessment in an age-appropriate manner as suggested by the first three outcomes of the review, teachers need to develop their diagnostic competence. This can enable them to make accurate judgements and plan appropriate support for their learners. It seems that the first three of the above features of assessment suitable for primary-aged language learners are reflected in the nature of AfL, as discussed in Chapter 2. However, at the time of writing this book, there is very little empirical evidence reported in literature which could confirm that. My own research, reported throughout this volume, provides those much-needed insights into the way in which these three features were enacted in lessons (see Part 2).

Studies investigating the use of AfL in lessons indicate that it can be enacted though self and peer assessment. Encouragingly, research suggests that learners can and do make accurate self-assessments, especially when assessment directly follows the task. Findings presented in Chapters 6 and 7 demonstrate how AfL was used in primary language classes which I observed not only for self and peer assessment but also to set clear goals, monitor progress and provide quality feedback.

An emerging strand of research points to an interesting relationship between the use of AfL and the teaching of productive skills. This focus is explored in Chapter 8. A discussion of the findings provides interesting explanations of the possible reasons for the usefulness of AfL when teaching productive skills.

Studies into the use of AfL in primary language teaching suggest that several inhibiting factors affect the practical implementation of AfL. These include externally mandated policies or exams, and little practical advice on the effective implementation of AfL in primary language teaching. The second inhibiting factor is directly addressed by the main aim of this volume. Detailed reports of practical implementation which provide useful guidance to practitioners are reported in Chapters 6 and 7. Further insights into factors which may facilitate or inhibit the implementation of AfL are discussed in Chapter 9.

Before we move on to discussing the practical implementation of AfL in primary language classroom, it is important to reflect on the specific characteristics of primary-aged children as language learners. Due to their age, children differ from adolescent and adult learners in terms of their cognitive, social and emotional development. These areas are discussed in Chapters 4 and 5, respectively.

4 Assessment and Cognitive Development in Childhood

> It is axiomatic that the way that children learn best be reflected in the way that they are assessed, and the knowledge of how young learners learn language is therefore fundamental for those involved in the language assessment of young learners.
>
> McKay (2006: 47)

Introduction

McKay (2006) highlights that in order to assess children in an age-appropriate manner, teachers and other professionals who are involved in language assessment need to have sound knowledge of how children learn. Consequently, it would seem important for a book on language assessment at the primary school level to consider what current research tells us about the way in which children learn languages. Such insights are helpful in deciding not only how to conduct assessment in an age-appropriate manner but also what progress can be expected, and consequently what should be assessed, in primary language programmes. Therefore, in Chapters 4 and 5, I provide an overview of the knowledge base which should inform decisions about researching, planning and conducting language assessment in primary classes.

It is important to note that while there seems to be agreement that age is a significant factor in language learning, 'scholars have not been able to establish the exact pattern or nature of age-related change, let alone identify the specific causes and mediators of the process' (Dörnyei, 2009a: 233). While, as Dörnyei (2009a) rightly argues, we have yet much to learn about the way in which age-related factors can affect language learning, research has so far indicated that age is important in many areas of cognitive development which play a significant role in language learning. These include: critical periods (CPs) and sensitive periods (SPs) (Bialystok & Hakuta, 1999; Long, 2013); memory (Wen, 2012; Wen & Skehan, 2011); attention (Bialystok, 2001); and metacognition (Flavell *et al.*, 2000).

In this chapter, I adopt the cognitive constructivist perspective on learning to explore the relevant findings of research in each of these four areas. The aim of the discussion is to tease out those considerations that should be taken into account by professionals who are involved in language assessment of primary-aged learners in order to satisfy the condition proposed by McKay (2006). It is important that all these implications are considered collectively as they are mutually complimentary.

A detailed discussion of the research into various aspects of cognitive development in childhood is beyond the scope of this volume and has been discussed elsewhere (e.g. Pinter, 2011). In order not to replicate existing publications but rather to offer a new perspective on applying the existing body of knowledge to assessment, only research which has implications for language assessment at the primary school level is discussed in this chapter. This satisfies the aims of this volume.

Critical Periods

Research which offers insights into the relationship between age and language learning has investigated the claims that the human brain loses plasticity as it matures and that 'children are better second language learners than adults because their brains are specially organized to learn language, whereas those of adults are not' (Bialystok & Hakuta, 1999: 176). This is referred to as the critical period hypothesis (CPH). The CPH proposes that there are *critical periods* (CPs) for developing specific language areas of phonology, morphosyntax, lexis and collocations. CPs are understood to have three stages of varied sensitivity to a certain type of learning: the onset (the beginning of sensitivity), the peak (when sensitivity is high) and the offset (a decline in sensitivity). Research from second language (L2) contexts suggests that with maturation, a more gradual decline towards a levelling out can be observed at the offset stage rather than a termination of sensitivity or the ability to learn an L2 or a foreign language (FL) (Long, 2013).

The length of the three stages of CPs may vary for pronunciation and accent; morphosyntactic competency; or lexis and collocations. Research which investigated the CPH suggests that if exposure to an L2 occurs before the age of 12, a learner is more likely to develop a native-like accent and pronunciation (Flege *et al.*, 1995, 1999; Long, 1990, 2005) as well as lexis and knowledge of collocations (Munnich & Landau, 2010; Spadaro, 2013). The above studies indicate that the peak periods occur between the ages of 0 and 6. With respect to the development of morphosyntactic skills, the offset period seems to be longer and has been shown to last until the ages of 16 or 17 (DeKeyser, 2000; Long, 1990).

Sensitive Periods

Studies which account for contextual factors indicate that people whose exposure to an L2 began in adolescence might be able to achieve very high levels of proficiency, given favourable conditions. These include the quality of the language environment (Jia & Fuse, 2007), specifically the 'amount of exposure, usually operationalised as length of residence (LOR), and the proportions of L1 to L2 use' (Long, 2013: 4). Consequently, it could be argued that the notion of a CP does not adequately capture the process of how age is related to language learning because it claims that after the offset stage, the various language competencies listed above are unlikely to develop. Instead, Long (2013) argues that the term *sensitive period* (SP) describes the differences in the ability to develop competency in an L2 or an FL more accurately than CPs. Bialystok and Hakuta (1999) suggest that SPs could be considered a weaker version of CPs.

The notion of SPs has implications for learning and assessment. Importantly, the existence of SPs proposes that learners whose exposure to an L2 commences after a certain age may be less successful at developing native-like proficiency (Granena & Long, 2013b). By definition, children in primary schools are younger than 12. Research into SPs suggests that at this age, children are better equipped to learn phonology, lexis and collocations than older learners (e.g. Long, 2005; Spadaro, 2013). Therefore, primary language education seems to offer a unique opportunity for developing learners' knowledge and skills in these areas, while morphosyntax can be learned effectively later, up to the age of 16 or 17 (e.g. DeKeyser, 2000). In order to monitor progress and evaluate achievements in phonology, lexis and collocations, these areas should be included in language teaching and assessment at the primary school level. Morphosyntax could become a more prominent focus of teaching and assessment of adolescents. This conclusion is supported by the outcomes of research into the rate of progression (e.g. Muñoz, 2006) discussed in the next section.

IMPLICATION #1: CONSTRUCT OF ASSESSMENT IN THE PRIMARY LANGUAGE TEACHING CONTEXT

Research into SPs and CPs suggests that learners are more capable of developing their competencies in phonology, lexis and collocations if they are exposed to an L2 before the age of 12. Therefore, it follows that these competencies should be taught and assessed at primary school level. Instruction in morphosyntactic knowledge and assessment in this area could be postponed until children are aged 12–16 or 17. This has significant implications for the construct of assessment, which is to say that it indicates what should be assessed in language education at the primary school level.

In addition to providing important guidance for the construct of assessment in primary language education, research into SPs also raises several pragmatic questions. These include, but are not limited to, the relationship between a teacher's language proficiency or accent and learners' development of phonological competency; the amount of exposure to an L2 that would be required and over what period of time in order to secure the benefits offered by SPs; and whether such an amount of exposure could actually be achieved in the instructed context, where teaching time is often limited to several hours per week. Discussing all the above questions in detail is beyond the scope of this volume. Therefore, only the research that is relevant to the focus of the current chapter is included in the review. This includes a focus on the rate of progression and ultimate attainment.

Ultimate Attainment

Ultimate attainment in primary language education can be a problematic concept for two reasons. Firstly, as Nikolov and Mihaljević Djigunović (2011: 97) rightly point out, 'YLs are not expected to achieve native levels of proficiency'. Secondly, research has yet to provide clear insights into what native proficiency looks like for children. For example, a child's non-grammatical output could be accepted as correct, if native speakers (NS) of the same age tend to make similar mistakes. Language corpora for different age groups would enable comparisons of the language produced by primary-aged learners with that of their peer NSs. Comparing non-native speaker (NNS) children interlanguages to those of adult NSs does not seem to be helpful in evaluating their ultimate attainment.

Available research into ultimate attainment tends to examine the language proficiency of adults and analyse it in the context of learners' acquisition history. Although the findings of this body of research are rather complex, they corroborate studies which indicate that exposure to an L2 in childhood and adolescence can be beneficial in the long-term development of pronunciation and accent (Flege *et al.*, 1995, 1999; Long, 2005) and of grammar (DeKeyser, 2000). Typically, age of onset (AO) is adopted as the variable that can predict ultimate attainment. Most research in this area has aimed to document SPs but rather limited research attention has been paid to the factors that could shape those SPs (Granena & Long, 2013a). Consequently, although we can describe many changes that occur within sensitivity to various areas of the language, we do not have enough evidence to demonstrate whether maturational processes in the brain account for the SPs. In fact, a study by Granena and Long (2013a) demonstrates that individual differences (IDs), such as aptitude, can account for some of the variation in language attainment, especially in phonology; and in the case of participants who started learning an L2 (Spanish) at the age of 16 or later, also with lexis and collocations. Another strand of research suggests that favourable contextual factors can be a stronger predictor than age in the acquisition of pronunciation and accent (Moyer, 2004) or grammar (Jia & Fuse, 2007). In instructed contexts, Enever (2011) reported that contextual factors and IDs can facilitate or inhibit progress in language learning.

IMPLICATION #2: FACTORS WHICH AFFECT ATTAINMENT IN PRIMARY LANGUAGE LEARNING

Children's language attainment can be affected by multiple factors which include length of exposure to an L2, IDs and contextual factors. Therefore, teachers and researchers should at the very least be aware of this when evaluating learners' attainment. Cognitive IDs include aptitude, memory and attention; and affective IDs include: motivation, anxiety and self-concept (see Chapter 5 for affective IDs).

Although research findings indicate that AO is an important factor in predicting ultimate attainment, it seems crucial to also consider the context in which AO occurs. Of special interest to the focus of this volume is the distinction between naturalistic settings and instructed FL contexts. The majority of research on SPs has been conducted in contexts where language is acquired in a naturalistic setting, whereas primary languages are predominantly taught in instructed contexts, sometimes with limited time of exposure. Therefore, the findings of available studies on ultimate attainment, which are referred to in the current section, cannot be applied directly to primary language teaching. Nonetheless, it is important that we consider them, as they provide useful insights into language learning in childhood. More relevant to the focus of this volume, in terms of contextual similarity, seem to be studies which have investigated the rates of progress of early and late beginners in instructed contexts. These are reviewed in the following section.

Rate of Progress

With the notable exception of the Early Language Learning in Europe (ELLiE) study (Enever, 2011), research has yet to explore what is realistically possible to achieve in instructed language teaching at the primary school level. The outcomes of this longitudinal, large-scale study, spanning seven European countries and over 1000 participants aged 7–10, suggest that children make slow progress. Significantly, the researchers argued that Common European Framework of Reference (CEFR) descriptors do not allow for capturing such progress. This finding is consistent with Nikolov and Mihaljevic Djigunovic (2011: 109) who convincingly argue that '(l)ow proficiency levels need to be defined and described along a continuum in small steps so that children's relatively slow development can be documented'. The authors add that such descriptors should also take into account the development of learners' first language (L1) literacy levels. Decidedly, further research is needed in order to guide the development of descriptors for such small steps. It should be noted that some work in this area has been done, for example, in Norway for adolescents (Hasselgreen, 2000, 2005) or for learners aged 6–14 as part of the Pearson Global Scale of English for Young Learners (Benigno & de Jong, 2016).

Findings from research that focused on evaluating attainment at the primary school level suggest that children who start FL instruction in primary school can meet or exceed attainment targets, achieving the A1 level of the CEFR or above after two years of instruction (Baumert *et al.*, 2020). These outcomes can be interpreted as evidence of the effectiveness of primary language learning programmes.

Although research to date offers only limited insights into what attainment could be expected in instructed primary language pro-grammes, the rate of progress remains an important consideration in dis-cussing assessment. Related research (Burstall *et al.*, 1974; Muñoz, 2006; Pfenninger & Singleton, 2017) suggests that older beginners may have an initial advantage over their younger counterparts. Therefore, it would be logical to expect different amounts of progress over the same period of time between young learners and adolescents.

Burstall *et al.* (1974) compared the performance of students who started language instruction at the ages of 8 and 11. They administered speaking, listening, reading and writing tests to learners of modern foreign languages (MFL) in England. Their findings indicate that at 13, younger beginners outperformed their older counterparts in speaking and listening; however, by the age of 16, only performance on listening tests remained better. Muñoz (2006) reported a large-scale longitudinal study, known as the Barcelona Age Factor (BAF), which tested the English lan-guage performance of circa 2000 learners who, similar to the participants in Burstall *et al.*'s (1974) study, started instruction at the ages of 8 or 11. Measures in the four skills (speaking, listening, reading and writing) were administered after 200, 416 and 726 hours of learning. The findings indicate that initially, older beginners outperformed their younger coun-terparts on all measures. As the number of hours of exposure increased, younger beginners improved their performance on tests which evaluated implicit learning. However, it should be noted that in the BAF study, the majority of the comparisons which were made between the two cohorts took place when learners were at different ages. Specifically, only at one point in the study was a comparison made between the attainment of the two cohorts when the learners were of the same age. This was at the end of Year 7. At that stage, early beginners had received 416 hours of instruction over 5 years, whereas late beginners had received 200 hours of instruction over 2 years. The results obtained at that stage indicated that the later starters did not catch up on any measure with the early starters. Baumert *et al.* (2020: 6) argue convincingly that when achievement was compared after 726 hours of learning (in Year 9 for the early starters and in Year 12 for the later starters) 'an estimate of whether the learning rate of later starters offset the greater exposure of early starters was not possible' due to the difference in learner ages. Therefore, the results of the BAF study remain open to the interpretation that factors other than the age of starting instruction may account for the differences in achievement.

Neither Burstall *et al.* (1974) nor Muñoz (2006) evaluated affective and cognitive IDs or contextual factors (e.g. the quality of provision; transition between different phases of schooling: from primary to secondary school; or exposure to an FL outside the classroom). Therefore, the findings remain open to the interpretation that IDs or contextual factors, other than length of exposure, could have influenced the findings. For example, Enever (2011) reports that, in contexts where primary-aged children were exposed to an FL outside the classroom, higher rates of progress could be observed. More recently, Pfenninger and Singleton (2019) proposed that factors such as (bi)literacy skills, language learning motivation, transition from primary to secondary school and the intensity of FL instruction can account for progress better than an early start in FL instruction. Biliteracy and the quality of provision in secondary school were also identified as important factors in a large-scale study in Germany (Baumert *et al.*, 2020).

Pfenninger and Singleton (2017) reported on a longitudinal study in which they compared the achievement of two cohorts of learners who started English instruction at the ages of 8 and 13. The results indicate an advantage for the later starters on measures of linguistic accuracy in written and oral production, while the earlier beginners outperformed the other group on language complexity and receptive vocabulary measures. These findings point to a complex nature of progress and its relationship to the age when instruction starts. They seem consistent with the outcomes of the BAF study in which Muñoz (2006: 32) concluded that children who started learning English at the age of 8 'seem to favour and be favoured by implicit learning'. However, Baumert *et al.* (2020) note that the initial advantage of older starters reported by Pfenninger and Singleton (2017) could be explained by family or learner characteristics (e.g. socioeconomic background), or the fact that secondary schools did not adapt their teaching to account for language learning at the primary level. Since early and late beginners followed the same programme, with the same objectives, delivered by the same teachers at the secondary school level, Baumert *et al.* (2020: 13) convincingly argue that 'findings that may suggest levelling-off effects (…) are potentially caused by a lack of adaptivity in secondary language instruction'. This highlights that many factors contribute to progress in language learning. In addition to starting age of instruction, these include transition between school phases (primary to secondary), contextual factors (including the socioeconomic situation of the learner's family) and bilingualism and (bi) literacy (Baumert *et al.*, 2020).

Nevertheless, it is important to note that younger children initially seem to progress at a somewhat slower rate than adolescents. Muñoz (2006) provides a partial explanation for this outcome, suggesting that schooling and the development of morphosyntactic ability could provide an initial advantage in language learning. This has implications for assessment. Therefore, in the following section, I consider the relationship between language assessment and literacy development.

> ### IMPLICATION #3: MEASURING PROGRESS
>
> Research suggests that while young learners' rate of progress may be slower than that of adolescents, they can expect to achieve higher language proficiency in the long term (ultimate attainment), providing that secondary schools adapt their teaching appropriately to account for the gains of primary language learning. Assessment methods should account for the slow rate of progress. Efforts should be made especially to evidence the small steps in learning, and to account for the development of learners' L1 literacy levels.

Literacy and Schooling

Several studies from various primary contexts have so far indicated that there exists a relationship between progress in language learning and learners' L1 literacy levels, which children tend to develop at school (Dimroth, 2008; García-Mayo & García-Lecumberri, 2003; Knell *et al.*, 2007; Mihaljević Djigunović, 2010; Wilden & Porsch, 2014).

In Germany, Wilden and Porsch (2014) assessed the listening and reading skills of children who started instruction in English at the ages of 6.5 and 8. The assessment took place when children were aged 9–10. A comparison of the progress made by the two groups indicated that development of reading skills in an L1 was related to foreign language learning (FLL). These findings are consistent with Muñoz (2006). Further evidence of the importance of the development of L1 literacy for FLL was provided by Mihaljević Djigunović (2010), Knell *et al.* (2007) and Baumert *et al.* (2020). The first study compared the performance of 14-year-olds who started language instruction at various ages and concluded that while literacy (reading and writing) and oracy (speaking and listening) skills in an L1 are important for FLL, the strongest relationship exists between reading ability in an L1 and FLL. The second study measured the letter knowledge, phoneme and vocabulary recognition of 6 to 9-year-old learners in two different programmes in China (immersion and non-immersion). The authors report that letter recognition in pinyin (a phonetic system of transcribing Mandarin into the Latin alphabet) and phonological awareness could facilitate learning both the L1 (Chinese) and the FL (English). Finally, the outcomes of the third study indicate that bilingual learners who had not developed literacy skills in the language of school instruction (German) were at a disadvantage when learning the third language (L3) (English), compared to those learners who were able to read and write in German.

Another study investigated the rate of morphosyntactic development by researching the grammaticality judgements of L3 (English) learners, whose L1s were Spanish and Basque (García-Mayo & García-Lecumberri, 2003). The authors compared the performance of learners who started learning English at the ages of 11–12 and 8–9. The older group outperformed the younger learners, even when the latter were given an additional 198 hours of teaching. These findings corroborate the outcomes of Muñoz's (2006) study, who argued that younger learners benefit from implicit learning and, hence, may not be explicitly aware of form and, as such, are likely to underperform on grammaticality judgement tests. The implicit nature of morphosyntactic development in childhood was also confirmed in a naturalistic setting with L2 (German) learners who started their exposure to the L2 at the ages 8 and 14 (Dimroth, 2008).

The discussion above suggests that children's literacy levels in their L1 and the language of school instruction, morphosyntactic knowledge and reading competency should be considered when designing and administering language assessment (see also Chapter 8).

IMPLICATION #4: LITERACY AND SCHOOLING

Schooling and literacy levels (especially reading and morphosyntactic knowledge) may be important for successful FLL in childhood and should be considered in assessment. For example, it would be important to account for children's L1 literacy levels when designing assessment tasks, paying particular attention to the language of instruction (L1 or L2); the mode in which instructions are communicated to learners (e.g. orally or in written form); the expected output from learners (e.g. oral or written; in L1, the language of instruction [L1 or L2] or FL); the form and mode of feedback; and how targets are set.

In addition to schooling and literacy levels, research suggests that *individual differences* can be important factors in learning a language in childhood. In the following section, I focus on cognitive IDs and their relationship to primary language learning.

Individual Differences

Many readers might agree with the statement that no two students are the same. This observation is supported by research findings which suggest that IDs can be categorised into cognitive IDs (attention, memory, metacognition or aptitude) or affective IDs (motivation, self-concept or anxiety). In this chapter, I explore the relationship between cognitive IDs and assessment. Affective IDs are discussed in Chapter 5.

Few studies provide insights into how primary-aged children process information that they are presented with in language classrooms. There-fore, in this section, insights specific to primary language contexts are supplemented with relevant findings from cognitive psychology and from adult and adolescent contexts, where appropriate. Understanding cogni-tive development in childhood will inform the discussion of feedback on performance (Chapter 7).

Attention and noticing

In this section, I review the significance of attention and how it develops in childhood. Furthermore, I consider the role that noticing (or directing attention) plays in helping children understand feedback and act on it.

Teachers or researchers working with primary-aged learners might sometimes feel that it is harder for children to focus and maintain their attention on the task at hand than it would be for adolescents or adults. Such classroom experiences are also reflected in research findings, which suggest that children have short attention spans which become longer as learners' cognitive inhibition skills improve (McKay, 2006). This is because, as they mature, children become more able to ignore unneces-sary information (Ridderinkhof & van der Molen, 1997) and control their own attention. 'Control refers to the level of attention and inhibi-tion recruited during cognitive processing' (Bialystok, 2001: 15). Better control improves learners' ability to focus their attention on a task pre-sented to them by the teacher.

With age, children develop strategies, such as focusing, dividing or switching (Gopher, 1993), which help them manage their own attention. Research in cognitive psychology suggests that children start to develop attention strategies around the age of 6 (e.g. Vurpillot, 1968). Therefore, professionals involved in assessment should carefully consider the degree to which their learners are able to use attention strategies needed for the types of tasks that they are required to perform as part of assessment. For example, Pinter (2011) suggests that problem-solving puzzles or 'spot the difference' tasks could be too difficult for children in the early years of primary school.

IMPLICATION #5 ATTENTION

Language assessment methods used at the primary school level should account for learners' short attention spans.

For attention strategies to be effectively used and '(b)efore any information can be stored or processed, individuals must notice it or attend to it' (Pinter, 2011: 22). Therefore, it is important to consider the implications of the noticing hypothesis (NH) (Schmidt, 1992, 2010) to learning and assessment in primary language contexts. Robinson (1995) suggests that learners can learn more effectively if they notice the specific language features that are being taught. This is a weaker version of the hypothesis initially proposed by Schmidt (1992, 2010: 721) who argues 'that input does not become intake for language learning unless it is noticed, that is, consciously registered'. For example, in order to be able to learn the meaning of a new word, learners need to notice what it signifies, and not just pay attention to its pronunciation or spelling.

Of special interest to the focus of this volume is the concept of 'noticing the gap' (Schmidt & Frota, 1986), i.e. 'the idea that in order to overcome errors, learners must make conscious comparisons between their own output and target language input' (Schmidt, 2010: 724). Such gaps can be highlighted to learners through feedback (see Chapter 7). Therefore, research which provides insights into the relationship between noticing and feedback on performance is of direct relevance to the focus of this volume.

A relatively large body of research provides support for the NH in adult contexts. For example, it has been demonstrated that increased awareness of irregular Spanish verb forms could lead to an increased degree of noticing and accurate written production (Leow, 2000) or that the level of awareness of Spanish conditional forms is positively related to the intake of those forms (Rosa & O'Neill, 1999). In an English as a second language (ESL) context, Mackey (2006) reported on a study which demonstrated a positive relationship between interactional feedback provided in response to learners' problems with L2 production and their ability to notice and learn question forms. However, such findings are not easily transferable to primary settings.

Insights into the applicability of the NH to primary language teaching come from a limited number of studies. Some related studies which have been conducted with adolescents are also of use here. This body of research has focused on exploring implicit and explicit feedback (Lyster & Ranta, 1997; Oliver & Mackey, 2003; Tsang, 2004) as well as planned and incidental focus on form (Alcón, 2007).

Implicit feedback can be provided either as recast 'where a teacher reformulates a learner's non-target-like form' (Oliver & Mackey, 2003: 519) or through negotiation for meaning, using strategies such as clarification requests, repetitions and comprehension checks. One of the studies to include the youngest participants was conducted with 9 to 10-year-olds in a French immersion setting in Canada (Lyster & Ranta, 1997). The findings, based on 18 hours of audio-recorded lessons, indicate that to correct mistakes in the use of lexis, teachers used negotiation strategies, and to rectify mistakes in pronunciation or grammar, they tended to use recast. The type of implicit feedback used by the teachers impacted on the degree to which children noticed their non-target production. The researchers concluded that while recasts could easily be missed by children, negotiation strategies required them to notice the mistakes in order to modify their outputs. A similar study was conducted in Hong Kong with 12 to 17-year-olds, yielding comparable results (Tsang, 2004). Learners' ability to notice the difference(s) between the target language and their own interlanguage is important to the effectiveness of the feedback. Notably, by indicating that children as young as 9 are able to notice their own non-target production if implicit feedback is provided in a way that engages a response from them, Lyster and Ranta's (1997) results have clear implications for feedback provision in primary language classes as they indicate that learners should and can be active participants of the assessment process.

It seems important to separately consider two features of implicit feedback: the technique (the how) and the content (the what). The research reviewed here suggests that the choice of a technique influences whether learners notice the content of feedback. The techniques used in the studies referred to above were recast and negotiation for meaning. While recast did not seem to have a positive effect on the language produced by 9 to 10-year-olds (Lyster & Ranta, 1997), it was reported to benefit the production of 11 to 14-year-olds (Doughty & Varela, 1998). This might suggest that adolescents are more capable of noticing and using implicit feedback in the form of recast than younger learners. Negotiating for meaning was reported to offer advantages to 9 to 10-year-olds (Lyster & Ranta, 1997), presumably because it provided some scaffolding through interaction (see also Chapter 10). This might have helped to focus the participants' attention on their non-target production. This interpretation is consistent with the findings of cognitive psychology research which suggests that children develop attention strategies as they mature (Gopher, 1993; Vurpillot, 1968).

Furthermore, research indicates that different feedback-giving techniques may be more suitable for different language areas. For example, teachers in Lyster and Ranta's (1997) study signalled mistakes in lexis with negotiation for meaning, which was observed to result in modifications of output. This is consistent with research on attention which suggests that primary-aged children devote greater attention to meaning than to form and shift their attention to meaning even when the teacher tries to focus it on form (Bialystok, 2001). Phonological and grammatical errors were corrected with recast but there was no evidence that this led to modification of output. It is impossible to say whether it was the technique (recast) or the content of feedback (phonology and grammar) or the combination of both, that did not lead to modifications of output. Evidently, more research into effective feedback provision in primary language contexts is needed, focusing on both the content and the techniques of feedback.

IMPLICATION #6 NOTICING

Feedback should be interactional, helping to draw the learners' attention to their own non-target production. This could help learners to notice the gap between their output and the expectations, and subsequently to modify their output.

Finally, it is also important to consider the educational context in which learning takes place. Lyster and Ranta (1997) conducted their study in an immersion context, where children receive significantly more exposure to the L2 than in an instructed context. If classroom time is limited, the context is less conducive to implicit learning, which has been shown to be the kind of learning which is favoured by primary-aged children (Muñoz, 2006). Therefore, research that provides support for the NH becomes very attractive in such contexts. Especially, because it suggests that by helping learners to notice the gap between the target language and their interlanguages, teachers could facilitate learning.

The present discussion evokes an important question as to whether assessment methods could support noticing the gap and contribute to modifications of output in primary language teaching. It is hoped that by reporting an analysis of the use of AfL in lessons, this volume can offer much needed insights into the use of AfL techniques in facilitating learning through feedback.

Although learners' ability to notice the gap could be valuable, there is insufficient evidence to demonstrate that primary-aged language learners are capable of doing so. Some additional insights into children's ability to notice how their performance compares to the target language come from research into metacognition. They are reviewed in the following section.

Metacognition

Metacognition is defined as 'reflection and evaluation of thinking that may result in making specific changes in how learning is managed, and in the strategies chosen for this purpose' (Anderson, 2005: 99). Research conducted in primary language contexts usually adopts Flavell's (Flavell *et al.*, 2000) model (e.g. Gu *et al.*, 2005; Vandergrift, 2002) which proposes that metacognition consists of *metacognitive knowledge* and *control*. The former comprises the knowledge of a person, task and strategy, while the latter denotes the use of strategies.

As is the case with research on attention and noticing, the number of studies on metacognition in primary language contexts is limited. The available literature indicates that training learners in the use of metacognitive strategies can benefit the development of reading (Chamot & El-Dinary, 1999), writing (Gu *et al.*, 2005) and listening (Goh & Taib, 2006; Vandergrift, 2002). These studies also provide insights into the types of metacognitive strategies used by primary-aged learners.

Goh and Taib (2006) investigated the use of metacognitive strategies by 11 to 12-year-olds during listening tasks. Based on an analysis of students' reports at the end of an eight-lesson intervention study, their findings indicate that individual reflections and process-based discussions can help learners to: (1) direct their attention to the speaker, ignoring distractions; (2) notice repetitions to identify emphasis placed on key information; (3) visualise what they can hear; (4) maintain interest even if the task seems boring; (5) infer meaning from key words; and (6) reassure themselves in case of negative feelings. Similarly, reflective tasks used after listening tasks were reported to help 9 to 12-year-old beginner learners of French in Canada develop an awareness of the metacognitive skills needed for effective listening (Vandergrift, 2002). These included predicting possible answers and evaluating task completion.

Further insights into metacognition come from studies which investigated the use of learning strategies by children. Gu *et al.* (2005) used reading, listening and writing tasks as prompts for think-aloud one-to-one interviews with learners aged 7–9. Importantly, the researchers acknowledge that it was challenging for children to verbalise their accounts of strategy use. Therefore, additional probing questions were used but these could have impacted on the data. The findings of the analysis highlight that when focusing on receptive skills (reading and listening), children used predicting. However, when focusing on a productive skill (writing), learners used monitoring. The results additionally indicate that 9-year-olds used a greater repertoire of strategies than the younger participants. This finding corroborates research in cognitive psychology which suggests that although young children aged 3–5 begin to develop metacognitive awareness, they are not able to effectively use metacognitive strategies until the ages of 8–10 (Flavell *et al.*, 1993; Nisbet & Shucksmith, 1986).

Similar to the study by Gu *et al.* (2005), a think-aloud protocol was used by Chamot and El-Dinary (1999) to research strategy use by 5 to 12-year-olds. Although the findings offer a comprehensive inventory of the metacognitive strategies used by children, they are not reported separately for different age subgroups of participants. As indicated earlier, awareness and control of metacognitive skills differ even between 7 and 9-year-olds (Gu *et al.*, 2005). However, the results reported by Chamot and El-Dinary (1999) do not provide an indication of when children develop metacognitive control. Nonetheless, they are useful as they offer insights into the differences between effective and less effective readers and writers in French, Spanish and Japanese immersion programmes in

Washington, DC. Children who performed better in reading and writing: (1) planned (previewed, read aloud and made predictions); (2) monitored their performance (checked meaning, self-corrected, self-questioned, verified predictions); and (3) used selective attention (identified key words, linguistic features, text features and pronunciation). These findings are consistent with research conducted in adult contexts which has shown that good learners regularly implement metacognitive strategies (Griffiths, 2003; O'Malley & Chamot, 1990) while less effective learners fail to accurately select and/or use strategies (Vann & Abraham, 1990).

The studies quoted above indicate that it is challenging to collect data about metacognitive strategy use from primary-aged children. This finding itself has implications for language assessment.

IMPLICATION #7 TALKING ABOUT LEARNING

Young children find it difficult to verbalise the process which they go through to arrive at answers and solutions for tasks. Therefore, in order to evaluate the progress which they are making in the learning process, children need scaffolding.

However, as is also shown by the studies quoted above, children can and should be trained in metacognitive awareness and control of strategies because it can help them develop more accurate awareness and a wider repertoire of strategies which can facilitate language learning. This poses an important question as to whether language assessment could support the development of metacognition, for example, through facilitating reflection and process-based discussions.

Importantly, many of the metacognitive strategies that were identified by research helped children to plan, monitor and evaluate their performance. This observation has two implications for assessment. Firstly, the expected outcomes should be clarified with the children so that they are aware of how their performance compares to expectations; that is, whether they have met the learning objective (LO) (see Chapter 6). Secondly, assessment techniques should facilitate drawing learners' attention to the discrepancies (the gap) between their performance and the expectations set for them (see Chapter 7). A discussion of the practical implementation of AfL in Chapters 6 and 7 illustrates how AfL could address those two considerations.

In addition to noticing their mistakes, learners may also need to rely on memory in order to correct the mistakes (Robinson, 1995). Therefore, it is important to review the findings of research on memory which are relevant to primary language teaching.

Memory

Primary language teachers may find that their learners can remember lyrics to a long song but may find it challenging to remember and apply a simple grammar or spelling rule. The reasons for this are linked to how memory develops in childhood. Specifically, *working memory* (WM) has been shown to be predictive of achievement in FLL (Wen, 2012; Wen & Skehan, 2011). This is consistent with research in cognitive psychology which connects WM with the ability to comprehend and process language (e.g. Case *et al.*, 1982; Gathercole & Baddeley, 1993). Therefore, in this section, I review what is known about memory in childhood, WM in particular.

WM is 'the cognitive capacity to simultaneously store and process information in real time' (Wen & Skehan, 2011: 21). As is the case with other IDs, the majority of research on WM was conducted with adults. The studies which inform practice in primary contexts come from the fields of cognitive psychology and applied linguistics.

In foreign language teaching, researchers conceptualise working memory as a dual processing system proposed by Skehan (1996, 1998). It comprises two components: the exemplar based (also referred to as memory based) and the rule based. The former helps a learner recall whole chunks of information verbatim, while the latter enables them to think analytically. In cognitive psychology, the rule-based system is referred to as processing and the exemplar based as storage.

Studies in cognitive psychology suggest that as children mature, the processing demands in the brain diminish and, as a result, more storage space is available (Case *et al.*, 1982). Moreover, a trade-off between processing and storage can occur if the demands of a task with which a learner is presented are high (Daneman & Carpenter, 1980; Daneman & Merikle, 1996). A large-scale study conducted with 1200 participants aged 6–49 who were required to process syntax and recall linguistic information simultaneously suggested that WM develops between the ages of 6 and 15 (Siegler, 1994). These studies suggest that as learners mature, their rule-based systems develop and operate more quickly, requiring less space within WM. Consequently, more storage space becomes available.

The findings of the research quoted above collectively suggest that a large portion of children's WM is taken up by ineffective processing, leaving limited capacity for storage. This interpretation corroborates findings of studies on the memory spans of children. For example, Wilson *et al.* (1987) report that adult-like visual and phonological memory spans do not develop until the ages of 10–12.

Studies in applied linguistics have shown that foreign language learners can use two modes of communication, each of which relies on a different component of the dual processing system. Research suggests that adult learners tend to rely more heavily on the exemplar-based system if they feel under time pressure (Skehan, 1996). This ensures faster recall and enables them to communicate in the lexical mode. In cases where learners prioritise exactness or creativity, they tend to use the rule-based system. These findings from adult contexts cannot be easily applied to primary settings. However, they are important to consider as they may have implications for the modes of communication which are more naturally suitable for primary-aged children. Research suggests that children rely on the exemplar-based system which Skehan (1996) has linked to a lexical mode of communication. Therefore, it could be inferred that the lexical communication mode is more appropriate for primary-aged language learners due to the developmental stages of their WM. This could help explain why children have been found to pay greater attention to meaning over form (Bialystok, 2001; García-Mayo & García-Lecumberri, 2003).

The outcomes of research discussed in this section have important implications for language teaching and assessment. First, they require that assessment tasks do not pose high processing demands on learners, as children may not be cognitively ready for them. Secondly, as children seem to rely on the exemplar-based system before their ability to effectively use the rule-based system develops, teaching and assessment tasks can make use of that system, remembering, however, that children's memory spans are rather limited. For example, it would be inappropriate to expect children to remember long instructions for a task (see Chapter 8). Thirdly, the focus of primary language teaching and assessment should be on meaning, with language form being introduced gradually, when learners are developmentally better prepared for it.

Another area within memory research has investigated the use of memory strategies by primary-aged language learners. These can be divided into short-term (e.g. organisation, rehearsal and elaboration) and long-term (recall, reconstruction and recognition) memory strategies (Black, 2005). Cognitive psychology research suggests that memory strategies develop between the ages of 5 and 10 (Flavell, 1992) and that they can be taught (Wood, 1998). The latest strategy to develop is elaboration, which can rarely be used by children younger than 11 (Schneider & Pressley, 2013).

IMPLICATION #8 MEMORY

Assessment tasks should not pose high processing demands on primary-aged language learners because children rely on the exemplar-based system. The focus of assessment should be meaning, with language form being introduced gradually, when learners are developmentally more prepared for it around the age of 10.

Summary of the Chapter

In this chapter, I have reviewed what is known about the relationship between assessment and development of cognitive IDs and metacognition. The key outcomes of the review include eight implications for assessment. These are highlighted in text boxes throughout the chapter.

Overall, the review indicates that the construct of assessment in primary language teaching should prioritise phonology, lexis and collocations over morphosyntactic skills. Moreover, as the initial rate of progress is slow, assessment methods should evidence that progress in a series of small steps, which enable teachers to guide learners along their individual learning trajectories to achieve the expected learning outcomes. The design of assessment tasks should account for children's developing L1 literacy, and for their short attention and memory spans. Additionally, feedback provided to primary-aged language learners should be interactional as this may encourage a greater rate of noticing the gap and modifying output in order to correct non-target production. Such feedback should focus on meaning over the form of the language, accounting for developments in WM. Finally, metacognitive strategies which enable learners to plan, monitor and evaluate their performance should be incorporated into teaching and assessment practices.

Our attention now shifts to discussing the relationship between affective IDs and assessment in primary language teaching.

5 The Importance of Interactions and Affect in Assessing Primary-Aged Language Learners

Introduction

In this chapter, I adopt the sociocultural perspective on learning. The discussion focuses on three areas that are relevant to assessment: affect, the zone of proximal development (ZPD) and interactions. The aim of the chapter is to discuss the characteristics of primary-aged children which should be considered when assessing their language skills, and which, therefore, are directly relevant to implementing assessment for learning (AfL).

Affect and Assessment

As they experience life, children build their own appraisal system with different levels of anxiety and motivation, and their unique attitudes and self-concepts (Schumann, 2001). Those affective *individual differences* (IDs) are present in each language classroom and therefore should be considered when teaching and assessing children.

The relationship between affect (motivation, anxiety, self-concept and attitude) and learning and assessment is recognised as an important area of research (e.g. Bacsa & Csíkos, 2016; Mihaljević Djigunović, 2016; Nikolov, 2016). In recent years, the relationship between affect and language learning and assessment in childhood has become a popular research focus (Mihaljević Djigunović, 2019). Of direct relevance to the focus of this volume is research which concentrates on the relationship between assessment and affect.

While discussing the current body of knowledge on the relationship between assessment and affect, Mihaljević Djigunović (2019: 29) emphasises that although the cause–effect aspects of the complex relationship need further investigation, '(w)hat emerges as quite definite, though, is that affect and assessment interact'. Overall, research in this area suggests that primary-aged learners start language education with an existing affective profile. This seems to include a high, or perhaps even overinflated, level of motivation which may decrease as learners build up their experiences of language learning (Mihaljević Djigunović & Lopriore, 2011). Motivation was also found to correlate positively with language achievement (e.g. Mihaljević Djigunović, 2007). Children can and do experience anxiety related to assessment but that can be mitigated by ensuring that the feedback they receive emphasises success (e.g. Chan & Wu, 2004). Importantly, studies also indicate that developing positive affective dispositions towards a second language (L2) and its speakers is often explicitly stated as an objective of primary language programmes (e.g. Edelenbos & Kubanek, 2009). Furthermore, some types of assessment, such as AfL, have been suggested to support the development of positive affective profiles better than others (Mihaljević Djigunović, 2019).

In this section, I explore what the published studies can tell us about the relationship between assessment and affect in primary language teaching contexts. For detailed reviews of the relationship between affect and language learning in childhood, the reader may wish to refer to Nikolov and Mihaljević Djigunović (2011), Edelenbos *et al.* (2006) or Britton (2015).

Anxiety

Nikolov and Mihaljević Djigunović (2011) note that in recent years it has been recognised that primary-aged children can experience *foreign language anxiety* (FLA), defined as 'the feelings of worry and negative, fear-related emotions associated with learning or using a language that is not an individual's mother tongue' (MacIntyre & Gregersen, 2012: 103). Research suggests that FLA can be effectively lowered by increasing children's feelings of success, for example, by implementing the formative function of assessment in lessons (Shaaban, 2001). Nonetheless, very little research has been reported in this area so far.

It should be noted that the existence of relationships between FLA and language performance, as well as learners' self-confidence and self-esteem is well established in foreign language learning (FLL) (Oxford, 1999). However, the evidence comes almost entirely from adult and adolescent contexts, with only a few studies based in primary classes.

The outcomes of anxiety research in primary language teaching contexts indicate that there is a relationship between learners' perception of their own language proficiency and their levels of anxiety. For example, Yim (2014) investigated anxiety in primary schools in Korea. Reporting on the findings from a study conducted with 537 learners, the author concluded 'that students should be encouraged to assess themselves more positively in English so as to reduce their levels of anxiety in learning English' (Yim, 2014: 344). This finding is corroborated by a study conducted in Greece, where out of 184 learners aged 12, those less proficient in writing demonstrated higher levels of anxiety than participants with a higher level of writing competence (Griva *et al.*, 2009). This is consistent with the outcomes reported by Chan and Wu (2004), who found that the anxiety experienced by fifth-grade learners in Taiwan was linked to their perception of low competence in English. These findings suggest that it would be valuable to incorporate opportunities for primary-aged learners to recognise their own achievement through assessment in order to lower FLA.

Griva *et al.* (2009) identified two strategies which were used by 12-year-olds to improve their self-confidence and to lower anxiety; children used self-encouragement and rewarded themselves while they were completing writing tasks. However, the researchers also noted that the learners in their study made very little use of those strategies. Therefore, it would be useful to implement such assessment methods which could promote children's skills of self-encouraging and rewarding their own achievements in order to help them lower their FLA.

Another study, which provided insights into anxiety experienced by first-grade Chinese language learners, focused on speaking (Sun *et al.*, 2017). The outcomes suggest that incorporating the use of social networking sites (SNS)[1] might help to lower primary school-aged learners' anxiety about speaking in a foreign language. This finding indicates that the choice of method used for teaching productive skills could be linked to the levels of FLA experienced by children. Although not directly relevant to AfL, the study is of interest to the focus of this volume because the findings presented in Chapters 6–8 confirm that AfL is an integral part of the teaching methods used in primary language classes and that AfL is most frequently used when teaching productive skills. Therefore, it could be argued that the choice of an assessment method might be linked to learners' anxiety levels. Specifically, the available studies suggest that methods which require an immediate response or direct contact with an interlocutor could be less effective at lowering FLA than those which allow for individual reflection before responding. Admittedly, further research is needed to better understand the nature of such relationships.

Research on anxiety related to receptive skills comes from adolescent contexts. In a study of anxiety experienced by 13 to 14-year-olds during listening tasks, Mihaljević Djigunović and Legac (2009) reported that learners who were bilingual in languages other than English, experienced less anxiety when completing listening tasks in English. This finding points to the complexity of factors which impact on FLA experienced by children, indicating that some of them are placed beyond the language classroom.

Test anxiety

The related concept of *test anxiety*, defined as 'the tendency to become alarmed about the consequences of inadequate performance on a test or other evaluation' (Sarason, 1984) has also been investigated in primary language contexts. Although testing is not an intrinsic part of AfL, evaluation is. It should therefore be acknowledged that by incorporating an element of evaluation, AfL techniques could cause test anxiety. However, Aydin (2013) reported that learners aged 9–14 generally experienced low levels of test anxiety. Additionally, from a cohort of 477, younger participants seemed to experience less test anxiety than their older counterparts. Overall, the findings indicate that feelings of success and being prepared and aware of an upcoming evaluation were connected with lower anxiety levels, but fear of poor performance contributed to increasing test anxiety.

The above findings confirm that the way in which assessment is implemented is related to the level of anxiety that children may experience. Consequently, it would seem that assessment methods which hope not to evoke test anxiety should support learners in developing positive perceptions of themselves as language learners (see also self-concept, in the next section). Additionally, the form in which the outcomes of assessment are communicated to learners should be carefully considered. Specifically, Aydin (2013) noted that if a learner expects a pass or fail outcome, they may be more anxious than in the situation when the outcomes identify their achievement and provide an indication of areas for improvement.

In order to support teachers in their efforts to lower anxiety experienced by young learners, assessment methods should:

(1) Enable learners to recognise their own achievement.
(2) Promote self-encouragement and rewards.
(3) Avoid the pass/fail outcome in favour of identifying success and steps for further learning.
(4) Be incorporated into teaching in order to support the three purposes stated above.

Chapters 6 and 7 offer detailed insights into implementing AfL in classes conducted with children aged 7–11. It is believed that by analysing the way in which AfL is used in primary language teaching, the discussion will indicate whether AfL techniques could contribute to lowering FLA by creating learning conditions which address the requirements listed in the box above.

Self-concept, motivation and attitude

The findings discussed in the previous section indicate that there is a relationship between anxiety and children's perceptions of their own proficiency (their task related *self-concept*). This links the research on anxiety to that on self-concept, defined as 'a person's notion of himself as a FL learner' (Laine, 1988: 10). Self-concept can be different in relation to FLL in general and to specific languages. It tends to be discussed in three dimensions: a learner's perceptions of the ideal self (their aspirations); the actual self (themselves currently); and the social self (how others see them) (e.g. Mihaljević Djigunović, 2006). Self-concept is often researched alongside other affective IDs, such as motivation and attitude.

Motivation and attitude are frequently thought of as interconnected (Mihaljević Djigunović, 2006). In defining motivation, Gardner (2010) includes a positive attitude towards learning a language and the learner's desire and effort devoted to that end. Attitude is understood to be either a negative or a positive feeling about FLL and what the learner associates with that language (Gardner & MacIntyre, 1993).

Children tend to begin FLL with unrealistically positive self-concepts, positive attitudes and high levels of motivation, and as they accumulate experiences of FLL, their affective dispositions tend to change (Enever, 2011; Matsuzaki Carreira, 2006; Mihaljević Djigunović & Lopriore, 2011). What becomes important in ensuring that positive affective profiles are maintained and developed in primary-aged language learners is good quality FLL experiences (Cenoz, 2003). This can be facilitated through: (1) ensuring that learners achieve success (Cable et al., 2010); (2) the length (Donato et al., 2000) or early starting age of instruction (Kennedy et al., 2000; Nikolov, 1999); (3) models received from significant adults (Szpotowicz et al., 2009); and (4) interactions with native speakers (NS) (Marschollek, 2002, cited in Mihaljević Djigunović, 2015). The first condition is directly related to the focus of our discussion as it could be argued that assessment methods should play an important role in ensuring that learners experience success in a language classroom.

The concept of the L2 learning experience is a part of the L2 motivational self system proposed by Dörnyei (2005) alongside two future guides (ideal L2 self and ought-to L2 self). Dörnyei (2019: 20) defines the L2 learning experience as 'the perceived quality of the learners' engagement with various aspects of the language learning process'. While this model has not been researched specifically in primary language teaching contexts, it has been validated with learners aged 11 and 12 in middle school settings in China and Iran (Taguchi et al., 2009). Empirical research conducted with adolescents suggests that the L2 learning experience is a strong predictor of motivated behaviour (Csizér & Kormos, 2009; Kormos & Csizér, 2008; Lamb, 2012). Therefore, it is an interesting notion to consider as part of the discussion in this chapter. This is especially because Dörnyei (2019) highlights the importance of learners' practical engagement in classroom activities as an integral part of their L2 learning experience. Such learner engagement is integral to AfL, especially when children are encouraged to reflect on the expectations and their achievement by providing or responding to feedback.

Research has pointed to a number of ways in which affective profiles are linked to language assessment. Firstly, outcomes of assessment can inform the development of self-concepts by impacting on learners' perceptions of their own progress and/or their recognition of their achievement (Mihaljević Djigunović, 2015). Self-perception has been linked to positive attitudes towards FLL (Masgoret *et al.*, 2001). This suggests that assessment methods which provide language learners with evidence of achievement could help them feel successful. The feeling of success is vital for motivating future learning (Vilke & Vrhovac, 1995, cited in Mihaljević Djigunović *et al.*, 2008). Mihaljević Djigunović (2015) argues that motivating and purposeful learning environments can be created by ensuring that learners are aware of expected outcomes. This has direct implications for assessment. It suggests that the learning objectives (LOs) against which children are assessed should be communicated to them as part of the teaching process.

Secondly, although no causal relationship has been established between affect and performance, it is generally accepted that a positive affective disposition is linked to language performance in productive as well as receptive skills (Mihaljević Djigunović, 2006, 2012, 2019; Mihaljević Djigunović & Lopriore, 2011). Suggestions have also been made that affective factors may have a stronger impact on achievement as learners mature and as they gain experience of FLL than at the initial phase of learning (Mihaljević Djigunović & Lopriore, 2011).

Thirdly, it has been suggested that developing a positive disposition towards FLL may be one of the most important goals of primary language programmes (Edelenbos *et al.*, 2006; Mihaljević Djigunović, 2015, 2019). This final consideration has implications for the construct of assessment in primary language teaching. Specifically, if the aim is to develop a positive affective profile, it should be explicitly included in the assessment criteria. The discussion in this section highlights the features that assessment should have in order to foster positive affective profiles of primary-aged language learners. The outcomes are summarised in the following box.

In order to promote the development of young learners' positive affective profiles, assessment methods should:

(1) Provide opportunities for learners to experience the feeling of success.
(2) Provide evidence to learners that helps them develop positive perceptions of their achievement.
(3) Communicate clear expectations of outcomes.
(4) Contribute to learners having positive language learning experiences.
(5) Evaluate the development of affective dispositions alongside language proficiency.

In Chapters 6 and 7, I discuss which of the requirements listed in the box above could be met by implementing AfL. In order to do so, I report in detail how AfL techniques were used in lessons which I observed during my own study (Britton, 2015). By providing empirical evidence about the way in which the use of AfL might contribute to creating a learning environment which could foster the development of positive affective factors, the present volume offers useful new insights into the relationship between AfL and affect. This research focus gains currency especially in light of suggestions that using AfL 'can enhance young learners' self-confidence and boost their motivation to a large extent' (Mihaljević Djigunović, 2019: 26).

Interactions and Assessment

Learning can be mediated through 'demonstration, leading questions, and by introducing the initial elements of the task's solution' (Vygotsky, 1987: 209). In that process, learners are offered opportunities to internalise actions and processes from the intermental level. As defined in Chapter 2, AfL is a type of assessment that aims to support learning. Therefore, of central importance to the focus of this volume is to explore how AfL may facilitate the process of mediation as defined by Vygotsky (1987). In the Vygotskian view, language itself is an integral tool of cognitive development and mediates it through interactions within the learner's ZPD. Consequently, our attention turns to the relationship between interactions and assessment.

Negotiation for meaning

The research reviewed in Chapter 4 indicates that children may benefit from being actively engaged in the assessment process, for example, when feedback allows for negotiation for meaning. It has been proposed that providing comprehensible input which is beyond the learner's current level of knowledge can facilitate learning (Krashen, 1985) and that an effective way of ensuring comprehensibility is through interactional modification of input (Long, 1981). Such modification can occur when interlocutors negotiate for meaning; that is to say, when they 'express and clarify their intentions, thoughts, opinions etc., in a way which permits them to arrive at a mutual understanding' (Lightbown & Spada, 2008: 122).

A series of studies conducted with adolescents in Japan (Ellis *et al.*, 1994) empirically linked interactional modification of meaning to improving learning outcomes. Importantly, similar gains were reported for those learners who only observed the modifications but did not partake in them. These outcomes become interesting to the focus of the present chapter in light of more recent research which suggests that young learners are able to successfully negotiate for meaning

(Oliver, 1998, 2000, 2002; Oliver & Mackey, 2003) even though they do not always adopt their interlocutor's perspective (Butler & Zeng, 2014).

Learners' proficiency in English can impact on the amount of negotiation for meaning. Specifically, non-native speaker (NNS) learners aged 8–13 with low levels of proficiency in English were reported to negotiate for meaning with greater frequency than their more proficient peers or NS during learner–learner (L–L) interactions (Oliver, 1998, 2000, 2002). This is a useful finding as it indicates that primary-aged learners are able to engage in interactional modification of meaning through negotiations despite their low levels of proficiency in English.

Arguably, more empirical evidence is needed to better understand the relationship between negotiation for meaning through L–L interactions and language learning in childhood. Currently, the majority of such evidence comes from adult and adolescent contexts, where it has been shown that FLL can happen through interaction (e.g. Gass, 2013; Mackey, 1999; Pica, 1994).

Modification of output

Negotiating for meaning can play a role in providing opportunities for children to modify their output in response to *negative feedback* (Mackey *et al.*, 2003). Negative feedback is information 'provided in response to learners' non-target-like production' (Oliver & Mackey, 2003: 519). Since it has been argued that 'the importance of output for learning could be that output pushes learners to process language more deeply – with more mental effort – than does input' (Swain, 2000: 99), it seems important to understand whether assessment methods used in primary language contexts could benefit learning by facilitating opportunities for negotiating for meaning and modifying output (see Chapter 10). It follows that in order to maximise opportunities for learners to modify their input and/or output through negotiation, teachers should promote L–L interactions. This can, however, be challenging in young learner classrooms because children tend to rely on interacting with their teacher when negotiating for meaning (Ellis & Heimbach, 1997). The findings about interactional patterns which occur during AfL are reported in Chapter 10.

Teacher–learner interactions

Admittedly, teacher–learner (T–L) interactions offer opportunities for modifying input and output. However, the amount of such interactions per learner is limited if children are taught in groups. Nonetheless, it seems valuable to consider the impact that such interactions could have on learning. Although research in primary contexts has yet to fully explore this interesting focus, it has been suggested that categorising interactions into the quadrants proposed by Storch (2002) could be informative for analysing the impact of dyadic interactions in primary language lessons (Butler & Zeng, 2014). The Storch (2002) model is already successfully used to analyse interactions in adolescent and adult contexts (e.g. Watanabe & Swain, 2007; Williams, 2001). It proposes that we should consider the level of mutuality and equality of each exchange. Mutuality focuses on the degree to which interlocutors work towards achieving a shared goal and respond to one another's points of view in the conversations. Equality is linked to the interlocutors' English proficiency, age or role in the class. A medium to high level of mutuality between interlocutors has been linked to gains in learning, regardless of the accompanying level of equality. This includes two interaction patterns: (1) *expert-novice* (low to medium equality and medium to high mutuality levels); and (2) *collaborative* (medium to high levels of equality and mutuality). The levels of mutuality and equality during interactions which occurred while AfL was being used are analysed in Chapter 10.

Other studies have reported that T–L interactions tend to focus on:

(1) Classroom management (Oliver & Mackey, 2003; Walsh, 2006).
(2) The non-linguistic content of the lessons in immersion programmes (Oliver & Mackey, 2003).
(3) Vocabulary and form of L2 ('explicit language focus' in Oliver & Mackey [2003] or 'skills and systems mode' in Walsh [2006]).
(4) Topics of interest to learners ('communication' in Oliver & Mackey [2003] or 'classroom context' in Walsh [2006]).
(5) The learning materials used in lessons ('materials mode' in Walsh [2006]).

Depending on which of the modes of communication listed above learners encounter, they experience different language environments in the classroom. Research in this area suggests that teachers tend to provide explicit feedback during T–L interactions in two contexts; when they focus on the non-linguistic topic of the lesson (content mode) or the language form (explicit language focus mode). However, they are unlikely to do so in communication or management contexts (Oliver & Mackey, 2003). Primary-aged language learners have been reported to use the feedback provided in the explicit language focus context most readily. This suggests that some linguistic contexts in the classroom are more conducive to learning which could occur as a response to feedback. Therefore, the analysis in Chapter 10 seeks to investigate whether AfL can offer opportunities for creating such contexts.

However, it may be challenging to identify the modes of classroom conversations, especially when a teacher's use of language is not aligned with the pedagogical aims of the conversation (Walsh, 2006). Furthermore, Walsh (2006: 88) observed that when 'teacher talk and learning objectives are incongruent – the teacher's use of language actually appears to hinder rather than facilitate learning opportunity'. Walsh (2006) argued convincingly that in order to create the type of linguistic environment that supports learning, teachers should aim to align their language use with the pedagogical objectives of conversations.

Fully investigating whether AfL could facilitate conditions for teachers to align their language use with the pedagogical aims of the conversations was beyond the scope of the study which informs this book. However, to gain preliminary insights in this area, examples of classroom discourse which occurred during the use of AfL were analysed. The outcomes of that analysis are discussed in Chapter 10.

Oliver and Mackey's (2003) study was conducted in an immersion context, whereas Walsh (2006) developed his categories in an adult teaching English as a foreign language (TEFL) context and subsequently used them to research young learner classrooms. The four modes proposed by Walsh (2006) are used for an analysis of classroom interactions (Chapter 10) and include: management, skills and systems, materials and classroom context. This choice is justified by the contextual similarity between Walsh's (2006) study and my own research: an instructed setting.

Learner–learner interactions

The second type of interaction characterised by a medium to high level of mutuality is the collaborative pattern. It also requires a medium to high level of equality. The findings discussed in Chapter 10 indicate collaborative interactions were observed between pairs of learners (L–L interactions). The lack of collaborative T–L interactions can be explained by the difference in the language proficiency levels and teachers' and learners' roles in the classroom.

Research into L–L interactions has suggested that language learning at the primary level might benefit from interactions with peers to a greater degree when learners are already familiar with the structure of the task at hand (Pinter, 2007). Pinter (2007) argues that this is because when learners do not need to concentrate on understanding the requirements of the task, they can focus on co-constructing the language needed to complete it. It could be argued that under such conditions, students are able to demonstrate their ability more accurately, thus enabling teachers to collect valid evidence of learning. The beneficial effects of familiarity with the task structure on performance were also reported in adult contexts (Bygate, 1996; Skehan & Foster, 1999). Similar observations were made in studies which involved adolescents (Swain, 2000; Swain & Lapkin, 1998), indicating that such co-construction occurs during *language-related episodes* (LREs). LREs are those parts of conversations during which learners discuss their speaking or writing output. Studies which explored the relationship between LREs and language learning were based predominantly in adult contexts. Overall, the outcomes of this area of research suggest that collaborative and expert-novice interaction patterns help to create conditions that are conducive to learning (Kim & McDonough, 2008; Ohta, 1995; van Lier, 2014; Watanabe & Swain, 2007; Williams, 2001).

The evidence that is emerging from the primary language context suggests that although similar gains could be expected, children may find it difficult to take the perspective of their interlocutor and therefore require scaffolding which would enable effective collaboration (Butler & Zeng, 2014). Such scaffolding could be provided through AfL in two ways. First, by clarifying the LOs and success criteria (SC), AfL could contribute to a higher level of mutuality of interactions (see also Chapter 10). Secondly, by incorporating AfL into day-to-day teaching, teachers can ensure that learners are familiar with the structure of the assessment techniques (see also Chapter 8).

Interactions and assessment

The outcomes of research into the relationship between interactions and assessment have important implications for primary language teaching. These are summarised in the following box.

In order to benefit learning through the interactional modification of output, assessment methods should:

(1) Facilitate dyadic interactions between learners.
(2) Provide opportunities for negotiation for meaning.
(3) Encourage interactions in those modes which facilitate LREs.

The criteria listed in the preceding box have implications for the way in which we conceive of the role of a learner in the assessment process. The processes of negotiating for meaning and modifying output through interactions require active involvement from the learner. Consequently, assessment methods which aim to create learning environments conducive to such processes should also engage learners' active participation in the assessment of their learning.

Researching AfL from the Sociocultural Perspective

The theoretical framework of AfL adopted in this volume (Chapter 2) incorporates five aspects. Table 5.1 sets out the links identified between each of those aspects and the research into affect and interactions in primary language teaching. Evidently, several connections exist. They should inform those investigations into the classroom use of AfL which aim to explore the relationship between AfL and affect or interactions.

Table 5.1 Considerations for researching the five aspects of AfL in primary language teaching

Aspect of AfL (Black & Wiliam, 2009: 8)	Outcomes of research on affect and interactions	Considerations for researching AfL
(1) Clarifying and understanding the learning intentions and the criteria for success	Motivating and purposeful learning environments can be created by ensuring that learners are aware of expected outcomes (Mihaljević Djigunović, 2015).	(1) Could AfL contribute to creating purposeful learning environments by communicating and clarifying expected outcomes?
(2) Eliciting evidence of student understanding	Only some of the modes in which classroom interactions happen have been shown to be conducive to learning. These include 'explicit language focus', 'skills and systems' and 'materials' modes (Oliver & Mackey, 2003; Walsh, 2006). The familiar structure of tasks can facilitate performance (Pinter, 2007; Swain, 2000) providing valid evidence of learning.	(2) Which modes of conversation can be observed during the use of AfL techniques? (3) Is there any evidence that these modes are conducive to learning? (4) Can AfL techniques provide a familiar structure of assessment?
(3) Providing feedback that moves learning forward	Negative feedback can lead to modifications of output (Mackey et al., 2003). This tends to happen during LREs (Oliver & Mackey, 2003).	(5) Can the use of AfL techniques provide opportunities for negative feedback? (6) Do primary-aged language learners tend to modify output in response to such feedback?
(4) Activating students as learning resources for one another	Primary-aged language learners can and do negotiate for meaning (Oliver, 1998, 2000, 2002; Oliver & Mackey, 2003) but may require support to adopt their interlocutor's perspective (Butler & Zeng, 2014).	(7) Can the use of AfL techniques provide opportunities for: (a) negotiation for meaning? (b) L–L interactions during lessons?
(5) Activating learners as owners of their own learning	Primary-aged language learners can use self-encouragement and reward themselves when they recognise their own achievement (Griva et al., 2009).	(8) Could AfL techniques be used to promote self-encouragement and rewards?

To address this research focus, I report a detailed account of the implementation of AfL gained through observations of 28 primary language lessons, taught over 5 months by eight experienced teachers, and an analysis of school records from 448 lessons. Insights from such a large sample were not available in the published research at the time of writing this book. Rich descriptions of the way in which teachers and learners used AfL provide useful insights into the relationship between AfL and the development of primary-aged language learners' positive affective dispositions. The discussion in Chapters 6 and 7 addresses questions 1, 4 and 8 in Table 5.1.

To investigate the relationship between AfL and interactions, extracts of classroom discourse were sourced from video-recorded lessons ($n = 26^2$), transcribed (see Appendix 1 for the transcribing convention) and analysed using the Storch (2002) model and the variable approach to analysing classroom discourse (Walsh, 2006). The analysis aimed to address questions 2, 3, 5, 6 and 7 in Table 5.1. The outcomes of this analysis are reported in Chapter 10.

Summary of the Chapter

In this chapter, I have considered the relationship between learning and assessment from the sociocultural perspective. Two areas have been identified as having special significance for assessment: (1) developing positive affective profiles and (2) facilitating learning through interactions.

The relationship between affect and assessment is complex. The picture that emerges from available research suggests that it is vital for primary-aged language learners to have positive experiences as they develop their affective dispositions. Of particular interest to the focus of this volume are the insights which suggest how assessment could be used in the classroom to lower learners' anxiety; develop their motivation and positive attitude towards FLL; and develop their positive self-concepts. Research discussed in this chapter suggests that it is important to enable learners to recognise their own achievement and experience the feeling of success. Consequently, the teaching and assessment methods should provide learners with opportunities to collect evidence which supports the development of positive perceptions of their own achievement. The review of studies included in this chapter revealed that this could be achieved by using techniques that promote self-encouragement and self-rewards, and help to communicate clear expectations of outcomes. The need for developing positive affective dispositions to language learning in childhood is emphasised by claims that such development should be included in the aims of primary language programmes (Edelenbos *et al.*, 2006; Mihaljević Djigunović, 2015, 2019).

The sociocultural perspective on learning proposes that educators can collect evidence of the potential development of learners from interactions with more capable peers (Swain, 2000). The second part of this chapter focused on the relationship between interactions and language assessment. The review of the research from primary language teaching contexts points to the importance of enabling L–L interactions in order to maximise opportunities for learners to negotiate for meaning. Furthermore, it suggests that teachers could promote learning by (1) using such teaching and assessment methods that promote medium to high levels of mutuality during interactions; (2) encouraging interactions in those modes which facilitate LREs; and (3) aligning their use of the L2 with the pedagogical aims of conversations.

In Part 2 of this volume, I report on the practical implementation of AfL. The discussion focuses on whether and, if so, how such implementation could address any of the implications for assessment discussed in this chapter.

Notes

(1) Using SNS with primary-aged children should always be approached with caution to ensure that children are safeguarded online and that the end-user policy of SNS platforms is adhered to. Such policies often include age restrictions.

(2) Out of the total of 28 lesson observations, 26 were video recorded. The remaining two were voice recorded due to parental preference not to video record their children as expressed in the process of gaining informed consent.

Part 2

Implementing AfL in the Classroom

6 Setting Expectations and Monitoring Progress

depending on the lesson plan we use the [AfL] techniques at different points throughout the lesson to help them get there and be able to do the can[1] (1) every single lesson they have at least one element of AfL
(T7/INT)

Introduction

In this chapter, I focus on the use of assessment for learning (AfL) for the purposes of setting expectations and monitoring learning. All examples are sourced from field notes recorded during 28 lesson observations. The lessons were conducted by eight experienced primary language teachers with learners aged 7–9 and 10–11 (14 lessons in each age group). The participating teachers had between 5 and 18 years of experience teaching English and between 2 and 12 years of experience teaching young learners. Each teacher had used AfL for at least one academic year before the study commenced. Out of the 28 observed lessons, 26[2] were also video recorded. This enabled later reviewing to capture additional detail and verify field notes. The findings provide unique insights into the practical implementation of AfL in language lessons conducted with primary-aged children.

As discussed in Chapter 3, purposes for use guide the implementation of AfL. The main purposes identified in primary language education include setting expectations, monitoring progress and evaluating achievement. Many of the techniques which were used for monitoring progress were also used for setting expectations, while most of the techniques used for evaluating achievement were used only for that purpose. In this chapter, I provide an inventory of those technique types which I observed to be used for setting expectations and monitoring progress. This is not intended as a complete list of all possible technique types which could be used for those purposes or as a comprehensive practical guide. For more examples of AfL techniques, readers may wish to consult practical guides such as Clarke (2005, 2014), Chappuis et al. (2004) and Hattie (2012). Here, the purpose for reporting how AfL was implemented in primary language lessons through techniques is to provide the reader with empirical insights into classroom use. This serves as a basis for discussing the relationship between language learning and the use of AfL, later in the chapter. The focus of the discussion is to consider what the findings presented in this chapter reveal about AfL's potential to help teachers create such conditions in lessons which the research discussed in Part 1 of this volume has shown to be beneficial to language learning in childhood. The outcomes of that discussion suggest that AfL could help teachers to account for learners' developing metacognition; to increase learners' familiarity with the task structure; and to develop children's responsibility for their own learning.

AfL Technique Types Used to Set Expectations and Monitor Progress

The data I collected by observing lessons provide unique insights into the practical use of AfL in a primary language teaching context. I became interested in how, why and when teachers use various AfL techniques because in the interviews and the focus group (FG) discussion, the teachers indicated that AfL could be implemented in primary language teaching through various AfL techniques. They reported that while 'the whole thing is about that (1) getting them [the learners] to understand what to do and then to figure out how well they have done' (T3/FG), 'what it involves is a series of tactics tools techniques and things that you can do to facilitate that' (T2/INT). The finding that AfL *can* be successfully implemented in primary language lessons through AfL techniques makes it interesting to explore how AfL techniques were used in lessons. Therefore, all the techniques that I observed are described in detail and illustrated with examples of how they were implemented. The AfL techniques described in this section include:

(1) Sharing two models (STM)
(2) Success criteria (SC)
(3) What are we learning today?–type questions (WALT)
(4) Learning partners (LP)
(5) Mind maps (MM)
(6) Increased thinking time (ITT)
(7) Thumbs up or down (THUD)

(1) Sharing two models (the STM technique)

This technique was observed with productive skills, predominantly when setting up writing tasks. A teacher presented the class with two completed models of the task. Usually, one of the models would provide an example of a high quality output, whereas the other would not meet the teacher's expectations or would only partially meet them. The teacher would then either introduce or elicit from the children the features which demonstrated that the expectations were met. This resulted in producing a list of criteria which ought to be met in order to produce output of the

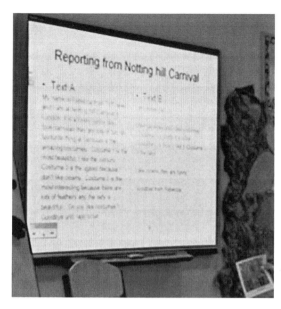

Photo 6.1 Sharing two models technique in action; two examples of short newspaper reports displayed in front of the class and being discussed by the teacher

expected quality. Teachers were observed to record a short list of such criteria and refer to them as success criteria. The STM technique was also observed to be used alongside other techniques: WALT-type questions, I can statements and SC.

Example 1: In Photo 6.1, the teacher is sharing two short newspaper reports about the Notting Hill Carnival with the class. The teacher had prepared the two texts before the lesson. They are displayed on the interactive whiteboard (IWB). The top line reads 'Reporting from Notting Hill Carnival' and below are 'Text A' on the left and 'Text B' on the right half of the IWB. In the bottom right corner of the photo, the teacher is holding a picture of street floats from Notting Hill Carnival, providing a visual prompt that accompanies the texts. In the previous lesson, students read about the carnival and completed a comprehension task based on a video; additionally, vocabulary related to this topic was introduced.

In the lesson pictured in Photo 6.1, the teacher elicited from a group of children ($n = 11$) what features made Text A superior to Text B. As a result of that process, a list of several bullet points was created. They constituted the SC for writing a newspaper report.

(2) Success criteria (the SC technique)

SC was one of the most frequently observed techniques. It was used for all three purposes: setting expectations, monitoring performance and evaluating achievement. Teachers also referred to this technique with two other names: criteria for success or steps to success. In the interview, T5 commented on the name of this technique by remarking that

> *I really like about success criteria is that it's called success criteria so they know what they have to do in order to achieve something so it gives them the sense of achievement* (T5/INT)

When setting expectations, SC were usually presented as a short list of criteria which ought to be met in order to produce output of the expected standard, or as a list of steps to take in order to complete a task. As they worked independently or with peers, learners would be encouraged to refer to the criteria in order to help them monitor their own work. Finally, SC were also used to guide evaluation, including peer and self-assessment. SC were recorded as words or in pictorial form as is evident in the following examples.

Example 2: The student marked the criteria which they met with ticks and the criterion which was not met with a cross (Photo 6.2). Each of the marks was made in a different colour and the same colour was also used to highlight evidence of the respective criterion being met in the student's writing (see also the colour coding technique in Chapter 7).

Photo 6.2 Success criteria for a writing task from a class of 7 to 9-year-olds

Example 3: Students had a copy of the SC stuck in their notebook and were able to refer to them while writing independently. The ticks and the cross were added later, in the process of evaluating the completed writing tasks.

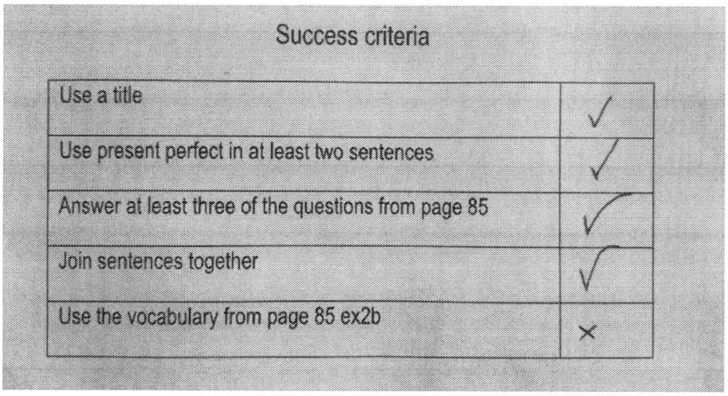

Success criteria	
Use a title	✓
Use present perfect in at least two sentences	✓
Answer at least three of the questions from page 85	✓
Join sentences together	✓
Use the vocabulary from page 85 ex2b	✗

Photo 6.3 Success criteria for a writing task from a class of 10 to 11-year-olds

Example 4: The learners' task was to write simple sentences to describe the weather in the pictures provided by the teacher. The criteria (Photo 6.4) were explained to the students by their teacher. The pictures stand for:

- 'eye' – look carefully at the picture;
- 'pen' – write your sentence;
- 'crossed stick figure' – do not call out for help from the teacher;
- 'pencils' – colour in.

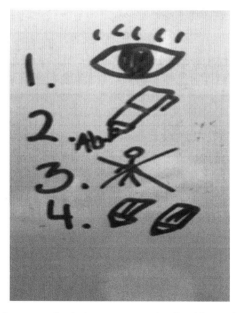

Photo 6.4 Pictorial success criteria for a sentence-level writing task from a class with 7 to 9-year-olds

These criteria were displayed on the whiteboard in front of the class. Students were asked to follow the order of the criteria, ensuring that they completed the language-focused work before moving on to colouring. Students were also encouraged to work independently without relying on the teacher's support.

(3) What are we learning today?–type questions (the WALT technique)

WALT was used by the teachers, who I observed, to stand for 'What are we learning today?'. In other contexts, the same acronym is sometimes used to mean 'We are learning to…'. This technique is mainly used at the initial stages of lessons and serves the purpose of introducing the learning objective (LO). It can be referred to during later stages to help students monitor their progress or as a prompt for students to reflect if they have met the LO. Some of the teachers in the study used cartoon creatures called WALT. Such a character would ask children a question at the beginning of the lesson. Photo 6.5 illustrates how a creature called WALT was presented to children in one of the younger groups (7 to 9-year-olds). On the computer screen, there is a frog-like cartoon creature which this particular teacher called WALT.

Example 5:

Photo 6.5 WALT displayed in a classroom

(4) Learning partners (the LP technique)

Learners were paired up or put in small groups referred to as learning partners for the duration of one or several lessons. After that time, new LPs were assigned. Some teachers allowed children to decide who their LP would be, while others were observed to dictate the pairing, either randomly, e.g. by drawing names from a hat, or purposefully, e.g. to aid differentiation. When introducing LPs, teachers explained to the children that their role was to help their peers learn and elicited from them how this could be achieved. The LP technique was used during pair work, especially to practice speaking, to prepare for independent writing or to peer assess. To aid memory, some teachers displayed LP pairings and the descriptions of LP's role in their classrooms (see following examples).

Example 6: Photo 6.5 shows a list of LPs in the bottom left corner of the flipchart. A close-up of this section of the photo cannot be produced here because it contains the names of the children. Instead, a blank template used to record LPs is presented in Photo 6.6.

Example 7: In Photo 6.7, the teacher recorded the role of the LP. The list reads: help, work, listen, learn, teacher. The teacher discussed with the class how children should help each other; work together; and listen to one another in order to learn more effectively. The teacher agreed with the group that their role was that of their peer's teacher. To the right of the list, the note reads: 2 weeks 4 lessons. This means that these sets of LPs were assigned for 2 weeks. Finally, below the rules, the teacher displayed a list of LPs.

Photo 6.6 A template used for recording learning partners

(5) Mind maps (the MM technique)

MMs can be used for formative purposes. When introducing a new unit of work, some teachers elicited what learners already knew and recorded it on the whiteboard or a flipchart using one colour. At this

Photo 6.7 Learning partners in a class of 7 to 9-year-olds

stage, the teacher would not correct any misconceptions. Next, the children were encouraged to share any questions they had about the new topic or ask about words which they would like to learn. These were added to the MM in a different colour. As a result, the teacher could collect some initial information about the knowledge and misconceptions which the group of children already had. Such insights could be used to inform the teaching.

A third colour was used at later stages. Some teachers were observed to use an MM as a working document, editing it by adding new knowledge, answering questions, adding new questions and correcting misconceptions as the work on the unit progressed. Others returned to the MM towards the end of that unit of work. The notes made using the third colour demonstrated to the learners and their teacher the learning that took place.

(6) Increased thinking time (the ITT technique)

Some teachers were observed to allow their learners time to think before they accepted answers from the children. For example, after asking a question, a teacher would explicitly instruct the class to have some thinking time in silence. The children were not allowed to raise their hands or offer answers at that time. This would normally only last for a short time and was sometimes followed by a pair-share; learners were asked to share the answers which they had just thought of with a partner. The pair-share stage was not always present. The

ITT technique was also implemented after learners received instructions but before they started working on their task, allowing learners some time to plan what they were going to do when they started working on the task.

(7) Thumbs up or down (the THUD technique)

The THUD technique was frequently used by the majority of the teachers in the study, predominantly for checking whether children understood the instructions which they had been given and/or whether the learners thought that they met the criteria for success. The whole class would be asked to simultaneously signal with their thumbs up ('correct'/'I agree'/'yes'), in the middle ('partly correct'/'not sure'/'maybe') or down ('incorrect'/'I don't know'/'no'). This technique was also implemented to enable learners to provide peer feedback.

Example 8: Teachers' accounts of how they implemented the THUD technique.

I also use thumbs (1) thumbs up for good things and feeling confident and moving thumbs around for different levels of confidence (T1/INT)

We also use thumbs up thumbs down and across to indicate if they know what they are about to do (T7/INT)

In this section, I have reported on the way in which teachers implemented the AfL techniques which were used predominantly to set expectations and to monitor progress. I will now move on to discuss insights into the nature of assessment which are offered by the description of these AfL techniques.

Discussion

In the first section of this chapter, I report on seven technique types which can be used to set expectations and to monitor progress in primary language lessons. In this section, I consider the insights into the teaching, learning and assessment which can be obtained from this evidence. The foci of the discussion are (1) the classroom processes which occurred while AfL techniques were being used; and (2) the age-specific characteristics of learners, as discussed in Part 1 of this volume. The discussion is supplemented with quotes from participating teachers, which were obtained from the interviews (INT), the FG discussion and the delayed questionnaire (DQ).

As reported in Chapter 2, individual semi-structured interviews were conducted with the teachers who participated in my study ($n = 8$). The findings were verified through a focus group discussion with all eight participants. Sixteen months after the cross-sectional data collection stage was completed, the teachers were approached again and asked to complete a delayed teacher questionnaire. The purpose of the questionnaire was to gain a longitudinal perspective. All participating teachers returned completed questionnaires.

Learning objectives

The outcomes of the review in Chapter 4 suggest that primary-aged language learners should be assessed against clear objectives and that these objectives should be communicated to children as part of the teaching process (Mihaljević Djigunović, 2015). As outlined in Table 5.1 in Chapter 5, one of the key aspects of AfL is for teachers to clarify and for learners to understand the learning intentions and criteria for success (Black & Wiliam, 2009). Therefore, it is interesting to carefully consider the first question in Table 5.1 (Chapter 5); it seeks to understand whether AfL could contribute to creating effective conditions for language learning by communicating and clarifying the expected outcomes to learners aged 7–11.

There is plenty of evidence in the data to suggest that teachers used AfL techniques such as SC, STM and WALT questions to make learners aware of the LOs. The usefulness of AfL techniques for sharing LOs was recognised by the teachers themselves. For example, T1 commented that AfL 'is giving them [learners] clearer targets and a sense of achievement' (T1/INT). T1 commented that the LOs are 'clearer' when using AfL. This can be explained by the additional information that teachers tended to share with learners while using SC, STM or WALT; the learners were provided with clarification on what they should do in order to meet the LOs (see examples in the first section of this chapter). T1's quote also points to another important characteristic which assessment methods used with primary-aged language learners should have, namely, they should ensure that children experience a feeling of success in language learning. The importance of learners' sense of achievement for lowering their foreign language anxiety levels and developing a positive affective disposition in learners is discussed in Chapter 7. Another teacher remarked that:

> *They [learners] know what to do and miraculously somehow are able to do it. Which is not to say that they do not make mistakes. Mistakes happen but at least there is an opportunity for them to make mistakes and get those corrected and not as I remember my pre-AfL teaching, you just didn't know what your student knew because it was hard to get anything out of them.* (T3/ DQ)

T3 explains how sharing clear LOs can help create learning conditions which could facilitate the provision of scaffolding and feedback on the ongoing learning. The quote indicates that when learners are aware of what is required from them ('They know what to do'), they seem to be more capable of completing the tasks at hand ('somehow are able to do it'). T3 continues by explaining that the learners' ability to do what is asked of them can be observed as learners attempt tasks more readily, not because they complete the tasks correctly. But it is that process of learners working on tasks and making mistakes that T3 considers beneficial to learning. This is because when learners are working on tasks they have opportunities to make mistakes and to collaborate with peers and/or the teacher to modify their output in order to correct these mistakes. The significance of modification of output to learning is discussed in Chapter 7.

Metacognition

Several of the AfL techniques reported in this chapter could help learners plan how to approach a task and subsequently monitor their own performance. They include ITT, SC, LPs and THUD. Although planning and monitoring are two metacognitive strategies which can be used by primary-aged learners (Chamot & El-Dinary, 1999), children may need scaffolding in order to use them effectively. Such support is especially important for younger learners who begin to develop their metacognitive awareness as early as 3 to 5-years-old but do not begin to exercise control over their metacognitive strategies until the age of 8–10 (Flavell *et al.*, 1993). Psychological research suggests that knowledge of strategies can facilitate control (Borkowski, 1985) and that children can be trained in strategy use (Ghatala, 1986). By providing age-appropriate scaffolding through AfL techniques, teachers may be able to train primary-aged language learners in using simple metacognitive strategies such as planning and monitoring. This could have implications for language learning as efficient strategy use has been shown to benefit learning for older learners (e.g. Griffiths, 2003). The limited evidence available from primary contexts confirms that learners who planned and monitored their own work performed better on reading and writing tasks (Chamot & El-Dinary, 1999). Another study suggested that monitoring may be especially benefi-cial for productive skills while predicting can help with tasks that focus on receptive skills (Gu *et al.*, 2005).

The view that AfL can support teachers in encouraging the use of metacognitive techniques by primary-aged language learners was reflected in the FG discussion.

EXTRACT 3
(From the FG discussion)

[1]   T1: I think for me for the young learners you're teaching them skills of (1)
[2]   before they start something to consider what will make it successful so instead
[3]   of launching into something and just doing it they pause and my primary
[4]   groups especially have learnt to think before they do things which is a skill they
[5]   didn't have before
[6]   T7: Yeah that's true generally raising their awareness that they have to think
[7]   before they say it and they really have to find these bullet points on paper or in
[8]   their heads

The conversation in Extract 3 indicates that teachers observed that when they used AfL, their learners developed the basic metacognitive skills of planning what to do before they started to work on a task. T7 mentioned 'these bullet points', most likely referring to the use of SC. The teacher explained that learners have to reflect on the demands of a task at hand to 'find these bullet points'. In other words, they have to decide what they need to do to complete the task to standard. By helping learners to develop skills for planning and monitoring their own performance, AfL techniques such as SC might be useful in helping primary-aged language learners develop metacognitive control.

Familiarity with task structure

Another question from Table 5.1 (Chapter 5) which could be answered by using the insights provided by the report on the practical implementa-tion of AfL is Question 4. It seeks to understand whether AfL techniques could provide a familiar structure to assessment tasks. Presumably, with experience of using AfL techniques, learners' familiarity with technique types would increase. Such knowledge could help learners construct their own SC such as those described by T7 in the previous section. Therefore, when they encounter familiar task structures, learners might be able to use this metacognitive strategy more efficiently. Because AfL is integrated into the teaching and learning activities, it would be possible to hypothesise that with consistent use of techniques such as SC, teachers can help learn-ers to become familiar with the structure of assessment used in lessons.

Such familiarity could facilitate language learning. According to Pinter (2007), when children do not focus their attention on the structure of a task, they perform better because they can concentrate on the language which they need to complete it. It could be argued that when students are not required to understand an unfamiliar task structure, they are better placed to demonstrate their language skills. As a result, they can provide more valid evidence of achievement. This is directly related to Aspect 2 of the theoretical framework of AfL as defined by Black and Wiliam (2009: 8) (Chapter 2), which specifies that AfL involves 'engineering effective classroom discussions and tasks to elicit evidence of student understanding'.

The study reported by Pinter (2007) focused on learning through dyadic interactions. However, it would also be interesting to explore if similar gains can be observed when learners work independently on tasks with a familiar structure. This focus for future inquiry gains currency in light of the well-established outcomes from adult contexts, which indicate that familiarity with the task structure can benefit language learning (Bygate, 1996; Skehan & Foster, 1999).

Responsibility

By clarifying LOs and expected standards of performance, and by facilitating the use of metacognitive strategies, AfL techniques could help to create classroom conditions in which children begin to take greater responsibility for their own learning. This was a strong theme in teachers' reports. For example, Extract 4 from the FG discussion illustrates that teachers recognised the existence of a relationship between clarifying the LOs ('everyone knows what they need to do') and encouraging children to take responsibility for their own learning ('kids can get involved and take responsibility').

EXTRACT 4
(From the FG discussion)

[1]   T2: (...) it seems to work very well so goals are easily established everyone
[2]   knows what they need to do and there is no concept of what did we do or
[3]   what haven't we done and everyone seems to have a clear idea of what's going on
[4]   at the simplest level it works (1)
[5]   T3: yeah and it also shows that kids can get involved and take responsibility
[6]   for their own learning and that applies to young children too (1) I've certainly
[7]   used it with my young ones
[8]   T7: Yes(...)

The theme of growing learner responsibility for their own learning was also evident in individual accounts.

> *it was amazing how quickly kids got used to taking some responsibility and when you think about young learners they still don't have that concept of taking responsibility for their learning until you start using AfL and then somehow it clicks for them so for me that does it (1) I no longer have to be responsible for everything in the classroom when I use AfL (T4/INT)*

> *they [learners] are more responsible for their learning and this is something very very important (1) this is something that when you use AfL really small kids start feeling (T5/INT)*

> *When I use these techniques, my students seem to notice the purpose of each lesson and they feel more responsible for their own learning. They take pride in their achievement. As their involvement increases, they enjoy the lessons more and, obviously, learn more. (T7/ DQ)*

The finding that using AfL might help to promote children's responsibility for their own learning is consistent with other reports from primary contexts. For example, based on a case study in Malaysian primary classrooms, Sardareh and Saad (2012) report that AfL could promote active learning and responsibility.

Summary of the Chapter

This chapter focuses on the practical implementation of AfL for the purposes of setting expectations and monitoring progress. The discussion of the processes which were included in using AfL illustrates how such implementation could contribute to creating favourable conditions for language learning in primary language classes. The four ways in which this could be achieved include (1) clarifying LOs and the level of expected performance; (2) providing familiarity with the structure of the task; (3) training primary-aged language learners in metacognitive strategy use; and (4) promoting learners' responsibility for their own learning.

Notes

(1) Saying 'the can', T7 is referring to 'Can I …?'-type questions which they often used to start the lessons, e.g. 'Can I tell my partner about ten things that I did yesterday?'
(2) Two of the lessons were audio recorded. This was due to a lack of parental permission for 1 out of 148 learners to be video recorded. Permission for audio recording was fully granted.

7 Evaluating Achievement

> the children get bits of feedback on what they've done correctly and what they have
> not done correctly which is meaningful to them
> (T4/INT)

Introduction

In this chapter, I continue to report on the practical implementation of assessment for learning (AfL). The focus is on the techniques that can be used for evaluating the achievement of primary-aged language learners. In the lessons I observed ($n = 28$), evaluation was done in the form of feedback provision either during monitoring of the ongoing learning or towards the end of a lesson or a task. As discussed in Chapter 2, feedback which facilitates learning is central to formative practices. However, as discussed in Chapter 4, children's cognitive and metacognitive skills, which are necessary for using feedback effectively, are not yet fully developed in childhood. In this chapter, I consider whether, and if so how, the AfL techniques which I observed being used with 7 to 11-year-olds could help learners notice and act on the feedback they receive. To provide empirical evidence for the discussion, the present chapter starts with a detailed report on the use of those AfL techniques which were predominantly used for feedback provision. As in Chapter 6, these findings come from a series of 28 lesson observations in 14 different groups, taught by 8 experienced teachers. For more information about the data collection and analysis, see the introduction to Chapter 6.

It is important to note that feedback can be provided either by the teacher, peers or the learners themselves. In the younger age group (7 to 9-year-olds), the feedback providers were predominantly teachers and peers. Self-assessment was implemented more frequently in the older age group (10 to 11-year-olds). For findings regarding the differences between the two age groups, see Chapter 8.

AfL Techniques: Feedback

Observational data indicate that 11 AfL techniques were used for providing feedback on learning:

(1) Colour coding (CC)
(2) Indicate mistakes without explanations (IMWE)
(3) Perfect purple and red to remember (PPRR)
(4) Smiley faces (SF)
(5) I can statements (ICS)
(6) Traffic lights (TL)
(7) Next steps (NST)
(8) Star charts (SCH)
(9) Two stars and a wish (TSAW)
(10)   Find the fib (FTF)
(11)   Sheriff's star (SST)

(1) Colour coding (the CC technique)

This technique can be used to provide feedback on written output at the word, sentence and/or text level. When using the CC technique, a feedback provider would refer to agreed criteria (see the success criteria [SC] technique in Chapter 6), highlighting evidence for each criterion in the learner's work. If there was insufficient evidence that a criterion had been met, the learner would be asked to perform a short additional task to improve their work (see the NST technique below). Such a sequence could lead to a learner modifying their written output. If the modifications resulted in a target production, the learner would demonstrate that they meet the criterion for success. Alternatively, if there was no modification of output or if the modification which was made by the learner resulted in another non-target production, then the teacher would get valuable insights into the gap in the learner's knowledge or understanding. Formative evidence collected in this way can inform teaching, fulfilling the pedagogic function of assessment (Rea-Dickins, 2001). Perhaps even more importantly, using the CC technique to encourage learners to modify their output could serve the learning function of assessment (Rea-Dickins, 2001), that is to say, it could help to facilitate learning through assessment.

Example 9: Photo 7.1 is a scan of a piece of written work marked with the CC technique. It is a description of a character written by an 8-year-old learner. The scan is annotated with numbers and explanations are provided below.[1]

(1) In the top left corner, there is a picture of the character that was described (covered here due to copyright regulations). Before the learners were asked to start writing, the whole class worked together

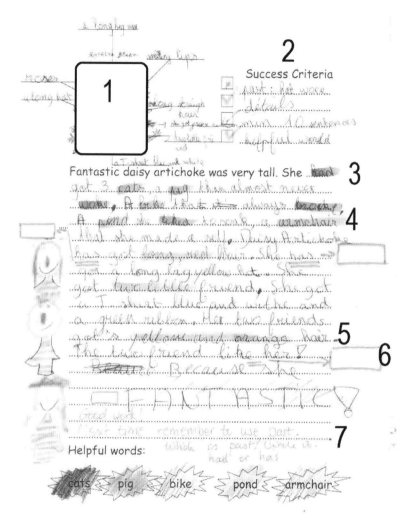

Photo 7.1 A piece of writing marked with the CC, the SC and the IMWE techniques

with the teacher to label the small picture in the top left corner with some key vocabulary. The children were asked to use some of that vocabulary to add detail to their descriptions.

(2) The SC (top right corner) for this task were recorded before learners started the independent writing.

(3) The CC technique was used by the learner to self-assess their own work by highlighting evidence for each of the criteria. This learner used purple to highlight the past tenses.

(4) The learner used green to indicate where they used the 'helpful words' provided by the teacher at the bottom of the page and/or from the labelled picture at the top.

(5) The learner also highlighted additional detail (in yellow in the original). In the line marked with number 5, the phrase 'yellow and orange' was highlighted; this provided extra detail about the character's hair. The learner used the same colours (purple, green and yellow) to put ticks or crosses in the little box by the respective SC. In the process of self-assessment, the learner identified that their use of the past tenses did not meet the SC. This is indicated with a cross in the box corresponding to that criterion.

(6) Subsequently, the teacher collected the written work and indicated where mistakes were, leaving three boxes, like the one marked with number 6, for the learner to provide the correct forms (see also the IMWE technique). In doing so, the teacher provided an opportunity for the learner to improve their skills of using the past forms correctly.

(7) The teacher also provided some further feedback at the bottom of the page (7). It consists of praise and a short task to support the learner in developing their skills of using the past tenses. The feedback reads: 'Great work! Next time remember to use past. Which is past? Circle it. had or has'.

When that work was returned to the learner, they had to respond to the teacher's prompts, thereby working towards developing their language skills further. This example shows the process of providing individualised feedback which indicates the next step on the child's learning path, which will take them closer to meeting the learning objective (LO). As a result, the learner's attention is focused on the form of the language, helping them to notice the discrepancy between their interlanguage and the correct form of the second language (L2). The importance of noticing for learning is discussed later in this chapter.

(2) Indicate mistakes without explanations (the IMWE technique)

This simple technique allowed the teacher to quickly provide feedback to students while they were working on any kind of task that was recorded in writing (grammar, spelling, writing tasks or reading comprehension tasks). The teacher would walk around the classroom with a coloured pen and circle or underline areas of students' work that required improvement, without explaining what needed to be changed. Learners had been informed about the meaning of such marks and the same colour would be used consistently. Once the teacher had marked a learner's work with the IMWE technique, it was the student's task to reflect on their output and modify it. Such modification would either remedy the problem or would indicate to the teacher that further pedagogical intervention was needed in order to address a gap in that student's understanding. This enabled the teacher to provide individualised feedback to learners while they were still working on tasks. This is an important point to note because it demonstrates how AfL techniques can be used to offer opportunities for learners to try to improve their performance as they are learning new skills. What is important to note is that as the lesson progressed, the teacher was able to revisit the corrections made by their students and, if need be, indicate success or the need for further improvement, thereby providing ongoing formative feedback to their learners (see also Chapter 11).

If mistakes were highlighted to learners through the IMWE technique, the reader might rightly wonder about the children's reactions to such practice. Although the lesson observation schedule did not include a section for systematic recordings of the learners' affective reactions to AfL techniques, it did include a column for recording the activity that took place in the classroom as well as the interaction patterns. The data from those sections suggest that children reacted keenly to that kind of feedback; they often either conferred with peers or compared their work with them to spot the mistake. The observations suggest that learners were pleased when they were able to discover the mistakes that their teachers circled. Some learners also tried to ask the teacher for an explanation, but teachers mostly encouraged children to 'figure out' the correction that was needed by themselves rather than providing it to them. It was also evident that children were eager to show off what they thought the teacher wanted them to spot. This can be explained by the positive and supportive way in which the teachers introduced the technique; by explaining to their students that it was a game and the learners' task was to guess what the teacher was thinking; to read the teacher's mind or to be a learning detective.

The IMWE technique was mostly used while children were working but sometimes also after a task had been completed (Photo 7.1, point 6). The IMWE technique was frequently implemented with either SC (Photo 7.1, point 1) or ICS (Photo 7.5).

Example 10: Photo 7.2 is a scan of a storyboard about Guy Fawkes. The annotation made by the teacher on the right of the scan says: 'What's wrong here?' and a box is provided for the learner to respond. The comment refers to the spelling of the verb 'traveled', spelled here with a single 'l' (US spelling) and not with a double 'l' (UK spelling). This illustrates an excellent opportunity for the teacher to use this point to increase the learners' awareness of various spelling conventions characteristic for different varieties of English. It is also interesting to note that the teacher did not draw the learners' attention to the incorrect use of the verb 'take' and

Photo 7.2 An example of the IMWE technique in a notebook

the lack of the word 'to' after 'travelled' in the same sentence. Instead, the teacher focused the feedback, and therefore the learners' attention, on just one language point. Arguably, the choice to focus feedback only on those features of performance which are key to meeting the LO not only supports learners in achieving that LO, but also results in a smaller amount of feedback. Effectively, such feedback may become more manageable for children to act upon.

(3) Perfect purple and red to remember (the PPRR technique)

The PPRR technique resembles the IMWE technique because it helps to indicate to the learner what needs to be amended in their work. Alliterated phrases are made up to help learners remember the significance of the colours used by their teacher. For example, red to remember would be used to mark areas that need improvement. Variations used by different teachers also included reflection red, improvement indigo and oh-dear orange.

The PPRR technique differs from the IMWE technique in that it uses a contrasting colour to indicate what has been done well. For example, perfect purple, brilliant blue, green to go were observed. Individual teachers tended to use just two colours, for example, purple and red. As a result, learners taught by one teacher knew that if something was circled in purple, it was done well and if something was circled in red, it needed improving.

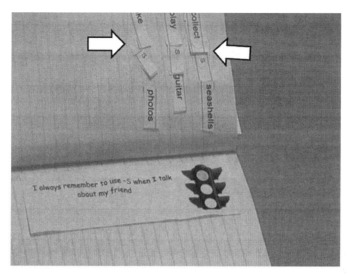

Photo 7.3 An example of self-marking, using the PPRR and the TL techniques

The PPRR technique was used with tasks that were recorded in books and with speaking. When used for speaking, the technique entailed the use of two laminated colour cards. One colour would be raised when the target language was used correctly or a success criterion had been met and the other when a mistake was made in the target language.

Example 11: Photo 7.3 illustrates how a learner self-marked a grammar-focused task using the PPRR technique. The learners were asked to stick in jumbled up sentences. They had to organise the individual word and letter cards to create grammatically correct sentences in the third-person singular of the present simple tense. The learner whose work we can see in Photo 7.3 has circled the verb and 's' in each sentence with a purple crayon. They have also stuck the LO, which reads: *I always remember to use –s when I talk about my friend*, into the notebook. The LO is accompanied by a TL template (see also Example 15). Having circled the evidence for meeting this LO (marked for the reader by the white arrows in Photo 7.3), the learner subsequently awarded themselves a green TL.

(4) Smiley faces (the SF technique)

The SF technique was used predominantly in the final stages of lessons to enable learners to reflect on the degree to which they met their LO. Children were invited to draw a smiley face if they thought they 'met their LO'; a neutral face for 'LO partially met'; and a sad face for 'LO not met'. Sometimes, teachers also referred learners to SC or ICS when using the SF technique.

A variation was also observed in one teacher's class; the children were asked to draw how they felt about their learning and could

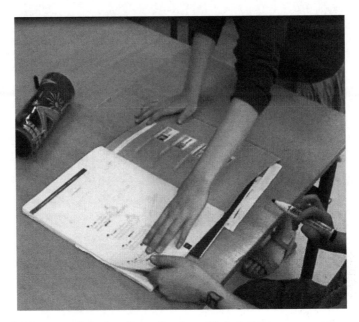

Photo 7.4 Learners discussing the smiley faces AfL technique

choose any emotion, not limited to the 'happy, neutral and sad' options. This allowed the learners to communicate their excitement or nervousness about a certain area of their learning to the teacher in a safe and personalised manner. The teacher explained that 'with respect to feedback they liked it when they were able to quantify how they felt about their learning (...) some time ago I did the smiley faces but I adapted it so that they could make any face expressions' (T2/INT). Such feelings help children build their experiences of foreign language learning (FLL). Research discussed in Chapter 5 suggests that this can play an important part in developing positive affective profiles of primary-aged language learners (Enever, 2011; Mihaljević Djigunović & Lopriore, 2011).

Example 12: Photo 7.4 shows two learners discussing which expression should be assigned to a smiley face. The teacher asked the children to explain to their partners why they had chosen their expressions. In the process of doing so, children were encouraged to reflect on the reasons for selecting an expression.

Example 13: Photo 7.5 is a scan of the back page of a learner's notebook where the SF technique was recorded together with ICS. After each lesson, children were given a sticker which they completed with an ICS. Next to each statement, learners recorded a SF. Evidently, the learner whose book this was seemed very happy with their progress in each of those lessons.

Photo 7.5 The SF technique recorded in a notebook

(5) I can statements (the ICS technique)

The ICS technique was used to evaluate whether the LOs were met by the learners. It was implemented either on its own or in conjunction with SF, CC or TL.

Example 14: Photo 7.5 illustrates five examples of ICS recorded in a learner's notebook. The statements read: 'I can remember places in town; I can talk about differences; I can write about my hero; I can describe people; I can sing the beach song'.

(6) Traffic lights (the TL technique)

Feedback providers used colours analogous to the road code to indicate the degree to which an LO had been met: green for 'LO met, you can move on'; amber for 'LO partially met, slow down and think'; red 'LO not met, stop and improve'. The meaning of each colour tended to be described with child-friendly and accessible phrases, using mostly positive statements and avoiding negative information which could discourage the children. Table 7.1 lists examples of such phrases, which were recorded in observed lessons when TL were implemented.

Table 7.1 Phrases used to describe the meaning of colours in the traffic lights technique

Green	Amber	Red
I can ... by myself/well	I can ... with some help	I will achieve ... next time
I know how to ...	I sometimes remember how to ...	I need to work on ...
I know this already	I know something about this	I don't know this yet

I can ask someone what they got for their birthday.

Green = I know this already.
Yellow = I know something about this.
Red = I don't know this yet.

Photo 7.6 An example of traffic lights recorded in a notebook

Example 15: Photo 7.6 illustrates one of the ways in which TL were recorded in students' notebooks. In this instance, the teacher provided a TL template with explanations of what each colour meant. Learners were asked to colour in one circle on the TL template. In Photo 7.6, the learner initially coloured in the middle circle with yellow. This indicated that they thought that they had partially met the LO. However, after the teacher reminded the learner what they did during one of the activities during that lesson, the learner changed their self-evaluation to green. Green pen was used to cross out the pale yellow shading of the middle circle and subsequently to colour in the top circle. This is an interesting example, illustrating how a teacher can use this AfL technique to help the learner recognise their own achievement and to reward themselves. Research discussed in Chapter 5 indicates that teachers can lower learners' foreign language anxiety (FLA) by encouraging learners to recognise their achievements and to reward themselves.

(7) Next steps (the NST technique)

The NST was a short task or a question with which teachers annotated learners' work. The purpose was usually to provide an opportunity for extra practice in response to a learner's non-target production. It was also sometimes used to provide a learner with an opportunity to extend their learning. The NST most commonly followed SC, TL or PPRR techniques. It was used by teachers when they were either monitoring or evaluating learners' work.

Example 16: In Photo 7.1, point 7, the teacher provided a NST, asking the student to indicate which of the two words was in the past tense. In doing so, the teacher provided an opportunity for the learner to practice the skill which the learner identified as a criterion that had not been met. In this piece of work, the learner did not demonstrate that they could correctly use verbs in the past simple tense. This was one of the SC. The teacher asked the learner to select which of the two verbs provided by the teacher in the NST (had or has) was in the past tense and to circle it. By completing this simple activity, the learner had an opportunity to start working on improving their skills and ultimately to meet the SC.

Example 17: In Photo 7.7, a learner from the older group (10 to 11-year-olds) set their own next steps task. First, the learner used the CC technique to identify where in the written text they met the SC. The SC are recorded in the top right corner. The learner was expected to use the grammatical construction 'to be going to' at least five times in the text; to write a long text which consists of at least 10 sentences; to use a simile with the words as…as… at least once; and to use at least one question in the text. The learner highlighted evidence of the SC which they had met and annotated the SC. For example, next to the 'Going to x5' criterion,

Photo 7.7 Next step set by a learner

they wrote the digit 7 in a circle. This indicated that they used the phrase 'going to' seven times in the text, thereby meeting the requirement set by the SC for a minimum of five 'going to' phrases. However, it should be noted that there actually are only three instances of correct use of 'going to' to describe future intentions, which was the intended use as modelled by the teacher. Interestingly, the learner ticked the criterion corresponding to the simile with 'as...as...'. Having received some oral feedback from the teacher, the learner realised that they had not use a correctly formed simile and therefore gave themselves a next step activity which reads: 'Next time I'm going to remember to write as...as'.

This example illustrates that learners can attempt to set their own next steps activities, even though they may need some guidance from the teacher in doing so. Importantly, the evidence identified by the child in the text allowed the teacher to help the learner address the incorrect use of 'as...as...'. In this lesson, every learner received individual feedback from the teacher. This was possible because the children were engaged in self-assessing and the teacher was able to use that time to provide individual feedback.

(8) Star charts (the SCH technique)

Some teachers were observed to use posters which helped them record and display a list of LOs for the whole term. Learners' names were listed in the first column and the LOs in the top row. After each lesson, those children who met their LO were awarded a gold star to stick in. Silver stars were used for 'LO partly met' and brown for 'LO not met'. Some teachers only awarded stars to those students who met their LO but withheld stars for the others, until they could demonstrate that they met the LO, for example, through homework, an NST activity or in subsequent lessons. As the term progressed, LOs were added to the poster. This helped to build a big picture of the learners' progress over a longer period of time.

Example 18: In Photo 7.8, a start chart is displayed on the flipchart (annotation 1). The photograph additionally illustrates how other AfL techniques were used within that lesson. On the same flipchart, there is a list of learning partners (3). In Photo 7.8, the teacher is in the process of recording the SC (2) which she elicited from the learners.

(9) Two stars and a wish (the TSAW technique)

The TSAW technique was used to provide feedback on writing. The feedback provider recorded two positive comments (two stars) and one point for development (a wish). This was often done with reference to the SC. The purpose was to inform the learner which of the criteria they met and which one required further practice. If all the SC were met, the wish would normally be a suggestion of how to extend the learning further. If more than one SC was not met, only one tended to be

Photo 7.8 A star chart displayed in the classroom, alongside the LP and SC

selected as an area for improvement (the wish). This type of feedback was provided predominantly by teachers with several instances of peer feedback also observed. The focus was clearly on highlighting achievement through the two stars and indicating the one key element which should be improved.

Example 19: Photo 7.9 shows a completed writing task in which the learner was asked to describe five photographs. The sentences written by the learner are (my comments in brackets):

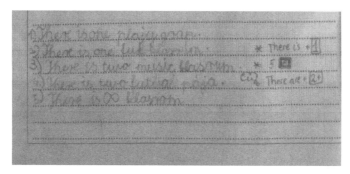

Photo 7.9 A piece of writing by a beginner 10-year old student, marked by the teacher with two stars and a wish

(1) *There is one playj gran* (playground).
(2) *There is one fud klasrum* (food classroom – canteen).
(3) *There is two music klasrum* (classrooms).
(4) *There is two futbal pája* (football pitches).
(5) *There is ∞ klasrom* (classrooms).

The teacher provided feedback on this performance using the TSAW technique. The stars read: '*There is +[1]*' and '5 ☐ (picture of a square)' while the wish reads: '*There are + [2+]*'. The teacher's comments written next to the stars mean that the learner used 'There + to be' correctly when they were describing one place in the school; and that all five photographs were described. The wish draws the learner's attention to the fact that when using plural nouns, they should use 'are', not 'is'. This simple feedback was provided to a learner aged 10 who was at the very initial stages of English. The teacher used only the target language (there is/are) and drawings to communicate with the child and to offer an opportunity to develop their understanding of grammar. This is a useful example illustrating how AfL techniques could be used to facilitate feedback provision in contexts where learners are at low levels of their L2 and do not share a first language (L1) with the teacher (see also Chapter 8).

It is also worth mentioning that the LO of that lesson was to use the phrase 'There + to be' correctly. It seems that the feedback was only provided on that aspect of the learner's performance and no other elements of their performance were included in the feedback. The following features of the output in Photo 7.9 were not commented on by the teacher: (1) mistakes in spelling; (2) the lack of –s at the end of the plural nouns; or (3) the creative use of the ∞ *sign* to replace a word the learner might have not known. This observation illustrates how an AfL technique might have supported the teacher in providing feedback which was focused on the skills that the learner was expected to develop in the lesson and which addressed the individual learning needs of the child. This is an important observation in light of research which suggests that learners may take individual trajectories to achieve attainment targets (Mihaljević Djigunović, 2015).

Example 20: Photo 7.10 illustrates how the TSAW technique was used to mark against SC. The students were given the SC before they started writing. The SC are recorded in the top left corner of the writing template in Photo 7.10. They read: *8 sentences; Always, Never, Usually; Once/twice a week; Words p.18.*

The class had received feedback through TSAW before and the learners were also used to providing peer feedback using this technique. In Photo 7.10, a peer provided feedback on the story about another child's daily routines. The feedback was recorded in pink under the completed task. It reads:

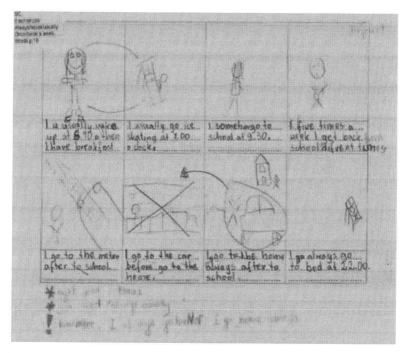

Photo 7.10 The TSAW technique used for peer-marking against SC

* Eight good sentences,
* You used always, usually,
! Remember: I always go home. NOT: I go home always.

By offering two pieces of positive information and only one point for further development, the feedback provider helps to highlight achievement. This is important information which may help to build a learner's positive self-concept and lower their FLA (see also Chapter 5). The point for development can help the learner notice the gap between their expected performance and their current performance. See Chapter 4 and the discussion later in this chapter on the importance of noticing in language education.

(10) Find the fib (the FTF technique)

This simple technique is an adaptation of the popular game 'Call my bluff'. Learners would be provided with several possible answers or solutions and would be asked to explain which one is incorrect (the fib) and to justify their choice. This technique was sometimes used orally after new target language was introduced or in a written form to practice spelling. The purpose was to identify gaps in understanding and address them. The FTF technique tended to be followed by the NST.

(11) Sheriff's star (the SST technique)

As they arrived for a lesson, children in some classes were given stars which looked like sheriff's badges. Learners attached these to their clothes to indicate that they were 'in charge' of their own learning. However, if at any point during the lesson, a child was feeling lost, they would take the badge off, indicating to the teacher in a quiet and safe way that they felt that they were losing control over their own learning and that they needed extra support. A teacher was able to support when needed, while the learners were given a way to ask for help, without stopping the flow of the lesson for the rest of the class and without having to state out loud that they did not understand something.

In this section, I have provided a detailed report of how teachers implemented AfL techniques to provide feedback to primary-aged language learners, together with a description of feedback provided through AfL techniques. I now move on to discuss whether, and if so how, such feedback could benefit language learning in childhood.

Features of Feedback Provided through AfL

In this section, I consider whether feedback provided through the AfL techniques described in this chapter is appropriate for primary-aged children and if it offers benefits to language learning. In order to do that, I compare the features of feedback that can be provided through AfL with the outcomes of a review of research on language learning in childhood (Chapters 4 and 5). The discussion is supplemented with quotes from the participating teachers. The outcomes of the discussion highlight how AfL could address the specific requirements of language assessment in primary contexts.

Based on tangible examples

An immediate observation that can be made about the feedback provided through AfL is that it is focused on output, rather than the processes involved in language learning. The focus seems to be predominantly on whether, or to what degree, the learner achieves the LO. This means that ongoing feedback tends to refer to concrete examples from children's performance. Such examples come from tasks that are either fully or partly completed. These can be used to exemplify whether children meet the predefined LOs and to offer guidance on how to improve performance. The observation that teachers tend to use concrete examples as a basis for the feedback which they provide to young learners can be explained by the findings of research that have indicated that children tend to find it difficult to discuss the learning process (Gu *et al.*, 2005).

Importantly, by using examples from each learner's performance to provide feedback to them, teachers are able to individualise it. This kind of feedback is relevant and meaningful to learners. As a result, children are informed about their achievements as well as which aspects of their performance need to be improved. Given such feedback, learners can be equipped with tools to take some ownership of their own learning. This is a practical way in which teachers could activate 'learners as learning resources' (Black & Wiliam, 2009: 8).

Relevant to concurrent learning – contextualised through teaching

As is evident in the field notes from observed lessons and from teachers' accounts of how they used AfL, the techniques used for providing feedback were implemented either during or directly after a task. Similar to Butler and Lee (2006), who argued that on-task self-assessment is more accurate than off-task self-assessment, primary language teachers reported that AfL techniques work better when children are given feedback on their performance in the task at hand. However, if the use of AfL is deferred until a later time, learners may not find it easy to reflect on their learning and achievement as effectively. For example, T2 recalled that once they used TL 'later and not straight after the task (1) and if it was a couple of weeks later (1) then they [learners] just couldn't remember'. This quote indicates that deferring the use of an AfL technique in time may result in it losing its potential to be an effective assessment tool. Therefore, it suggests that the techniques themselves may not be helpful if they are not contextualised through teaching activities. This interpretation resonates with T1's belief that AfL is 'continuous and it's more meaningful because they know it's about the things we learnt to do that lesson and not something that they did a while ago and now perhaps cannot remember' (T1/INT).

Implementing assessment alongside teaching and learning and providing feedback on the ongoing learning has implications for the type of evidence that can be collected. Research suggests that by using continuous assessment which is contextualised through age-appropriate tasks, teachers are more likely to collect valid evidence of learning (Hasselgreen, 2000; Hasselgreen & Caudwell, 2016) as opposed to relying on a one-off summative test.

Sense of success

The techniques described in this chapter provide learners with opportunities to obtain information about their progress and to recognise their own achievement. This is evident in the way that SC, perfect purple, two stars, TL and SCH can be used. This is an important feature of AfL as it takes into account the initial slow rate of progress of primary-aged language learners (e.g. Muñoz, 2006). Pragmatically, it offers teachers a tool which can be used to evidence the slow progress by building up a bank of small steps that children take in their learning.

However, perhaps even more importantly, the techniques listed above could support learners in recognising their own achievement because they can explicitly see what they have already achieved: purple highlighting in PPRR; stars in TSAW, etc. This is a significant finding because as Dörnyei (2009b: 29) convincingly argues '(f)or some language learners the initial motivation to learn a language does not come from internally or externally generated self-images but rather from success-ful engagement with the actual language learning process (e.g., because they discover that they are good at it)'. Empirical research has suggested that fostering a sense of success in such a way can lower FLA (Griva *et al.*, 2009; Yim, 2014), inform the development of positive self-concepts (Mihaljević Djigunović, 2015) and help to motivate learners (Vilke & Vrhovac, 1995, cited in Mihaljević Djigunović *et al.*, 2008). It has also been reported that experiencing success in a language classroom can help children develop positive affective dispositions towards FLL (Cable *et al.*, 2010) which, itself, is considered an important aim of primary language programmes (Edelenbos *et al.*, 2006; Mihaljević Djigunović, 2015).

Some of the participating teachers recognised the need for evaluat-ing their learners' affective profiles and indicated that they used AfL techniques for that purpose. For example, T1 explained that they used 'thumbs up for good things and feeling confident and moving thumbs around for different levels of confidence' (T1/INT) and T8 also reported that they used AfL 'for checking how they've done their work and how they felt about their work' (T8/INT).

The feedback-giving techniques discussed in this chapter can be used for teacher feedback and for self and peer assessment. They offer oppor-tunities for learners not only to recognise their own achievements but also to have them recognised by their peers. T1 commented that primary-aged children engaged with each other in a positive and supportive manner when using AfL. They said that 'the biggest benefit for my groups has been the peer learning (1) working together and not being competitive in their English but being supportive of each other's learning' (T1/INT). By offer-ing opportunities to notice their own and their classmates' achievements, AfL techniques could help primary-aged children build realistic self-con-cepts as language learners. Additionally, they seem to offer opportunities for learners to practically engage in classroom activities. Dörnyei (2019) considers engagement to be an important component of the L2 learning experience, itself a powerful predictor of motivated behaviour.

While self-assessing, learners are encouraged to refer to examples from their own work, for instance, by highlighting in the text they have written where they meet a criterion for success. Such practice could help children learn how to recognise their own achievement. This is an important point in the discussion because research has shown that self-encouragement and self-rewarding techniques can improve self-confi-dence and lower anxiety but are rarely used by learners (Griva *et al.*,

2009). It would be interesting for future studies to explore the relationship between AfL and anxiety, especially focusing on whether embedding AfL in teaching and learning could help to lower learners' anxiety.

Noticing the gap

Through AfL techniques, primary-aged language learners are encouraged not just to recognise their own progress but also to notice the discrepancies (the gap) between the target production and their own interlanguage(s). The techniques which can be used for that purpose include IMWE and red to remember. Teachers observed that their learners were able to recognise both their achievements and the gap. For example, T1 commented that 'I think that they can recognise what they're strong at and weak at which is really impressive especially with our young learners' (T1/INT). As discussed in Chapter 4, it could be beneficial to design the assessment process in such a way that it offers young learners opportunities for noticing the gap. This could create conditions in which primary-aged language learners can attempt to modify their output. Otherwise, if a child does not notice that they have made a mistake, they would not be aware that they should attempt to correct it. Consequently, they would be missing an important learning opportunity.

When a non-target production is noticed, the learner can attempt to modify their output. AfL seems to facilitate that process; many of the techniques helped the teachers provide feedback to which learners had to respond. For example, they could be asked to complete a next steps task. This kind of interaction could be repeated in a continuous manner more than once while a child was still working on a task, offering multiple opportunities to modify output through interactions (written or oral). The outcomes of the quantitative analysis reported in Chapter 9 indicate that this was possible even three times within one lesson. Such practice could contribute to language learning because 'output pushes learners to process language more deeply – with more mental effort – than does input' (Swain, 2000: 99).

Teachers explained that AfL techniques helped learners to notice the gap because they explicitly indicated it to the children. This is exemplified by T3 and T6's comments about providing feedback on writing through AfL.

> *certainly has impact on the way I mark writing because in a way it just makes it easier to mark and more useful because you're actually focusing on things that they've done well and on the things that they need to improve in the future which is more meaningful than just calling four out of five for writing good which at the end of the day doesn't mean very much at all* (T3/INT)

> *a really good way to make them focus on a few different things in their writing rather than you know (1) 'my writing sucks I can't write very well' (1) and the students can then focus on just a few key things and get a good grade, whereas before it was not up to standard and you just had to fail them based on that but then here you can actually say (1) well you did this this and this (1) this was what was the most important and that's why they got a bad grade and they understand that (1) and I think that's good* (T6/INT)

These two teachers draw our attention to the importance of the information that primary-aged language learners are provided with through feedback. Both teachers indicate that AfL helps them to focus their learners' efforts on those language points that will help to close the gap between their current performance and the expected level of performance. These two accounts also contrast feedback on writing provided through AfL techniques with summative grading. Specifically, they explain that with AfL, the teacher is able to help the learner understand the reasons for a grade when the grade is also provided alongside the feedback. This is an important point to note as other studies have indicated that teachers should avoid simply providing a pass/fail outcome in order to lower the anxiety levels which might be experienced by children (Aydin, 2013).

Visual – suitable for low levels and non-literate children

Another important characteristic of AfL techniques is that some of them relied on either visual elements (SC in Photo 6.4, TL in Photo 7.6, SF in Photo 7.5) or the use of very basic words or expressions (SC in Photo 6.2, TSAW in Photo 7.9). This is an important observation which illustrates how feedback could be made accessible to children who are at early stages of L2 learning and do not share a lingua franca with their teacher, or to those who have not yet developed literacy skills in their L1. The need for learners to understand the feedback which they are given would seem to be a prerequisite for the potential benefits which providing the kind of feedback discussed above could have on language learning. On the other hand, there were examples of techniques which required a fairly high level of literacy or understanding of some metalanguage (e.g. SC and TSAW in Photo 7.10). It would seem that the techniques can be adapted to various levels of language proficiency and literacy levels to suit the needs of learners (see also Chapter 8).

Summary of the Chapter

In this chapter, I have reported on the practical implementation of those AfL techniques that can be used to provide feedback on learning. There are 11 techniques in this group. The examples and detailed descriptions, which are based on data from lesson observations, are supplemented with quotes from the participating teachers, who explained how they implemented AfL in their classes.

The discussion revealed that those AfL techniques have several features which make them particularly appropriate for primary contexts. First, they offer children opportunities to recognise their own achievement and experience success in language learning. Second, children can be guided to notice and address the gap between their current performance and the expected level of performance. Third, the techniques are flexible and can be adapted to suit learners' levels of L2 and literacy. Fourth, the feedback provided through AfL techniques is contextualised through teaching activities.

These features seem to be especially appropriate for primary contexts as they address a number of characteristics which assessment of language learning in childhood should contain. Most significantly, the discussion indicates that feedback provided with AfL techniques could help to (1) allow for children's short attention spans by facilitating immediate feedback; (2) use performance as a basis for feedback, accounting for primary-aged language learners' limited ability to reflect on the learning processes; (3) enable children to notice non-target production and promote opportunities for correcting their mistakes and/or improving performance; (4) offer opportunities to lower learners' anxiety by fostering their sense of success in language learning and avoiding pass/fail results; (5) build positive affective dispositions towards FLL and motivate learners.

Importantly, the discussion also reveals that it is not just the nature of the AfL techniques but also the timing of implementation that together may offer the benefits to learning. Therefore, the attention will now shift to discussing the process of implementing AfL techniques, in particular, to the use of AfL when teaching different language skills (Chapter 8); to the between-age group variance in the use of AfL (Chapter 8); and to the frequency and diversity in the use of various technique types (Chapter 9).

Note

(1)   A colour version of Photo 7.1 is available in the ebook version of this publication.

8 Teaching and AfL: Tasks, Skills and Age-Related Differences

teachers can use AfL to present tasks and material in a clear way to kids who speak hardly any English
T5/INT

Introduction

In this chapter, I focus on the relationship between assessment for learning (AfL) and teaching. First, I discuss how AfL was used in the lessons which I observed with the four language skills: speaking, listening, reading and writing. Subsequently, I explore the relationship between typical tasks which tend to be used in primary language classes and AfL techniques. Finally, I report on the differences in implementation of AfL in the two age groups: 7 to 9 and 10 to 11-year-olds. The findings from my own research discussed in this chapter illustrate how AfL techniques were used to provide scaffolding. They also suggest that AfL was used predominantly in those activities during which learners were expected to produce output in second language (L2) either in writing or orally. The differences in the use of AfL between the two age groups highlight the relationships between first language (L1) literacy, metacognitive control and assessment.

AfL across Language Skills and Lesson Activities

I acknowledge that language skills are not taught entirely on their own and that many activities are likely to include the use of more than one, if not all four, skills. However, developing a particular skill may be the focus of an activity and that skill may need to be used to a greater degree than others in order to complete a particular activity. In fact, the learning objectives (LOs) for lessons which I observed during my own research suggested that developing one specific skill was the pedagogical aim of lessons. For example, the LOs in Photo 8.1 read: 'I can remember places in the town'; 'I can talk about differences'; 'I can write about my hero'; 'I can describe a friend'; 'I can sing the beach song'. Out of these five LOs, three refer to skills, either writing ('I can write', 'I can describe')

116

Photo 8.1 Learning objectives from a learner's book

or speaking ('I can talk', 'I can describe'). This provides a justification for selecting a language skill as a unit of analysis.

An additional reason for analysing how AfL was used across the four language skills came from the analysis of interview data. Some of the teachers referred to the four skills when describing the way in which they implemented AfL. For example, T5 reported that:

> initially I used it just for writing with good models bad models and then I started using it for speaking tasks and then I was impressed with how well it worked and I wanted to use it more so I started using especially success criteria for listening tasks with how they have to approach it how they have to do it (T5/INT)

In order to explore how AfL was used across the four language skills, the field notes from lesson observations were scrutinised. The analysis included annotating each technique with the type of activity it was used for and *the focal skill*; this was one of the four language skills which were either stated in the LO or perceived by the researcher as the pedagogical aim of the activity. The outcomes of this analysis are summarised in Table 8.1.

Table 8.1 AfL techniques and language skills

Column A	Column B: Name of AfL technique	Column C: Types of learning activities with which the technique was used	Column D: Skills with which the technique was used
1	Success criteria (SC)	Arts and crafts, classroom instructions	Writing
2	Learning partners (LP)	Vocabulary learning	Speaking
3	What are we learning today?–type questions (WALT)	Learning objectives	
4	Traffic lights (TL)	Vocabulary learning, learning objectives	Speaking
5	Thumbs up or down (THUD)	Classroom instructions, arts and crafts	
6	Two stars and a wish (TSAW)		Writing
7	Sharing a good and a bad model (SGBM)		Writing
8	Smiley faces (SF)		Writing, speaking
9	'I can' statements (ICS)	Learning objectives	
10	Perfect purple and red to remember (PPRR)	Grammar	Writing (often with grammar focus)
11	Next steps (NST)	Vocabulary learning, grammar	Writing
12	Colour coding (CC)		Writing
13	Find the fib (FTF)	Vocabulary, grammar	Speaking
14	Increased thinking time (ITT)	Comprehension tasks	Speaking, reading
15	Star charts (SCH)	Learning objectives	
16	Indicate mistakes without explanations (IMWE)	Grammar, spelling, comprehension tasks	Writing, reading
17	Sheriff's star (SST)	Learning objectives	
18	Mind maps (MM)	Projects, vocabulary	

Source: Adapted from Britton (2015).

Similar to T5, other teachers also reported that with time, they expanded their use of AfL from one skill (predominantly writing) to other skills. For example, T1 reported that 'initially I just used it for writing but now I've used it for all parts of the lesson' (T1/INT). I was interested to know more about the way in which the teachers' practice changed over time. To gain that longitudinal perspective, 16 months after all the interviews and lesson observations had been completed, I asked the teachers to complete a delayed questionnaire. One of the questions sought to understand how they used AfL with various language skills and activities. Those insights are summarised in Table 8.2.

As can be observed from the findings presented in Tables 8.1 and 8.2, AfL was implemented predominantly when the focus was on productive skills: writing and speaking. The longitudinal data confirm that

Table 8.2 Use of AfL with task types and language skills – a longitudinal perspective

AFL	Types of activities	Skills
WALT	Introduction to the lesson (T1, T2, T5, T7) With any activity to keep learners focused on what they are learning (T1, T7)	
SC	Arts and crafts (T2, T6) Classroom management (T4, T6)	Writing (T2, T4, T8) Speaking (T4, T5)
ICS	With any activity to introduce or reflect on the learning objective (T1, T2, T3, T6)	
LP		Speaking (T3, T4, T8)
SF	After any task (T4, T8)	
TSAW		Writing (T5, T6)
IMWE		Writing (T7)
ITT		Speaking (T7)

Source: Adapted from Britton (2015).

this finding was stable over time. The usefulness of AfL techniques for teaching productive skills could be explained by their potential to provide scaffolding (see next section) and/or feedback which encourages modifications of output (see Chapter 7). Gan and Leung (2020) convincingly argue that formative assessment is compatible with task-based language teaching. They use productive skills to exemplify how such compatibility looks in practice.

AfL as a Tool for Scaffolding L2 Production

In order to better understand why AfL was used with productive rather than with receptive skills, it would be useful to consider what tasks are typically used for practising the four language skills in primary language classes. Therefore, a list of tasks was sourced from an authoritative methodological guide for teachers (Szpotowicz & Szulc-Kurpacka, 2009). This book was selected for the following reasons: (1) it was the most frequently signed-out book from the resource cupboard in the school where I conducted my research; (2) it was published in Poland, where the study was based, for the educational context of that country; (3) it provides a recent perspective on teaching primary-aged language learners. The task types were organised into four lists; one to illustrate typical tasks used to teach each of the four language skills (Columns A and B in Table 8.3). It is acknowledged that Table 8.3 does not include an exhaustive list of all task types which could be used. However, the aim of this analysis was to consider the nature of typical tasks (not all task

Table 8.3 Typical tasks in primary language lessons and use of AfL techniques

Skill		Tasks types used in primary language lessons (based on Szpotowicz & Szulc-Kurpaska, 2009)		AfL techniques used for each purpose in the study classrooms		
		Column A: Task types that are likely to require on-line processing	Column B: Task types that are likely to have an inherent structure	Column C: Setting objectives and expectations	Column D: Monitoring performance	Column E: Checking achievement
Productive skills	Speaking	1. Role plays 2. Information gap activities 3. Describing people and objects (narrative)	1. Singing 2. Class surveys 3. Asking and answering questions	Success criteria Increased thinking time Learning partners	Increased thinking time Learning partners	Smiley faces Find the fib Traffic lights Learning partners
	Writing	1. Creative writing: descriptions and stories 2. Functional writing: letters, postcards, film/book reviews 3. Dialogue journals	1. Writing labels on pictures/objects 2. Copy/write words in different categories 3. Copy/write a sentence and add a missing word 4. Running dictations	Success criteria Sharing two models	Indicating mistakes without explanation Perfect purple and red to remember	Two stars and a wish Perfect purple and red to remember Next steps Colour coding Learning partners
Receptive skills	Listening	–	1. 'Listen and do' activities 2. Bingo 3. Simon Says 4. Chinese whispers 5. Picture dictation 6. Mime what you can hear 7. Follow the route 8. Listening grids 9. Listen and point	–	–	–
	Reading	–	1. Matching words and phrases 2. Labelling pictures/objects with words 3. Predicting words from initial sounds 4. Rearranging jumbled words/letters 5. Guess the missing word 6. Arranging sentences in a text 7. Memory games 8. Clapping syllables		Increased thinking time Indicating mistakes without explanation	

types) that can be used with primary-aged language learners. Therefore, this set of tasks is considered to be a representative selection of typical tasks used in primary language classes. Consequently, it satisfies the aim of the analysis.

Subsequently, the tasks were subdivided into two categories by applying Skehan and Foster's (1999) distinction between: (1) tasks that require on-line processing from learners; and (2) those which are inherently more structured. The decision to adopt the internal task structure as a criterion seems justified by the participating teachers' comments that 'it [AfL] helps to teach (1) you could say (1) because it gives you structure (...) I think it's also very helpful for learners in completing tasks' (T5/INT). Finally, AfL technique types were mapped out against all the skills according to the purpose which they were used for in the study classrooms. The results of that analysis are summarised in Table 8.3.

The results suggest that the majority of tasks used in primary language lessons have an inherent structure (Column B). However, there is a noticeable difference in the distribution of tasks in Columns A and B between receptive and productive skills. This indicates that there is a difference in the amount of structure that is provided and the amount of on-line processing required from learners, depending on whether the focal language skill of a task is receptive (reading and listening) or productive (writing and speaking). In the former group, all the tasks described by Szpotowicz and Szulc-Kurpacka (2009) seem to have greater inherent structure and require less on-line processing than those in the latter group.

Furthermore, the results of the analysis presented in Table 8.3 illustrate that AfL techniques were used for all three purposes when either writing or speaking was the focal skill of a task (Columns C–E). This could be interpreted as evidence that when the tasks did not have inherent structure, teachers used AfL techniques to provide additional scaffolding for learners. The data presented in Table 8.3 indicate that they did so when setting up tasks, monitoring performance and evaluating learners' achievement. There was also evidence in the interviews with teachers that they considered some AfL techniques to be useful when providing scaffolding for completing tasks. For example, T3 reported that 'the good thing about success criteria is that it gives them a clear framework to complete the task' (T3/INT) and T8 declared that (s)he used AfL techniques 'sometimes for more kind of role play speaking tasks so that they know exactly what they're doing' (T8/INT). While it was previously proposed that AfL could be linked to effective instructional scaffolding (Shepard, 2005), there is a need for empirical evidence of how this could practically be achieved in various educational contexts. The finding that AfL could be used to provide scaffolding in primary language education when teaching productive skills is very useful, especially in light of initial reports from adolescent contexts where peer-assessment (an integral part of AfL) has been shown to have a positive impact on learners' writing, including 'better performance, learner autonomy, self- and metacognitive awareness' (Tsagari & Meletiadou, 2015: 317). Benefits of peer assessment for the writing performance and autonomy were also reported from adult contexts (Birjandi & Hadidi Tamjid, 2012; Plutsky & Wilson, 2004).

A possible explanation for the usefulness of AfL techniques in scaffolding production could be inferred from some teachers reporting that they had their preferred techniques for teaching different language skills. For example, T3 said that the technique (s)he 'used the most is probably the success criteria (1) this was for different writing tasks' (T3/INT). This might suggest his/her learners were consistently exposed to some techniques. Under such conditions, children could become familiar with the structure of those techniques. As discussed in Chapter 6, such familiarity might render a similar positive impact on measures of fluency, complexity and/or accuracy as learners' familiarity with task structure reported from adult contexts (e.g. Bygate, 1996; Skehan & Foster, 1999). This interpretation seems to corroborate the limited evidence available from primary language contexts which suggests that learners' familiarity with task structure may have a positive impact on their performance (Pinter, 2007).

It is also worth noting that the participating teachers made some observations regarding the impact of the repeated use of AfL techniques on learners' performance. For example, T5 reported that using AfL techniques 'makes them [learners] much faster (1) so once they get used to the procedure they immediately (...) know what to do' (T5/INT). Perhaps T5's observation could be explained by the quantitative findings pertaining to the frequency of use of AfL (Chapter 9). T5 used AfL techniques in almost every lesson. (S)he implemented a total of 12 different technique types in one academic year. This suggests that individual technique types were repeated relatively frequently in the teacher's lessons and therefore, the learners had ample opportunities to become familiar with those techniques.

Admittedly, further research is needed to help us better understand the nature of scaffolding provided through AfL and its implications for language learning in childhood. For example, the above findings pose the question of whether learners' familiarity with technique types that were integrated into tasks could increase their familiarity with task structure and, consequently, whether it could have a positive impact on language learning in childhood. This would be an interesting area for future research to explore, especially as it could provide insights into the relationship between the use of AfL and improved achievement.

With regards to receptive skills, the use of AfL techniques was only observed for the purpose of monitoring progress when reading. It should also be acknowledged that although T5 reported that having implemented AfL with writing and speaking tasks, (s)he also 'started using especially success criteria for listening tasks' (T5/INT), there was no empirical evidence to corroborate this declared use of AfL for listening. This quote is reported here in the interest of providing a thorough account of the findings about the use of AfL. Regardless of whether T5 did start to experiment with AfL when focusing on listening skills, the key finding that AfL techniques were predominantly implemented when teaching productive skills remains unchanged.

In this section, I have focused on discussing the relationship between teaching and AfL by focusing on various language skills and task types. As learners' age is an important factor that influences how teaching is designed, the discussion will now continue by exploring the relationship between learners' ages and AfL.

Age as a Factor in Implementing AfL

To explore whether there were any differences in the way that AfL was implemented according to learners' ages, I compared the findings obtained from classes with 7 to 9 and 10 to 11-year-olds. The field notes from observed lessons ($n = 28$, $n = 14$ in each age group) were scrutinised to identify which AfL technique types were used in each age group and how they were implemented. Subsequently, the technique types were subdivided into three mutually exclusive categories according to whether they were used (1) in both age groups, (2) with 7 to 9-year-olds only or (3) with 10 to 11-year-olds only. The outcomes of a comparative analysis indicate that learners' ages were a factor in how teachers implemented AfL. The differences can be attributed to learners developing their literacy and metacognitive skills.

In both age groups, AfL was used for all three purposes: setting expectations and objectives; monitoring performance; and evaluating achievement. However, the ways in which it was implemented for each purpose differed. The outcomes are summarised in Table 8.4.

Across all three purposes

The most significant difference was the way in which the techniques were presented and recorded in both age groups. Across all three purposes for using AfL, a greater reliance on literacy skills was observed in the older age group (10 to 11-year-olds). It should be noted that in the educational context in which my research was conducted, formal literacy instruction started when children were 7 years old. Therefore, some of the learners in the younger age category were only just beginning to learn letters and sounds. By the time they turned 10, children would be fluent readers who routinely completed longer writing assignments. As might be expected, the use of AfL did not rely heavily on the written word in the younger age group. Some examples which illustrate this finding

Table 8.4 Differences in technique use between classes of 7 to 9 and 10 to 11-year-olds

Purpose	Description of the purpose	Age-related differences	
		Specific for 7 to 9-year-olds	**Specific for 10 to 11-year-olds**
Setting objectives and expectations	Used to clarify expectations of outcomes or explicitly raise students' awareness of what they were learning.	• The purpose of giving and clarifying instructions, reported by teachers, was observed only in the 7–9 year group.	• A wider range of techniques was used in the older age group to explicitly raise the students' awareness of what they were learning.
Monitoring performance	Often referred to the expectations set earlier in that lesson. Used to provide feedback on the learners' performance in real time.	• A greater reliance on monitoring by the teacher. • AfL techniques were used to gauge students' confidence.	• A wider range of technique types was used to encourage self-monitoring.
Evaluating achievement	This included self-reflection or peer- and/or teacher feedback. The AfL techniques which were deployed for teacher feedback were also used for peer feedback while those used for self-assessment were different.	• There was a wider range of technique types used to provide teacher and peer feedback.	• There was a wider range of technique types used to facilitate self-assessment and reflection on learning and areas for improvement.
Across all purposes	Differences which occurred in the use of AfL technique types regardless of the purpose.	• AfL technique types were less reliant on literacy skills; there was a greater reliance on pictorial representations.	• There was a greater reliance on reading and writing in the way AfL techniques were presented and recorded.

Source: Adapted from Britton (2015).

include: (1) success criteria (Chapter 6) tended to be presented as pictures rather than words; (2) when traffic lights and smiley faces (Chapter 7) were used for feedback, they were accompanied by either oral feedback or very simple written statements; (3) other techniques which did not involve a significant amount of reading or writing were commonly used, including colour coding, perfect purple and red to remember and thumbs up or down (Chapter 7). The techniques which relied predominantly on the learners' ability to read and/or write were observed in the older age group. These included, for example, two stars and a wish, I can statements or mind maps. Examples of SC from the two age groups provided in Table 8.5 illustrate this finding well.

The examples in Table 8.5 suggest that according to the learners' literacy levels, teachers were able to adapt some AfL techniques. This helped them cater to the age-related needs of their learners. Importantly, this finding indicates that AfL can be implemented with learners at initial stages of literacy development if suitable technique types are selected. Since research into FLL in childhood has indicated that L1 literacy levels

Table 8.5 Examples of SC in the two age groups: 7 to 9 and 10 to 11-year-olds

Success criteria with learners aged 7–9	Success criteria with learners aged 10–11

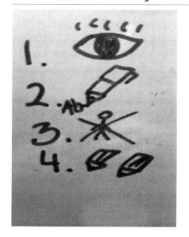

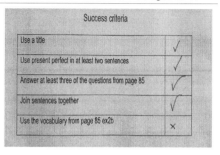

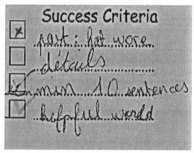

can be linked to success in language learning (e.g. Knell *et al.*, 2007), it would be worth investigating whether adopting non-literacy dependent assessment methods could benefit language learning in childhood.

Setting expectations and objectives

In both age groups, teachers used AfL techniques to raise learners' awareness of the objectives for the lesson and to communicate expectations for the level of performance. In the older age group (10–11), teachers tended to provide information about the LOs more explicitly, using a variety of techniques. In the younger age group, this purpose was fulfilled predominantly by using the what are we learning today?–type questions (WALT) (Chapter 6). However, four other technique types (SF, SC, TL and THUD) were also used by six out of the eight participating teachers before children started working on their task for a slightly different purpose, namely to clarify instructions. This use of AfL was only observed in the lessons with 7 to 9-year-olds.

In the process of synthesising findings, the purpose of clarifying instructions was included within the broader aim of setting expectations and objectives. However, it seems useful to take a step back and consider the nuances within that main purpose for using AfL. The finding that AfL was used in the younger group to clarify instructions for tasks provides an interesting insight into the methods used to help the learners manage the cognitive demands of instructions. It seems that in the older group, the teachers did not need any extra help to set tasks and that sharing the LO and clarifying the expected level of performance was sufficient for learners to attempt completing tasks independently or with partners.

The processes which occurred in the younger age group differed. It would seem that learners needed a different type of scaffolding. Teachers tended to provide instructions with the use of AfL techniques. Importantly, these were often recorded either on the whiteboard (see Photo 7.8 in Chapter 7) or in learners' books. Importantly, the techniques were made visible to learners while they were working on their tasks. During that time, teachers were also observed to actively encourage children to refer to the techniques to remind themselves of the expectations. This helped to account for children's short attention spans.

Teachers reported a positive impact of using AfL to clarify instructions. For example:

> As for teaching, giving instructions became more efficient and assessing students' work too. I was amazed how honest the kids were about their own results. (T5/DQ)

> we use thumbs up thumbs down and across to indicate if they know what they are about to do (T7/INT)

Research suggests that the clarity of instructions can be related to adult learners' performance (Winer et al., 1992). As discussed in Chapter 3, as children's processing ability develops throughout childhood, they tend to rely on the exemplar-based memory to a greater degree than adults (Wen & Skehan, 2011). Additionally, children have limited memory spans (Wilson et al., 1987). These two characteristics may explain why primary-aged children could benefit from scaffolding for more complicated sets of instructions. In language learning, this area seems even more important especially in immersion contexts and in those instructed primary language contexts where teachers and learners do not share an L1.

Monitoring performance and evaluating achievement

Learners aged 10–11 were encouraged to self-monitor and self-evaluate more frequently than their younger counterparts, who relied predominantly on the feedback from their teachers and peers. In total, eight technique types were used for self-monitoring and evaluation in the older age group, as compared to only two in classes with the younger learners. This was the main difference between the two age groups within the second and third purpose (monitoring performance and evaluating achievement, respectively). This finding can be explained by children's growing ability to self-monitor and self-evaluate as they develop metacognitively. This interpretation is consistent with findings of research which demonstrated that around the age of 10, children were able to perform more accurate self-assessments than younger learners (Butler & Lee, 2006).

Both processes, monitoring and evaluating, require learners to compare their own performance to either the requirements of the task (when monitoring) or the expected level of performance (when evaluating). This can be done by children who have developed at least some metacognitive control. As discussed in Chapter 4, children develop their ability to use metacognitive skills around the ages of 8–10 (Flavell *et al.*, 1993). However, research also suggests that children can be trained to use metacognitive strategies (Ghatala, 1986). Therefore, it would be interesting to explore whether embedded use of AfL (see Chapter 9) could help learners develop greater metacognitive control, therefore contributing to learning.

Finally, there was some evidence in lesson observations that teachers also used traffic lights, smiley faces and thumbs up or down to gauge how confident learners were about their performance and language skills. This was only observed in the younger age group (7 to 9-year-olds). This is an interesting finding which indicates that in addition to language proficiency, teachers also used AfL to evaluate their learners' affective responses. This theme occurred in the interviews and was mentioned by three out of the eight participating teachers. While not a very strong theme, this is certainly an interesting one when considered in light of research into the relationship between affective dispositions and language learning (Chapter 5). This finding suggests that AfL could be used to evaluate learners' affective responses to learning. Such insights could then be used to plan interventions and support the development of positive affective profiles. This is an important finding in light of research that indicates that positive affect can be linked to achievement in primary language learning (e.g. Mihaljević Djigunović & Lopriore, 2011).

Additionally, this finding indicates that affect can be included in the construct of assessment.

Summary of the Chapter

In this chapter, I have explored the relationship between teaching and AfL. The findings indicate that teachers used AfL predominantly with productive skills. The analysis suggests that this may be due to the additional scaffolding which AfL techniques provided, especially if tasks did not have a high degree of inherent structure and/or required on-line processing from learners.

The teaching across the whole cohort incorporated the use of AfL for three main purposes: sharing objectives and expectations, monitoring progress, and evaluating achievement. However, there were some differences in the way the techniques were implemented across the two age groups. The differences include the amount of scaffolding within the first purpose; the roles of teachers and learners; the visual representation of techniques; and the construct of assessment. These can be linked to learners' cognitive and metacognitive development and their literacy levels. All age-related differences in the use of AfL are summarised in Table 8.6.

Table 8.6 Age-related differences in the use of AfL

Area of differences	7 to 9-year-olds	10 to 11-year-olds
Roles	Dominance of teacher and peer monitoring and evaluation	Use of self-monitoring and self-evaluation in addition to teacher and peer monitoring and evaluation
Representation	Pictorial Single words and digits	Longer phrases
Instructions for tasks	AfL used	AfL not used
Construct	Affect and academic performance	Academic performance

9 Types of Implementation of AfL

Introduction

The discussions in Chapters 6–8 offer interesting insights into how assessment for learning (AfL) can be used in lessons. To better understand the nature of AfL in primary language education, we should also consider differences in the practices of individual teachers. For example, a teacher could use the same technique every lesson while a colleague next door implements various technique types. In such a case, the *diversity* of use of AfL (the number of different AfL technique types) would be different between those two teachers, while both could still say that they used AfL. Yet another teacher might use AfL techniques less frequently, perhaps only in a few lessons per term. Consequently, they would be implementing AfL with lower *frequency*. In order to better understand whether there was any between-teacher variance in the way that AfL was implemented, I analysed the frequency and diversity in the use of AfL.

The data to address this research focus came from the school records of work ($n = 448$), lesson observations ($n = 28$) and, to include the longitudinal perspective, from the delayed teacher questionnaire ($n = 8$). The findings were triangulated through the data from teacher interviews ($n = 8$) and one focus group.

School documents (Appendix 3) were identified as a useful source of data as they provided insights into the use of AfL in a large number of lessons ($n = 448$). These records were a part of the school's practice; teachers used them to record what was covered in each lesson and what assessment techniques were used. As can be observed in the example in Appendix 3, there was a box for recording AfL. Teachers tended to write down what AfL techniques they implemented in each lesson. Therefore, AfL techniques were selected as a unit of analysis of the frequency of use. This methodological choice is further justified by teachers' understanding of AfL as a type of assessment that can be implemented through a variety of techniques (Chapter 2).

School documents were analysed quantitatively by calculating frequency counts of techniques and deploying descriptive statistics in SPSS v19, including mean, median, standard deviation and maximum and minimum values. The aim was to investigate how often teachers used AfL across and within lessons (frequency) and how many different types of techniques they implemented (diversity).

Frequency of use was measured within lessons (intra-lesson frequency), focusing on how many techniques were used on average in one lesson. Additionally, this was also calculated across all 448 lessons (inter-lesson frequency), focusing on how many of them featured AfL. It was also possible to include a longitudinal perspective on the inter-lesson frequency by incorporating a question in the delayed questionnaire which asked the teachers to self-report how often they used AfL 16 months after the empirical data were collected. Both types of frequency are discussed for the whole sample and for individual teachers.

The analysis sought to establish whether any particular frequency or diversity in the use of AfL was favoured by the primary language teachers. Furthermore, the analysis aimed to identify factors that might explain the suitability of the preferred type(s) of implementation to primary language classes. The findings reveal that there were four types of implementation, depending on the frequency and diversity of use.

Frequency of Use

As discussed in Chapter 6, familiarity with the structure of tasks is an important consideration for language learning (Pinter, 2007). The outcomes reported in Chapters 6 and 7 indicate that AfL techniques tend to be used within tasks and that they should be considered an integral part of the task structure. Therefore, it becomes important to explore the frequency with which learners are given opportunities to use AfL techniques. Arguably, the more often learners are exposed to AfL techniques, the more chances they have to become familiar with their structure. For example, Pinter (2007) reports that as few as three instances when 10-year-olds used the same task structure had positive impact on performance.

As teachers were the ones who made decisions about the frequency of use, in my study I focused on between-teacher variance in the implementation of AfL. I also considered whether learners' age could be linked to frequency of use but found that there was no significant difference between the two age groups of learners. For example, T1 used AfL in 89% of their lessons, including 92% of lessons with 7 to 9-year-olds and 85% with 10 to 11-year-olds. During the same time, T2 used AfL in 18% of their lessons, accounting for exactly 18% of lessons in each age group. Similar results were obtained for all other participating teachers on measures of frequency and diversity. This illustrates that learners' age does not seem to be related to the frequency and diversity of AfL used in lessons.

I report the findings about the inter-lesson frequency before moving on to the intra-lesson frequency, and subsequently, to diversity of use.

Inter-lesson frequency

Inter-lesson frequency was investigated by applying the frequency function on SPSS v19 to the data from 448 lessons recorded by teachers. The findings offer insights into how systematically learners were exposed to AfL. First, the outcomes of the analysis provided an overview of the whole cohort. Then the inter-lesson frequency for individual teachers was explored. Finally, changes over time are also discussed to provide a longitudinal perspective.

Table 9.1 Inter-lesson frequency for the whole cohort

Number of AfL techniques used within one lesson	Number of lessons (inter-lesson frequency)	Percentage	Cumulative percentage
4	17	3.8	3.8
3	69	15.4	19.2
2	59	13.2	32.4
1	49	10.9	43.3
0	254	56.7	100.0
Total	448	100.0	

Source: Adapted from Britton (2015).

The findings reported in Table 9.1 reveal the percentage of lessons in which AfL was implemented. The findings indicate that 43.3% featured at least one AfL technique. The maximum number of techniques used in one lesson was four (in 3.8% of lessons). Just under one-third of all lessons included either two (13.2%) or three (15.4%) AfL techniques. These outcomes indicate that taken as a whole, this cohort of teachers used AfL in slightly less than one out of every two lessons on average. The analysis proceeded to investigate whether the same was true for individual teachers.

Inter-lesson frequency for individual teachers

The frequency counts calculated for individual teachers (Britton, 2015) reveal significant between-teacher variance in the inter-lesson frequency of use. Overall, the teachers could be categorised into three groups according to the inter-lesson frequency of use (Table 9.2).

Given the low percentage point in the last row of Table 9.2, it could convincingly be argued that T8 did not actually implement AfL in his/her lessons. The remaining teachers seemed to implement AfL with the average frequency of between 'one in five lessons' to 'almost in every lesson'. A visual representation of the above results illustrates well how significant the differences in inter-lesson frequency were (Figure 9.1).

Table 9.2 Categories of inter-lesson frequency of use

	Inter-lesson frequency	Category description	Teacher code	Percentage of lessons during which AfL was used
Category 1	Frequent use	In more than half of all lessons	T5	91
			T1	89
Category 2	Moderate use	In between a quarter and one-half of all lessons	T7	50
			T3	38
			T6	31
Category 3	Rare use	In one-quarter or fewer of all lessons	T4	23
			T2	18
			T8	5

Source: Adapted from Britton (2015).

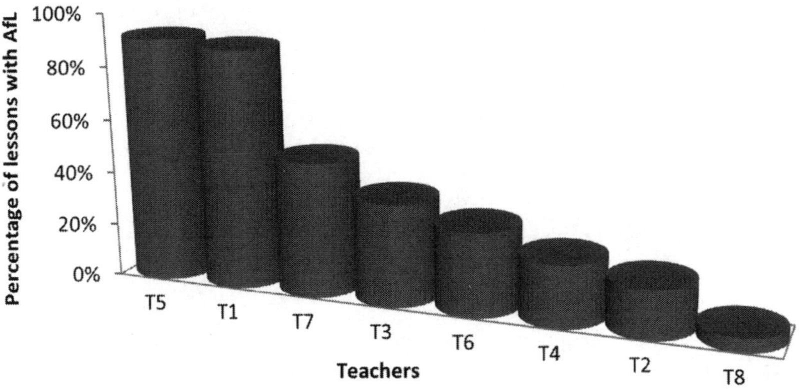

Figure 9.1 A visual representation of the inter-lesson frequency of use of AfL by eight teachers

After examining the inter-lesson frequency, the analysis focused on exploring the intra-lesson frequency. It is believed that reporting the findings about both kinds of frequency will contribute to providing a more accurate and detailed picture of the use of AfL in the study classrooms.

Intra-lesson frequency

Intra-lesson frequency was analysed in SPSS v19 by applying descriptive statistics (median, mean, standard deviation and frequency counts) to the data collected from 448 school records of work and separately to data from 28 lesson observations. The observed lessons are a subset of all lessons. The values calculated for the whole cohort are reported first.

Intra-lesson frequency values are reported only for the lessons in which AfL was used. By definition, the intra-lesson frequency in all remaining lessons is zero. The number of lessons in which AfL was not used was included in calculating the inter-lesson frequency, as reported

Table 9.3 Intra-lesson frequency for the whole cohort, excluding the lessons which did not include AfL

Number of AfL techniques used within one lesson	Number of lessons	Percentage	Cumulative percentage
4	17	8.8	8.8
3	69	35.6	44.4
2	59	30.4	74.8
1	49	25.2	100.0
Total	194	100.0	

Source: Adapted from Britton (2015).

in the previous section. The number of lessons in which AfL was implemented is reported for each teacher in Table 9.4.

The first finding from analysing the intra-lesson frequency across the whole cohort is that AfL techniques tend to be used more than once in a lesson or not at all. As is evident from Table 9.3, in 74.8% of the lessons during which AfL was implemented, the teachers used it at least twice. The observation that the majority of lessons during which AfL was used featured more than one instance of using AfL is confirmed through the median value of two in the final row of Table 9.4. It signifies that in at least half of all lessons during which AfL was used, it was used at least twice.

This is a very interesting finding as it points to the continuous nature of AfL. This means that the formative function tends to be revisited more than once in one lesson (see also Chapter 11). It is also consistent with teachers' reports of their own understanding of AfL. They stressed 'that AfL is a kind of philosophy' (T2/FG) which 'is the means to an end (1)

Table 9.4 Intra-lesson frequency – individual teachers

Category	Description	Teacher	No. of lessons	Min	Max	Median	Mean	Std. deviation
Category A – Frequent use	At least 50% of the lessons feature three or more AfL techniques	T1	50	1	4	3	3	0.756
		T5	52	1	4	3	2.83	0.585
Category B – Moderate use	At least 50% of the lessons feature two AfL techniques, but excluding Cat. A	T6	17	1	3	2	2.41	0.618
		T3	21	1	2	2	1.76	0.436
Category C – Infrequent use	Fewer than 50% of lessons feature more than one AfL technique	T4	13	1	2	1	1.31	0.48
		T7	28	1	2	1	1.25	0.441
		T2	10	1	2	1	1.2	0.422
		T8	3	1	1	1	1	0
All lessons in which AfL was used			194	1	4	2	2.28	0.941

just a part of what you're doing anyway with them (1) just teaching them in a slightly different way' (T6/INT) and that it can be implemented with various 'tactics tools techniques' (T2/INT). Such a nature of assessment is especially relevant to primary contexts, in which learners have been shown to benefit from a continuous approach to assessment (Edelenbos & Vinje, 2000; Hasselgreen, 2000).

The median values for individual teachers (Table 9.4) indicate the number of occasions on which AfL was used in at least half of those of their lessons during which they used AfL. These values were used to define the three categories of intra-lesson frequency. Category A comprises teachers who used AfL three or more times. The two teachers in this category (T1 and T5) are the ones who also implemented AfL with high inter-lesson frequency. Category B includes those teachers who used AfL twice in at least half of their lessons which featured AfL. The remaining teachers, who are classified as Category C, used AfL once in at least half of those lessons in which they implemented AfL.

The categorisation proposed above was confirmed through the mean and standard deviation values. The mean values of around three, accompanied by standard deviations below one, for teachers T1 and T5 confirm that when T1 and T5 implemented AfL, they tended to use it between two and four times per lesson. In the case of teachers T3 and T6, the mean and standard deviation values suggest that the intra-lesson frequency was lower than in the case of T1 and T5 but higher than in the case of the remaining four teachers. T3 and T6 used AfL around twice in those lessons that featured AfL, while for the remaining teachers, it was just one instance of AfL use.

As is evident from Table 9.4, T8 implemented AfL in three lessons in total, once in each lesson. The analysis of the diversity of use (see next section) illustrates that, through the whole of the cross-sectional phase, T8 used one technique type twice and another once. This evidence supports the previously proposed claim that T8 did not actually use AfL in his/her lessons. This is a valid and useful finding in itself. It indicates that even given the same conditions in a school and the same profile of learners, some teachers will adopt AfL while others may not. It suggests that other contextual or individual factors may facilitate or inhibit implementation. These are discussed later in this chapter.

The findings discussed so far are based on the data collected from school documents. The value of including them is linked to the relatively large number of lessons in the data set ($n = 448$). This allowed for a meaningful statistical analysis. However, it should be noted that the information in those was recorded by the teachers during or soon after each lesson. As such, the data provide insights into the use of AfL as self-reported by the teachers. In order to triangulate the findings empirically, field notes from 28 lesson observations were scrutinised. The same descriptive statistics were applied to the data obtained in this way. Because each teacher was observed only a limited number of times (two or four[1]), it would not be informative to calculate the inter-lesson frequency. Therefore, only the intra-lesson frequency was analysed based on lesson observations.

The main purpose of reporting the numerical values from the rather small sample of 28 lesson observations is to verify the findings from the analysis of the data self-reported through school documentation. The results are summarised in Table 9.5.

AfL was observed in all but one lesson. Overall, the findings confirm that AfL was used at least twice in at least half of all lessons taught by five out of eight teachers (T1, T3, T5, T6, T7). Furthermore, they confirm that there exists between-teacher variance. The categorisation of teachers into those who use AfL frequently (T1 and T5), moderately frequently (T3, T6 and T7) and rarely (T2, T4 and T8) is also confirmed by the findings presented in Table 9.5. The fact that some teachers seem to be in a different category of frequency of use here (T2 and T7, compared with Table 9.4) can be explained by the difference in the size of the sample in both analyses. This seems of secondary importance, as the main finding here is that there are three categories for frequency of use of AfL in which teachers can be placed. It should be noted that the numerical values for the statistical measures are higher than those obtained from the analysis of school documents (Table 9.4). This can be explained by three factors:

(1) A smaller sample size: 28 vs 448 lessons.
(2) The Hawthorne effect (Cohen *et al.*, 2007): lesson observations were overt and the teachers knew that the study looked at AfL but were not informed about the focus of observations.
(3) The difference in recording of the data by the teachers (as part of their work, in school documents) and by the observer (in the fieldnotes); the observer focused on the frequency of implementation and made sure to record every instance of AfL implementation that occurred.

Table 9.5 Intra-lesson frequency – lesson observations

Category of use	Teacher	Number of observed lessons	Min	Max	Median	Mean	Std. deviation
Frequent	T5	4	2	6	4.5	4.25	1.708
	T1	4	2	5	4	3.75	1.5
Moderate	T3	4	2	4	2	2.5	1
	T7	2	2	3	2.5	2.5	0.707
	T6	4	1	4	2	2.25	1.5
Infrequent	T2	4	1	2	1.5	1.5	0.577
	T4	2	1	1	1	1	0
	T8	4	0	1	1	0.75	0.5
	All lessons in which AfL was used	28	0	6	2	2.39	1.571

Source: Reproduced from Britton (2015: 168).

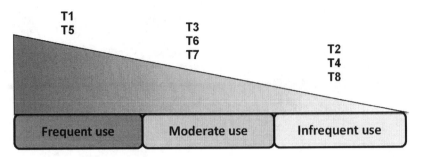

Figure 9.2 A sliding scale of the frequency of use of AfL
Source: Reproduced from Britton, 2015: 169

Overall, the outcomes of the analysis suggest that frequency of use could be conceptualised as a continuum, with those teachers who adopt high inter- and intra-lesson frequency at one end, and those who use AfL with low inter- and intra-lesson frequency at the other. The picture is somewhat more complex in the middle of the continuum; some teachers use AfL relatively frequently across lessons but tend to use it once in each lesson (T7), while others use AfL in about a third of their lessons but when they do, they tend to use it twice in a lesson (T3 and T6). The findings about frequency obtained during the cross-sectional phase were used to create a sliding scale of use of AfL (Figure 9.2). It visually illustrates the differences in frequency, as reported so far in this chapter.

To gain a more in-depth understanding of the frequency of use of AfL, I aimed to supplement the findings reported so far in this chapter with longitudinal insights. The next section reports the findings about how frequency changed 16 months later.

Frequency of use – changes over time

A longitudinal perspective was included in my research in order to build a more comprehensive picture of how AfL was implemented. Data that provide insights into the changes over time were collected 16 months after the initial set of data were collected. At that time, in accordance with the site access agreement, I was able to contact the teachers but had no access to school documentation or classrooms. Therefore, a delayed teacher questionnaire was selected as an appropriate method of data collection. All eight teachers who were involved in the initial study responded. The delayed questionnaire aimed to collect their accounts of the frequency and diversity of the use of AfL.

Question 2 (Q2) of the delayed teacher questionnaire was based on the finding reported in the previous section which suggests that the frequency of use could be conceptualised as a scale from '(almost) every lesson' to '(almost) never'. Respondents were asked to report how often

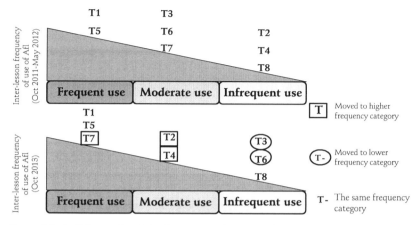

Figure 9.3 A sliding scale of the frequency of use of AfL showing changes over time
Source: Adapted from Britton, 2015

they used any of the AfL techniques identified in the initial study. The findings from analysing the responses to Q2 are presented in Figure 9.3. They confirm the existence of the three categories of frequency of use: frequent, moderate and infrequent. Interestingly, however, the distribution of teachers changed over time. Those who moved to a different frequency category are marked with rectangles and ovals in Figure 9.3. This finding suggests that while the categories seem stable, the practice of individual teachers changes over time. This provides useful evidence which informs the development of the model of implementation of AfL in primary language education.

Comparative analysis of the two sliding scales (Figure 9.3) indicates that all those teachers who were in the moderate category moved towards one of the ends of the scale. T7 joined T1 and T5 in the frequent use category, while T3 and T6 moved to the infrequent use category, where T8 remained. Two of the teachers who used AfL with low frequency moved up to the moderate category. This finding illustrates that as teachers gain experience of using AfL, their practice changes with respect to the frequency of use. This finding corroborates the claims that teachers need to develop their competence in using assessments such as AfL (Lefever, 2019).

It is important to understand what factors might have impacted those changes in the frequency of use of AfL. The delayed teacher questionnaire provided teachers with opportunities to identify the factors which in their view facilitated or hindered the frequent and diverse use of AfL. This was done through Q3 and Q4, respectively. It is important to note that it would have not been possible to distinguish between reasons relating to frequency and diversity from answers to those open-ended questions. Therefore, the findings from that section of the questionnaire are reported after the discussion of diversity.

The findings presented so far strongly suggested that individual teachers differed in the frequency of using AfL. Admittedly, frequency is not the only measure worth considering as it does not provide information about the diversity in AfL technique types which the teachers implement. Without that insight, it would be possible to claim, for example, that the teachers used just one AfL technique type. Such use would be rather limited in scope regardless of its frequency. Therefore, to better understand how AfL was used in the study classrooms, the analysis also sought to establish if teachers employed diverse AfL techniques. This is discussed in the following section.

Diversity in the Use of AfL

Diversity in the use of AfL refers to the number of different technique types implemented in lessons. The data to address this research focus came from school documents (records of 448 lessons) and 28 lesson observations. The findings are summarised in Table 9.6. Each number represents how many different technique types each teacher used. For instance, if traffic lights was recorded 15 times by a teacher in the school record, this would be counted as one type of AfL technique.

Overall, the teachers could be categorised into three groups: diverse use (T5 and T1), moderately diverse use (T6 and T3) and limited diversity of use (T7, T2, T4 and T8). The distribution of teachers into those three categories resembles that obtained from the analysis of the intra-lesson frequency. Specifically, those teachers who were categorised in the high and moderate intra-lesson frequency categories seemed to use significantly more technique types than those whose practice was characterised by low intra-lesson frequency of use. It seems logical for the intra-lesson frequency and the diversity in technique type to be linked. This means that if AfL techniques were used more than once per lesson, then these were likely to be different technique types. This could be explained by the ways in which teachers understood AfL. They reported that the purposes guided implementation (Chapter 2). Furthermore, different technique types were observed to serve the three purposes of use (Chapters 6 and 7). In fact, as discussed in Chapters 6 and 7, teachers tended to use similar technique types when setting expectations and monitoring progress but different ones when providing feedback. Therefore, in the lessons where moderate to high diversity and intra-lesson frequency were observed, teachers were most likely using AfL techniques to serve at least two of the three purposes for using AfL. This highlights the previously discussed nature of AfL in primary language teaching as a way of teaching which incorporates opportunities for processes integral to assessment such as gathering data, making judgements and providing feedback on progress. Similar pictures emerge from the self-reported data in school documents and the observational data from the lessons. This triangulation of evidence contributes to increasing the validity of findings.

Table 9.6 The number of diverse technique types used by teachers

Data source	Number of different AfL techniques							
Teachers	T5	T1	T6	T3	T7	T2	T4	T8
The number of different AfL techniques observed in 28 lessons (May 2012)	10	8	5	5	3	3	3	2
The number of different AfL techniques self-reported in 448 lessons (May 2012)	12	14	10	9	5	3	3	2
Number of technique types recorded in the longitudinal phase (October 2013)	15	14	8	8	13	10	14	4

Source: Adapted from Britton (2015).

The technique types identified by teachers in Q2 of the delayed teacher questionnaire provided insights into the changes in diversity over time. The techniques which were marked with 'sometimes', 'often', and 'almost every lesson' were considered representative of the diversity of use. The techniques marked as 'never' and 'rarely' in Q2 were excluded from this analysis.

Overall, the number of diverse technique types seemed to have increased in the practice of the majority of the teachers ($n = 6$) and only slightly decreased in the case of T3 and T6. The increase could be explained by teachers gaining experience in using AfL and developing their familiarity with using a greater number of technique types. The decrease in diversity in the case of the two teachers was paired with a decrease in the frequency of use of AfL by those two teachers. This points to a possible relationship between frequency and diversity in the use of AfL.

In the next section, I report the findings about the reasons for the changes in frequency and diversity over time.

Reasons for Changes over Time

The reasons for changes in frequency and diversity of use of AfL over time were investigated with three questions (Q1, Q3 and Q4) in the delayed teacher questionnaire, as reported below.

First, in Q1, teachers were asked to account for professional development (PD) that they participated in between the end of the initial study and completing the questionnaire. The findings indicate that those teachers whose frequency of use of AfL:

- Remained high or increased had all observed AfL being used in lessons by colleagues. The remaining teachers had not.
- Increased from 'infrequent' to 'moderate' had participated in training about AfL.

- Decreased had participated in training about a different form of assessment.

These findings indicate that PD activities such as training or lesson observations that focus on AfL can support teachers in developing their own practice. They also point to the relationship between implementation of AfL and other forms of assessment, suggesting that if the focus of PD activities is on assessment methods other than AfL, then it may hinder the implementation of AfL. These findings corroborate recent suggestions that teachers need training in order to be able to use AfL (Lefever, 2019).

The findings based on the data collected from Q3 and Q4 are summarised in Table 9.7, together with examples of teachers' reports, quoted verbatim from the questionnaire data. The most notable finding is that the majority of reasons appear to be teacher-centred; they clarify teachers' preferences or beliefs and do not describe the learners' experiences or attitudes towards AfL. This suggests that in this context, it was the teachers' choices that guided the decisions about how they implemented AfL.

Furthermore, the findings indicate that there were a number of factors that contributed to the teachers choosing whether to use AfL or not. Those that can facilitate the use of AfL are:

- The teachers' beliefs that AfL helped to raise learners' awareness of their own achievement.
- The perceived compatibility of AfL techniques with the teaching methods used.
- The teachers' familiarity with and/or their experience of using or seeing AfL techniques being used in the classroom.

According to the participants, the factors which might hinder implementation are:

- The teachers' lack of familiarity with technique types.
- The perceived or actual lack of time.

The insights from the delayed teacher questionnaire help to contextualise the statistical findings discussed earlier in this chapter. Specifically, they can account for the differences observed in the frequency and diversity of use of AfL by primary language teachers.

Frequency and Diversity Considered Together

The findings discussed so far strongly suggest the existence of between-teacher variance in frequency and diversity of use of AfL. Furthermore, they point to the usefulness of considering diversity and frequency of use together. For example, it seems that the teachers who implemented AfL with high intra-lesson frequency also used a greater diversity of technique

Table 9.7 Reasons for changes in diversity and frequency over time

	Teachers' reasons for choosing to use AfL	Teachers' reasons for choosing *not* to use AfL
High ↑ **Frequency and diversity in AfL use** ↓ **Limited**	• **Familiarity with AfL techniques gained through training, observations and experience of using AfL** *'I chose the techniques I used most often because I had learned about them from input sessions and from further background reading. I tried them and they worked best for me and my students.'* (T1/Q3) • **AfL techniques were an integral part of the teaching style** *'Some of the techniques I use are an essential part of my teaching style and I do not necessarily make a conscious decision to use them.'* (T7/Q3) • **AfL was considered an effective tool to focus students on expectations of outcomes and on students' own achievement** *'They [AfL techniques] give students an appreciation for what was achieved in the lesson as well as a sense of accomplishment. It is extremely simple and effective, and they can understand how to improve.'* (T2/Q3) • **Satisfaction with the amount of AfL that teachers used** *'I thought they [the AfL techniques that this teacher used] did the job and there was no need for other techniques.'* (T8/Q3) • **Ease of use** *'I used these techniques because these are the ones that I am most happy with, and I find them easy to set up and use.'* (T3/Q3)	• **Lack of familiarity with a given technique** *'The main reason that I've not used these techniques is that I am (or was) unfamiliar with them.'* (T3/Q4) *'I may not have seen them [the AfL techniques that I do not use] in action. I usually have to witness the effectiveness of a technique first-hand in a language lesson in order to gain a full appreciation for it.'* (T4/Q4) • **Time constraints (on preparation and within lessons)** *'This could be time consuming to prepare.'* (T6/Q4) *'Colour coding is sometimes too time consuming with small kids.'* (T5/Q4) *'The idea of learning partners was not particularly practical due to limited time in class.'* (T7/Q4)

Source: Reproduced from Britton (2015: 176).

types. Those who implemented AfL rarely used a low diversity of technique type. It should be noted that due to the small sample of participants ($n = 8$), these findings cannot easily be generalised beyond this sample. Further research in this area is needed to enable generalisations.

Between-learner age group variance in the use of AfL

To investigate whether age was also a factor in the frequency and diversity of use of AfL, the whole data set was subdivided according to the learners' ages into 7 to 9 and 10 to 11-year-olds. The same measures were applied to the two subsets. The results show no significant differences between the two cohorts. This finding suggests that in the age group 7–11, age does not seem to be related to the frequency and diversity of use of AfL. This could lead to an interpretation that teachers make decisions about the use of AfL based on factors other than the learners' ages. This has important pedagogical implications as it highlights the significance of teachers as mediators of assessment practices.

Towards a Model of Implementation

Although some claims for the significant impact of AfL on achievement have been made (Black & Wiliam, 1998; Wiliam, 2011), it has
also been argued that establishing links between AfL and achievement
is challenging. This is because research into AfL seems to be hindered
by the lack of a commonly accepted theoretical framework (Bennett,
2011). Furthermore, no models of implementation which are grounded
in empirical data have been proposed in primary language education.
The study which informs much of this book seems uniquely positioned
to address this gap by reporting findings from a significant data set. I
believe that grounding the proposed model of implementation in the
empirical findings warrants a claim for its validity. Although the model
of implementation which is proposed here may need to be revised in light
of future research findings, I hope that by proposing this model, the present volume can contribute to facilitating future research into AfL and
consequently, to informing classroom practice.

By applying the criteria of frequency and diversity, we might theorise
that there could be at least four types of implementation (Figure 9.4). In
Type 1 and Type 2, teachers would use AfL techniques frequently, for

Frequency	
High	**Low**
Type 1 High frequency and diversity	**Type 3** Low frequency but high diversity
Type 2 High frequency but low diversity	**Type 4** Low frequency and low diversity

Figure 9.4 Possible types of implementation of AfL with regard to frequency and diversity of use

example, almost every lesson. The difference between those two types of implementation is in the number of different technique types that are used; while Type 1 implementation entails the use of a diverse repertoire of AfL techniques, in Type 2 the number of different technique types is limited. It might be argued that either of these two types of implementation would offer systematic opportunities for the learners to experience AfL and to become familiar with it. In Type 1 implementation, teachers would probably use AfL for all three purposes of use: setting objectives and expectations, monitoring progress and evaluating achievement. Whereas, in Type 2 implementation, teachers would probably focus on fewer purposes, for example, only on providing feedback. Therefore, it would seem that Type 1 implementation would be a more comprehensive way of implementing AfL. Type 2 would be a more diluted version of it, focusing on using just certain aspects of AfL but not the whole approach.

The other two types of implementation offer less frequent or perhaps only occasional opportunities for learners to use AfL. Type 3 refers to the practice of a teacher who uses a relatively large repertoire of technique types but does not use them frequently. Perhaps such a teacher is experimenting with using AfL for various purposes to see how this might work in their context. Finally, Type 4 implementation entails infrequent use of a limited number of AfL technique types. However, if implementation is infrequent and only a limited number of technique types are used, it could be argued that the Type 4 scenario represents a context in which AfL is implemented in a tokenistic manner and may not offer any of the potential benefits to learning.

A model of implementation for AfL in primary language education

In this chapter, I propose that the values of frequency and diversity should be considered when developing a model for the practical implementation of AfL. The choice of those two characteristics is supported by the empirical findings related to the nature and practical use of AfL in primary language classes (Chapters 2, 6 and 7), and by research that suggests that language learning at primary school can be facilitated by children's familiarity with task structure. Specifically, as is evident from the findings discussed in Chapter 2, fitness for purpose guides the practical implementation of AfL. To fit various purposes of use, teachers tend to choose different technique types, as reported in Chapters 6 and 7. Such choices contribute to high diversity in the use of AfL. Consequently, the types of implementation which are characterised by high diversity of technique type (Types 1 and 3), might offer opportunities for implementing AfL in a more comprehensive manner than those types in which diversity is low.

Additionally, the findings demonstrate that AfL techniques can be incorporated into the structure of the tasks during which they are used.

	May 2012			October 2013		
	High Frequency	Medium Frequency	Low Frequency	High Frequency	Medium Frequency	Low Frequency
High Diversity	T1 T5	T3 T6	-	T1 T5 T7	T2 T4	-
Medium Diversity	-	-	-	-	-	T3 T6
Low Diversity	-	T7	T2 T4 T8	-	-	T8

Figure 9.5 Frequency and diversity in the use of AfL: Longitudinal perspective
Source: Reproduced from Britton, 2015: 174

If learners are offered frequent opportunities for using certain technique types, they can become familiar with their structure. Consequently, learners' familiarity with technique types could contribute to their familiarity with the structure of tasks during which the familiar AfL techniques are used.

The findings about the diversity and frequency of use based on data collected in May 2012 and in October 2013 are presented in Figure 9.5. The outcome illustrates which types of implementation were preferred by the teachers in my study. In both phases, the majority of teachers used AfL with medium to high frequency, and over time all but one used medium to high diversity.

As is evident from Figure 9.5, the high frequency and high diversity category seemed to be stable; both teachers who were in that group in the cross-sectional phase remained there after 16 months. This suggests that the teachers in this category sustained the high frequency and high diversity of use because they *embedded* AfL into their practice.

The remaining categories seem less stable, as most teachers changed their places after 16 months. With regard to the low frequency and low diversity category, there was evidence that some teachers might continue to implement AfL in a very limited form and may not develop their practice to the same level as others over time. Such implementation is characterised by low frequency and low diversity of use; teachers in this category make only a symbolic effort to implement AfL. Therefore, such implementation could be referred to as *tokenistic.*

The teachers who moved out of the low frequency and low diversity category in October 2013 (T2 and T4) both significantly increased the diversity of technique type to high, while also increasing the frequency of use from low to medium. This is an interesting finding in light of the possible existence of a relationship between diversity and the range of purposes which AfL was used for. It suggests that this group of teachers were implementing it in an increasingly more comprehensive way, using AfL to serve a wider range of purposes. These findings suggest that in their practice, T2 and T4 were experimenting with an increasing number of technique types but were not (yet) implementing AfL as frequently as the teachers in the embedded category. Therefore, the way they were implementing AfL could be referred to as *experimental*.

One teacher who significantly increased the diversity of use and also moderately increased their already relatively high (50%) inter-lesson frequency of use was T7. That teacher developed their practice in the direction of embedded implementation, therefore, this type of use is referred to as *developing*.

The remaining two teachers (T3 and T6) could be placed in the experimental category in May 2012. However, over time, the frequency with which they implemented AfL decreased from medium to low. This change was accompanied by a lower diversity as well, resulting in the way they implemented AfL resembling the tokenistic category. This finding is consistent with the interpretation that teachers in this category experiment with AfL in their lessons but, in the case of these two teachers, the results of their experiments led them towards decreasing the frequency and diversity of use.

Four types of implementation

Based on the findings discussed above, the proposed model of implementation for AfL in primary language education encompasses four types of use: embedded, developing, experimental and tokenistic.

The embedded type, which is characterised by high levels of diversity and frequency of use (within and across lessons), seems to be the most stable over time. Additionally, it seems that the practice of teachers with increased measures of frequency or diversity or both resembled the embedded type of use over time. Teachers in this category use AfL in almost all their lessons and do so for all three purposes: setting objectives and expectations, monitoring progress and evaluating achievement.

The experimental type of implementation incorporates teachers who use AfL with low inter-lesson frequency but medium to high intra-lesson frequency and diversity. Overall, the frequency of use in that group can be judged as low due to the low inter-lesson frequency values. The teachers in this category used AfL on average in one out of three lessons. It is interesting to note that in those lessons which included AfL, the teachers in the experimental category tended to use AfL on more than one occasion within a lesson. For example, the median value of 2 was obtained for teachers in this category across 448 lessons in school records, while for those in the embedded category the median was 3. Those two values indicate that, while the teachers in the embedded category tended to use AfL on more occasions within a lesson than those in the experimental category, the difference in the intra-lesson frequency was not significant between those two groups. Additionally, the differences in diversity of use across the 448 lessons in school documents were not significant either; they included between 8 and 10 technique types for teachers in the experimental category and between 12 and 14 for teachers in the embedded category.

The above findings suggest that the way in which teachers in the experimental category implement AfL within a lesson resembles the type of implementation in the embedded type. The main difference is that in the former category, there seem to be two types of lessons: (1) those in which no AfL is used; and (2) those in which the use of AfL resembles that of the embedded type of implementation. For the purposes of the present discussion, I will refer to these two types of lessons as 'non-AfL lessons' and 'AfL lessons', respectively. In the experimental type of implementation, 'AfL lessons' account for only about a third of all lessons. In contrast, almost all lessons in the embedded category are 'AfL lessons'. Importantly, during 'AfL lessons' in the embedded and experimental types, teachers seemed to use AfL in a similar way. This conclusion was verified through field notes from lesson observations. This is an important outcome as it suggests that ensuring medium to high diversity and intra-lesson frequency are important considerations for the implementation of AfL in primary language teaching (see the next section for further discussion).

Importantly, teachers who increased the number of 'AfL lessons' over time (T2 and T4) changed their practice in a way that resembled the embedded type of implementation. However, the practice of those who increased the number of 'non-AfL lessons' (T3 and T6) moved closer to the tokenistic type of implementation. The factors which might have affected such changes in practice are discussed earlier in this chapter.

The tokenistic type describes the practice of teachers who do not actually implement AfL, but instead they might have selected to use an aspect of AfL occasionally, perhaps in order to comply with an externally imposed policy. Such interpretation is consistent with Rixon (2017) who demonstrated convincingly that teachers may find it challenging to implement a new pedagogical policy in their classrooms if they do not receive appropriate training and support.

The developing type of implementation is characterised by relatively high inter-lesson frequency but low diversity and intra-lesson frequency. On average, one in every two lessons includes an aspect of AfL. However, the lessons in which AfL is used do not resemble 'AfL lessons' as defined above. This is because a rather diluted version of AfL is used in them, serving just one of the three purposes of use. This is confirmed by quantitative data (median value of 1 from 448 lessons, accompanied by an average of 1.25 and an SD of 0.441). The teacher who used the developing type of implementation in May 2012 (T7) increased the diversity of technique type over time. This could have contributed to them teaching more genuine 'AfL lessons'. They also increased the inter-lesson frequency of use. Effectively, in October 2013, that teacher was using the embedded type of implementation. The four types of implementation which constitute the model of practical use of AfL in primary language teaching are presented in Figure 9.6.

As illustrated by the discussion above and by Figure 9.5, the changes which happened over time suggest that the proposed model is dynamic in nature. This means that the type of implementation preferred by a teacher may change. The reasons for such changes are discussed earlier in this chapter.

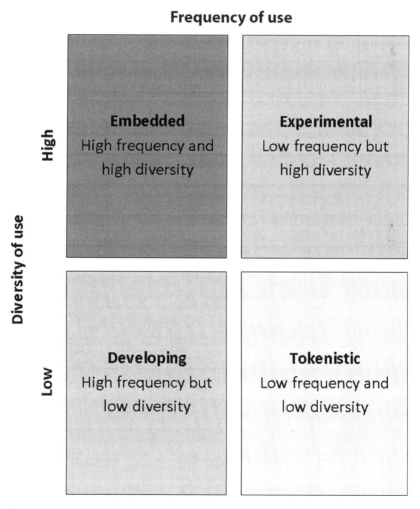

Figure 9.6 A model of implementation of AfL in primary language education

The optimal type of implementation of AfL in primary language education

The discussion so far has indicated that out of the four types of implementation the embedded type is not only stable over time, but importantly, it seems to be the type of practical implementation towards which teachers tend to develop their practice, given favourable conditions. In this section, I consider whether, and if so why, the embedded type of implementation is the most optimal for primary language education.

Inevitably, different levels of frequency and diversity would result in creating various learning environments. This could affect whether learners become familiar with the structure of AfL technique types or not. Consequently, different levels of learners' familiarity with the structure of the AfL techniques which are used as part of tasks would have implications for the potential benefits of using AfL to support learning. Moreover, diversity of use could be linked to the number of purposes that AfL is used for. For example, the teaching and learning processes would differ in classes where AfL is used predominantly for providing feedback on performance because learners in such classes would not be engaging in preparatory formative assessment (Gan & Leung, 2020) through clarifying expectations or planning how to complete tasks according to criteria of success. Arguably, various learning environments resulting from different levels of frequency and diversity might have a different impact on the quality of language learning that takes place.

In the embedded type of implementations teachers and learners used AfL frequently, using a high diversity of technique types. High diversity can be linked to the number of purposes that AfL is used for. For example, field notes from lesson observations indicate that in those lessons in which teachers used two or more AfL techniques, each of these techniques was used to serve a different purpose; one technique might have been used for sharing objectives and expectations and a different one for providing feedback. In classes where AfL techniques are implemented for all three purposes (sharing objectives and expectations; monitoring progress; and evaluating achievement), the assessment processes which they serve to implement could help to fulfil the requirements for effective assessment of young learners, discussed in Chapters 4 and 5. Additionally, when teachers and learners use AfL frequently, children have ample opportunities to become familiar with the structure of AfL techniques. As previously discussed, this could facilitate learning. Consequently, it seems that through the embedded type of implementation, teachers might be able to create conditions that are more conducive to language learning in childhood.

Learners whose teachers' practice fits the developing type would have relatively frequent opportunities to become familiar with a smaller number of different technique types. Therefore, it is plausible that the developing category of use could also help to create conditions in which learners' familiarity with technique structure was good and could facilitate learning. However, the teachers in the developing category might not offer their learners all the potential benefits of AfL if they do not fulfil all the purposes of AfL, by limiting their practice to a narrower range of technique types.

The teachers who use the experimental type of implementation could facilitate learning through assessment during the 'AfL lessons', namely those lessons in which they use AfL in a way that resembles the embedded type. Those teachers do not tend to use AfL in their remaining lessons ('non-AfL lessons') and would therefore be unable to offer any benefits to learning through AfL in those lessons. Admittedly, a similar lack of gains to learning could be expected in the tokenistic type of use of AfL, where teachers only occasionally use a very narrow range of techniques.

The discussion in this section suggests that the embedded type of implementation is the most optimal for ensuring that assessment facilitates learning in primary language education. This is due to two reasons. First, high frequency of implementation can help to ensure learners' familiarity with the structure of techniques that are implemented within teaching tasks. Secondly, by ensuring that assessment serves all three purposes of AfL, teachers can ensure that assessment fulfils the conditions for assessment appropriate for primary-aged learners, as discussed in Chapters 4 and 5. Most importantly, such implementation of AfL could facilitate 'setting clear goals, sequencing materials, frequent questions to monitor progress in the learning process, opportunity to learn, testing and quality feedback [which] are all important characteristics from which early foreign language learning can benefit tremendously' (Edelenbos & Vinje, 2000: 160).

Summary of the Chapter

As is evident from the data reported in this chapter, there exists between-teacher variance in the frequency and diversity of use of AfL. Over time, the diversity and frequency of use tend to increase, provided favourable conditions. The data suggest that the reasons for this are linked to teachers' familiarity with the technique types; their experience and the compatibility of AfL techniques with the teaching methods; and being given opportunities to experiment with AfL and receive training in this area.

The discussion also considered whether the way in which teachers implemented AfL could offer benefits to learning. The outcomes suggest that opportunities for learners to become familiar with the structure of techniques and to engage in all three purposes of AfL could help to design learning environments that are conducive to primary language learning. The outcomes suggest that teachers can implement AfL in four different ways according to the frequency and diversity of use and that one of them – the embedded type of implementation – could be optimal for primary language education as it could help to facilitate learning.

One interesting focus for future research would be to analyse the achievement of learners who experienced the four types of implementation of AfL. The findings of such studies could provide interesting insights into the relationship between AfL and improving achievement.

This chapter concludes Part 2, which has focused on the practical implementation of AfL. In the next part, I explore the impact of AfL on language teaching and learning.

Note

(1)   Each of the 14 groups of children was observed twice.

Part 3
Impact of AfL on Learning

10 Interactions through Assessment

Introduction

The findings reported in Chapters 6 and 7 suggest that the practical implementation of assessment for learning (AfL) entails frequent interactions between learners and teachers, and among learners. As discussed in Chapter 5, the quality of oral interactions is an important consideration for language learning in childhood. Therefore, I decided to analyse the observable impact of interactions which happen while AfL techniques are being used. The types of interaction discussed in this chapter include L–L (pairs), T–1L (teacher–individual student), T–C (teacher–whole class), IND (individual work), L–C (learner–whole class), T–xLL (teacher–group of students, e.g. T–4LL) and LL (groups).

The data came from individual interviews ($n = 8$), a focus group with teachers, lesson observation field notes ($n = 28$), and transcripts of extracts from video-recorded lessons ($n = 26$).[1] In the process of analysis, transcripts of the interviews were content-analysed (see Appendix 1 for the transcribing convention). The preliminary findings were verified through the focus group. Empirical data from lesson observations were analysed quantitatively using descriptive statistics. The outcomes were used to triangulate findings from the interviews and the focus group. The interaction patterns observed in lessons were recorded in the field notes, adopting the schedule and coding used in the ELLiE study (Enever, 2012: personal communication).

Subsequently, nine extracts of classroom discourse were transcribed and analysed in two ways. Firstly, Storch's (2002) model was used to identify holistic patterns of dyadic interactions. Secondly, the variable approach (Walsh, 2006) to classroom discourse analysis was used. Each extract was categorised according to the following: the mode of interaction; the occurrence of negative feedback; the resulting modifications of output; the alignment of teacher language use with pedagogical aims; and/or the occurrence of language-related episodes (LREs). The analysis was informed by the outcomes of the literature review in Chapter 5.

Teachers' Perceptions about Interactions

During the interviews and focus group discussion, teachers reported that they observed an increase in the number of one-to-one interactions between teachers, learners and peers when AfL techniques were being used.

Perceptions about Teacher–Learner interactions (T–1L)

It seemed to be a shared perception that children were less reliant on teacher support to sustain work on the task at hand when AfL techniques were used. Consequently, teachers were able to focus their attention on facilitating learning. Most significantly, they were able to devote more time to monitoring, during which they provided individual support and guidance to learners. This explains the positive correlation between the use of AfL and the number of T–1L interactions during lessons (Table 10.1). As the exchange between T1, T2 and T4 (Extract 5) illustrates, the quality of monitoring and the support given through T–1L interactions improved.

Extract 5
(From the focus group discussion)

[1] **T2:** *with time input from teacher should be smaller (...) because they know their*
[2] *success criteria how to do it or they should be aware of what is expected but I think*
[3] *at that point monitoring becomes more effective to make sure that they're actually*
[4] *doing it properly*
[5] **T4:** *I think this is a very good point=*
[6] **T1:** *=yes more time to monitor better (...)*
[7] **T2:** *yes and how you would do that is an important element of this discussion*
[8] *when you monitor and how you monitor and what you say to individual students*

T2 reports that the quality of T–1L interactions is important to consider. I was interested in knowing what the teachers actually said to their learners during such interactions. The outcomes of the discourse analysis – which are reported in the second part of this chapter – provide further insights into the content of T–1L interactions.

Perceptions about Learner–Learner interactions (L–L)

Some of the teachers reported the impact of using AfL techniques on L–L interactions. Most notably, teachers believed that it was easier to introduce pair work in those lessons during which they used AfL techniques such as learning partners. Teachers commented that:

> *the one that I also found the most useful has been the learning partners idea (1) obviously there is benefit to the students in taking a bit of the control themselves and in doing that helping each other* (T4/INT)

> *I used this with primaries mainly to involve more pair work and it sort of helps them get what pair work is about* (T7/INT)

This finding suggests that some AfL techniques may facilitate L–L interactions. As indicated in Chapter 5, such interactions may be an important vehicle for language learning. The outcomes of quantitative analysis, reported later in this chapter, provide further insights into the relationship between using AfL and the number of L–L interactions in lessons.

Another perception reported by some teachers was linked to the quality of L–L interactions. It was indicated that children were able to collaborate, instead of competing, when working together.

> *I think the biggest benefit for my groups has been the peer learning working together and not being competitive in their English but being supportive of each other's learning (T1/INT)*

The suggestion seems to be that AfL techniques may be used to facilitate collaboration. While it would certainly warrant further investigation, this finding is very interesting because, as discussed in Chapter 5, collaborative dialogues may be beneficial to language learning (Swain, 2000) but primary-aged language learners may need support from teachers to engage with a peer with a medium to high level of mutuality (Butler & Zeng, 2014).

Relationships between AfL and Types of Interactions

Quantitative analysis (bivariate correlations calculated with SPSS v19) provided insights into the relationships between the use of AfL and the types of interactions which occurred in lessons. Seven types of interaction were observed in lessons T–1L, T–xLL, T–C, LL, L–C, L–L and IND[2] (all interval scales). The Pearson-product moment correlation coefficient was used to determine existence of any relationships between each of the interaction types and the use of AfL techniques in lessons. The outcomes point to strong positive correlations between frequent use of AfL and a large number of L–L and T–1L interactions, both significant to the 0.01 level. Additionally, a moderate negative correlation between frequent use of AfL and the T–C interactions, significant to 0.05 level was found in the younger group (7 to 9-year-olds). No other correlations were identified (Table 10.1).

Table 10.1 Relationships between classroom interactions and the use of AfL: Pearson-product moment correlation coefficients

Measure	L–L	T–1L	T–C
Use of AfL in both groups	0.719**	0.703**	−0.405*
Use of AfL in 7 to 9-year-olds	0.707**	0.684**	−0.561*
Use of AfL in 10 to 11-year-olds	0.753**	0.731**	−0.443

* Correlation is significant at the 0.05 level (two-tailed).
** Correlation is significant at the 0.01 level (two-tailed).

These results point to the conclusion that there is a relationship between frequent use of AfL techniques and the type of interactions which take place. More specifically, dyadic interactions seem to occur more frequently when AfL is used. This might mean that there exist conditions in some lessons that facilitate both a large number of L–L and T–1L interactions and the frequent use of AfL. As the Pearson-product correlation neither shows nor excludes causation, no claims of causation are being made here. Causation could be investigated with a different study design.

As the results of my research point to the increased number of dyadic interactions during the use of AfL, it would seem valuable to consider whether such interactional environment could facilitate learning. To provide some exploratory insights into this research focus, the *richness* (the quality) of interactions was evaluated. As discussed in Chapter 5, learning could be supported by creating certain interactional environments: (1) by providing opportunities for collaborative and expert–novice interactions (Butler & Zeng, 2014); (2) by aligning teachers' use of a second language (L2) with the pedagogical aims for each conversation (Walsh, 2006); and (3) when LREs occur (Swain & Lapkin, 1998). In the remaining part of this chapter, I consider whether AfL could contribute to any of these processes.

Nine conversations, which occurred during the use of AfL, were sourced from the video-recorded lessons. Similar to Walsh (2006: 165), the interactions were recorded 'under normal classroom conditions with no specialist equipment'. The resulting sample was particularly useful as it provided examples of classroom discourse which naturally occurred in lessons. Consequently, the extracts discussed in this chapter serve as examples of classroom discourse which occurs when AfL is used. The data are not intended to provide systematic insights into all the classroom discourse which occurred in the observed lessons. Each of the nine conversations was transcribed (see Appendix 1 for the transcribing convention).

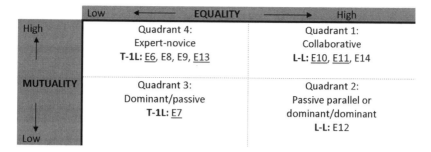

Figure 10.1 Findings from applying Storch's (2002) model to dyadic interactions which occurred during the use of AfL (Note: Extracts sourced from the younger age group are underlined)

Collaborative and expert–novice types of interactions

Storch's (2002) model for analysing dyadic interactions focuses on the perceived levels of equality and mutuality displayed by the interlocutors. The analysis resulted in categorising the nine extracts in the data set into four categories (Figure 10.1). Details of this analysis can be reviewed in Appendix 4.

Perhaps unsurprisingly, the level of equality was at the medium to high level in the majority of L–L interactions, as they occurred between peers of similar age and language ability (Quadrants 1 and 2). The level of equality in the T–1L interactions was medium to low as teachers tended to control the exchanges (Quadrants 3 and 4). Importantly, the majority of the conversations which occurred during the use of AfL had medium to high levels of mutuality. As is evident in Figure 10.1, three out of four L–L exchanges were of the collaborative type (Quadrant 1) and four out of five of the T–1L conversations displayed the expert–novice type (Quadrant 4). This finding suggests that when AfL was being used, learners assumed active roles during classroom conversations with their teachers or peers. These two types of interaction (collaborative and expert–novice) have been reported to support learning (Butler & Zeng, 2014; Swain, 2000). Therefore, it can be concluded that the present findings highlight how AfL can help to create interactional environments conducive to learning, with medium to high mutuality between learners (L–L collaborative interactions) and between learners and their teachers (T–1L expert–novice interactions).

Teachers' Use of L2 in Relation to the Learning Objectives

The second stage of analysing the classroom discourse employed a variable approach to investigating FL interactions. It involved using conversation analysis (CA) methodology, analysing turns and sequences of transcribed speech and categorising each exchange into one of the modes of conversation discussed by Walsh (2006).

The outcomes of the second stage of analysis are summarised in Table 10.2. The aim was to investigate the relationship between learning and discourse which occurs during the use of AfL. The focus was on evaluating whether:

(1) Teachers' use of language was aligned (Column IV) with the perceived pedagogical aims of each conversation (Column II).
(2) The perceived pedagogical aims of conversations offered opportunities to support learners in achieving the lesson objectives recorded by teachers in school documents (Columns III and V).
(3) Such opportunities appeared to be effectively used (Column VI).
(4) LREs occurred (Column VII).

The data presented in Table 10.2 led to three main findings.

> Finding 1: Limited alignment of teacher language use with aims of conversations

The analysis presented in Column IV suggests that teachers' use of language was not congruent with the aims of the conversations. This is a similar finding to that reported by Walsh (2006). It suggests that AfL does not play a role in facilitating the alignment of teacher language use with the perceived aims of the conversations.

> Finding 2: AfL might help to create conditions for supporting learners in achieving learning objectives (LOs)

As is evident from Column V, all the interactions which occurred during the use of AfL provided opportunities for teachers and learners to move learning towards the predefined LOs. Encouragingly, in almost all of the exchanges, such opportunities were effectively used (Column VI). It seems especially interesting to note that such opportunities were used not only in the T–1L interactions but also in the L–L interactions. By activating learners as instructional resources for one another (Black & Wiliam, 2009), teachers can offer significantly more opportunities for practising L2 and negotiating for meaning, than they would through just teacher-led conversations. This is simply because many L–L interactions

Table 10.2 Outcomes of applying the Variable Approach to analysing classroom interactions which occurred during the use of AfL

1. Extract	2. Perceived aim(s) of the conversation	3. Learning objectives recorded in school documentation	4. Alignment	5. Opportunity to support the lesson aims	6. Effective use of opportunity	7. Language-related episodes
Managerial mode						
E6 T–1L	To draw the learner's attention to a success in the criterion for writing.	To write an interesting newspaper article about Notting Hill Carnival	Yes	Yes	Yes	No
E7 T–1L	To support the learners in assigning themselves a traffic light	To use eight or more phrases about hobbies	No	Yes	No	No
Skills and systems mode						
E8 T–1L	L: To find out how to spell 'throwing' T: To elicit a correct question structure and to support with spelling	To use was/were + ing to talk about the past	No	Yes	Yes	Grammar
E9 T–1L	L: To check if 'too much fans' was correct; T: To correct a mistake: 'too much fans'	To use (too) much/many, not enough with countable and uncountable nouns	Yes	Yes	Yes	Grammar
Materials mode						
E10 L–L	To negotiate the meaning of 'pm'	To make suggestions using 'Why don't we...?', 'Shall we...?' and 'Let's'.	N/A	Yes	Yes	Lexical
E11 L–L	To select a colour for a Christmas tree	To practice speaking through games	N/A	Yes	Yes	Lexical
Mode side sequences						
E12 L–L	To correct a mistake of using 'have' with a singular third-person pronoun	To ask grammatically correct questions using has/have...yet?	N/A	Yes	Yes	Grammar
E13 T–1L	To correct a mistake in the following sentence: I like to sleeping	To practice 'like/love plus ing' structure	No	Yes	Yes	Grammar
E14 L–L	To decide whether to start a question with 'what time' or 'when'	To ask eight questions correctly, about activities that a person did yesterday	N/A	Yes	Yes	Grammar

Source: Mode side sequences: E12 and E14 – Mode: Materials-Skills and systems-Materials; E13 – Mode: Skills and systems-Materials. Skills and systems: E8 and E9 – Mode: Skills and systems-Classroom context- Skills and systems.

could occur simultaneously as opposed to just one interaction involving the teacher at any one time. This is an especially useful finding in light of research which suggests that primary-aged language learners can and do negotiate for meaning effectively (Oliver, 1998, 2000, 2002; Oliver & Mackey, 2003).

Finding 3: AfL might help to facilitate learning by creating opportunities for LREs

---

As discussed in Chapter 5, LREs, which are those parts of conversations during which learners discuss their speaking or writing output, can offer opportunities for language learning. The data reported in Table 10.2 illustrate that when the interactions took place in the materials mode, learners engaged in LREs which focused on lexical items (Column VII). In the skills and systems mode and side sequences which contained that mode, children's interactions focused on grammar. This observation demonstrates that when AfL was used, LREs occurred in two modes: skills and systems ($n = 3$), and materials ($n = 4$). This suggests that using AfL might help to encourage learners to engage in LREs in those two conversational modes. The nature of modifications which occurred during such LREs was also analysed and is reported in the next section.

Negative Feedback and Modifications of Output

The data reported in Table 10.3 suggest that in all seven conversations in which LREs occurred, they were preceded by one of the interlocutors signalling that something was wrong, unclear or not understood by him/her, providing negative feedback (e.g. Line 3 in Extract 10, Appendix 4). Negative feedback is feedback 'provided in response to learners' non-target-like production' (Oliver & Mackey, 2003: 519). Through LREs, learners were offered opportunities to modify their initial output (Extracts 8, 9, 10, 13,) and such opportunities led to output actually being modified in all T–1L and one L–L interactions (Table 10.3), especially in the skills and systems mode. This finding suggests that through T–1L interactions which occur when AfL is used, teachers can support primary-aged language learners in modifying their non-target production.

The data reported in Table 10.3 indicate that learners tended to engage in LREs in the materials mode. This is an interesting finding which may be linked to a role that materials, such as various types of visual (E10, E11 and E12) or lexical (E14) prompts, could play in facilitating LREs. On the contrary, the T1–L interactions (E8, E9 and E13) did

Table 10.3 Negative feedback and modifications of output

Extract	Mode	Type	Negative feedback	Outcome: Modification of output	Outcome: Output but no modification	Outcome: Lack of output
E8	SS	T–1L	Yes	Yes		
E9			Yes	Yes		
E13	SS–CC–SS		Yes	Yes		
E10	MAT	L–L	Yes	Yes		
E11			Yes			Yes
E12	MAT–SS–MAT		Yes		Yes	
E14			Yes		Yes	

Source: Adapted from Britton (2015).
Modes: MAT - Materials; SS - Skills and systems; CC - Classroom context.

not refer directly to lesson materials. They were all initiated by teachers who were either monitoring learners' work and noticed a non-target production (E8 and E9) or demonstrating how to conduct a self-assessment (E13). This highlights the important role of teachers (or perhaps that of more capable peers) in facilitating LREs. The one characteristic that all these exchanges have in common is that they occurred alongside an AfL technique being implemented.

The discussion in this part of the chapter suggests that when implementing AfL, teachers might be able to facilitate the occurrence of LREs. During LREs, learners are offered opportunities to modify their output, which has been shown to contribute to language learning. This finding points to a possible relationship between the use of AfL and opportunities for modifications of output, which were observed especially in T–1L interactions.

Summary of the Chapter

In this chapter, I have focused on the observable impact of AfL on classroom interactions. The findings indicate four ways in which AfL could help engineer conditions conducive to learning in primary language lessons through interactions:

(1) There was a strong positive correlation between the frequency of using AfL techniques and the number of learner–learner and teacher–learner interactions. In the younger age group (7 to 9-year-olds), the use of AfL was also negatively correlated with the teacher–whole class interactions. Together, these two findings suggest that when AfL is used, there are more dyadic interactions as compared to lessons without AfL. Importantly, the dyadic interactions which occurred during the use of AfL displayed holistic patterns that had been shown in previous research to facilitate L2 learning (Butler &

Zeng, 2014; Swain, 2000). Most significantly, the medium to high levels of mutuality observed in those interactions point to an active role of learners in the assessment process.

(2) By using AfL, learners were offered support in meeting the learning objectives. The findings of the conversation analysis indicate that when AfL was used, interactions offered opportunities for supporting the pedagogical aims of the lesson or task. Importantly, the majority of such opportunities were used in teacher–learner and learner–learner interactions.

(3) Using AfL techniques seems to be linked to the occurrence of LREs in the observed lessons. The LREs focused on grammar when conversations were centred around practising and clarifying language rules and meaning (the skills and systems mode) and on lexis when the conversations were guided by the materials which the learners were using (the materials mode).

(4) Using AfL techniques may facilitate conditions for modification of output by providing learners with negative feedback. The findings indicate that negative feedback was provided and used to modify output most frequently when conversations were centred around practising and clarifying language rules and meaning through teacher–learner interactions. There was also evidence of negative feedback provided through learner–learner interactions when the conversations were guided by the materials which the learners were using. However, in those types of interactions, negative feedback resulted in modification of output less frequently.

The findings discussed in the present chapter corroborate those from Part 2 by indicating that when AfL is used in primary language classes, various processes which may benefit learning occur in lessons. In order to understand how AfL can facilitate learning, further research is needed to investigate the impact of each of those processes on language learning.

Notes

(1) Out of the 28 lesson observations, 26 were video-recorded. The remaining two were voice-recorded due to parental preference not to video record their children as expressed in the process of gaining informed consent.

(2) Interaction codes: L–L (Pairs), T–1L (teacher–individual student), T–C (teacher–whole class), IND (individual work), L–C (learner–whole class), T–xLL (teacher – group of students, e.g. T–4LL), (LL) groups.

11 Assessment Spiral

AfL creates a kind of a circle when everybody knows where everybody is (1) and then it involves a series of tactic tools techniques and things that you can do to facilitate that
T2/INT

Introduction

In this volume, I have adopted the premise that assessment methods should take into account the ways children learn best (McKay, 2006). In the current chapter, I aim to relate the outcomes of my research, discussed throughout this volume, to the current body of knowledge about the intersection of learning and assessment in primary language education. In order to satisfy this goal, I consider what the outcomes my study reveal about how assessment for learning (AfL) can be integrated into those classroom processes which have been shown to benefit learning. Grounding the discussion in the empirical findings, I propose that teachers could satisfy the requirements for effective, age-appropriate assessment through the embedded use of AfL (Chapter 8). Moreover, I demonstrate how this would result in creating an *assessment spiral* (Wehlburg, 2007) in primary language classes.

Assessment Spiral

The embedded type of use of AfL (Chapter 8) offers opportunities for creating a process which T2 describes as 'a kind of a circle when everybody knows where everybody is'. I refer to this process as the assessment spiral. The term assessment spiral has been used in higher education to mean a move 'away from the two dimensions of the feedback circle' (Wehlburg, 2007: 1) and towards 'thinking of assessment as an upward spiral, still identifying goals and outcomes, still measuring those outcomes, but with ever-increasing improvement in the quality of student learning as the spiral moves upward' (Wehlburg, 2007: 1). This definition implies that assessment should be continuous, and that evidence of learning should be collected and acted upon in an ongoing manner. Specifically, steps for further development should be identified by teachers or learners themselves and they should be used to guide ever-increasing development in learners' knowledge, skills and understanding.

Defined as such, the assessment spiral resembles the core principles of the Growth Mindset philosophy (Dweck, 2006). More specifically, it shares the belief that knowledge, skills and/or understanding are not fixed attributes of a learner but that they can be improved and developed. For example, a learner could be working towards an LO which is 'to talk about six things which I did when I went on holidays' but would be unable to meet that objective. Using AfL techniques such as traffic lights (TLs) or two stars and a wish (TSAW) (see Part 2), their teacher, peer or the learner themselves could identify what they can already do and what steps to take in order to move their learning forward. It could be that this learner is able to describe six things that they normally do but is unsure of how to communicate similar information about the past. This next step could then be identified and acted upon, whereby the learner extends their knowledge of verb forms to include the past. The learner could initially say to themselves: 'I can't do this yet', demonstrating the Growth Mindset, rather than saying to themselves 'I'm not good at English because I can't meet that learning objective'. The key concept seems to be captured by the word 'yet' which indicates that the learner's inability to meet the learning objective (LO) is temporary and can be improved upon. A different next step in learning would be set for a learner who may already be able to demonstrate language skills which would allow them to meet such an LO. If they are able to describe what they did during their holidays with simple verbs like 'walked, ate, saw', they could be encouraged to explore synonyms and extend their vocabulary, for example, to include words such as 'sauntered, strolled, nibbled on, consumed, observed, witnessed'. As yet another step, students could be encouraged to modify such verbs with appropriate adverbs. The key principle of organising the learning process in that way would be the belief that with effort and commitment, learners can meet the LOs which are set for them, and that their performance could always be improved upon to exceed the LO. The LO would serve the purpose of signposting the direction of the learner's learning trajectory but would not constitute an end of that path. Such a process would promote learners' recognition of what they already know or can do and how to move towards their objectives and beyond them in order to ensure ever-increasing improvements in learning.

This conceptualisation suggests that feedback provision is only one of the steps in the process of assessment. Consequently, it would seem that having provided a learner with feedback on their performance, a teacher should then set out the next steps required for that learner to improve their performance. Following that, the learner's performance should be evaluated again and further steps outlined. According to Wehlburg's (2007) definition, there is no limit to how many times the cycle repeats, effectively creating a spiral of assessment.

Several classroom processes are integral to the practical implementation of the assessment spiral. Firstly, teachers would have to design conditions for ongoing feedback provision and follow up activities. Secondly, the types of interactions which can benefit learning should be encouraged. And finally, in addition to taking into account the learners' current level of skills and knowledge, the next steps activities should guide children towards the attainment targets, specifying what the learner needs to master next to meet a target and could also offer opportunities to stretch the learning beyond such targets.

In this chapter, I demonstrate how AfL could be used to create the assessment spiral in primary language classes. To achieve this, I compare the relevant outcomes of the review of research into the relationship between assessment and learning (Chapters 4 and 5) to the findings about the implementation of AfL (Part 2). The discussion is divided into four sections, focusing on (1) classroom processes; (2) assessment processes; (3) interactions; and (4) attainment. Finally, I discuss how the concept of an assessment spiral could be used in the future to design studies which explore the impact of AfL on learning. This focus gains currency in the face of the limited empirical evidence of the impact which using AfL could have on achievement.

Classroom Processes

Research into the ways that children learn languages suggests that 'setting clear goals, sequencing materials, frequent questions to monitor progress in the learning process, opportunity to learn, testing and quality feedback are all important characteristics from which early foreign language learning can benefit tremendously' (Edelenbos & Vinje, 2000: 160). In this section, I consider what the findings of my research reveal about the use of AfL within the classroom processes listed by Edelenbos and Vinje (2000). The outcomes are summarised in Table 11.1.

Setting clear objectives

The first classroom process, as identified by Edelenbos and Vinje (2000), is setting clear goals for learners. As is evident from the findings reported in Chapter 6, teachers used a variety of child-friendly techniques not only to make their learners aware of the objectives for each lesson but also to clarify the standard of performance which would demonstrate that a child has met their LO. While explaining AfL, T1 commented that 'it's a way of students and teacher establishing clear goals and working together to achieve those goals' (T1/INT). This was seconded by T2, who remarked that when a teacher uses AfL 'it [a lesson] has a much clearer purpose they [learners] know what is happening' (T2/INT). Evidently,

Table 11.1 AfL and classroom processes

Classroom processes beneficial to learning (Edelenbos & Vinje, 2000)	AfL processes identified in my research on AfL
Setting clear goals	AfL techniques can be used for the purpose of setting learning objectives and expectations of performance (Chapter 6)
Sequencing materials	No empirical evidence directly corresponding to this – but see discussion below.
Frequent questions to monitor progress	AfL techniques can be used for the purpose of monitoring progress (Chapter 6)
Opportunity to learn	AfL techniques allowed for building in 'next steps' activities in order to further learning (Chapter 7)
Testing	AfL techniques can be used for the purpose of evaluating achievement (Chapter 7)
Quality feedback	Eleven technique types were identified as suitable vehicles for providing quality feedback to learners (Chapter 7)

by implementing AfL in their practice, teachers were able to facilitate the first of the processes specified in Table 11.1.

Monitoring progress

Teachers also believed that setting clear goals was linked to the quality of support which they were able to provide while monitoring. T2 explained that when learners are aware of the expectations, 'at that point monitoring becomes more effective' (T2/FG). T1 concurred, explaining that teachers had 'more time to monitor better' (T1/FG). Monitoring progress is another process which can support learning (Table 11.1). While Edelenbos and Vinje (2000) suggest that this could be efficiently enacted by frequent questioning, the evidence from my own research identifies a wider range of techniques which can be successfully implemented in primary language lessons to monitor progress (Chapter 6).

Testing

Another classroom process, which Edelenbos and Vinje (2000) argue is beneficial to language learning, is testing. While AfL, as defined in this volume, does not incorporate testing, it is worth noting that Nikolov (2016) points out that the terms 'testing' and 'assessment' are sometimes used interchangeably in literature. This is predominantly when a summative assessment is discussed. As discussed in Chapter 2, in addition to its primarily formative function, AfL has a secondary summative function; it collects evidence of what has been learnt (summative) with the aim of supporting further learning (formative). Such secondary summative function was especially evident in those techniques which were used to evaluate achievement (Chapter 7).

Opportunity to learn

Notably, during monitoring progress and/or evaluating achievement, teachers were able to incorporate opportunities for learning. This was done by incorporating 'next steps' into AfL techniques (Chapter 7). 'Next steps' refer to opportunities for learners to address the gaps in their knowledge, skills or understanding identified in the process of monitoring and/or evaluation. Furthermore, for those learners who already demonstrate the standard of performance which meets the LOs, 'next steps' included short activities or questions which aim to extend the learning beyond the LOs. The finding that AfL techniques allow for building in 'next step' type activities provides direct empirical evidence which illustrates how the assessment spiral could be practically enacted in primary language education. Importantly, the findings reported in Chapter 7 also indicate that learners respond to such practices in a positive manner.

Quality feedback

Finally, quality feedback is also believed to benefit language learning in childhood (Table 11.1). Feedback provision is such an important component of AfL that Chapter 7 of this volume is entirely devoted to this area. Most significantly, the findings of my research indicate that teachers who have embedded AfL in their practice provide feedback continuously, and are always trying to improve their learners' outcomes. Important to the focus of the present discussions, the findings indicate that learners may receive feedback several times during one session (Chapter 9), each time identifying an achievement as well as an area for further development. Chapter 7 provides a detailed account of those AfL techniques which I observed being used to provide this type of feedback to primary-aged language learners. This adds further empirical evidence of how the assessment spiral can be enacted in primary language education.

Sequencing materials

There was one classroom process listed by Edelenbos and Vinje (2000) which was not directly identified by this study as part of AfL, which is sequencing materials. However, it seems likely that if teachers collect ongoing evidence of learning, they are able to use that information to inform the way in which they sequence materials. It would be interesting for future studies to investigate how the evidence collected through AfL informs teachers' decisions in this area.

Assessment Processes

Assessment is defined in this volume as a process of making judgements based on the evidence of learning collected from students (Part 1).

Research from primary language contexts shows that valid evidence of language learning can be collected when assessment is continuous and when it is contextualised through age-appropriate tasks (Hasselgreen, 2000). In this section, I consider what the empirical findings discussed in Part 2 of this volume reveal about AfL's potential to support collecting valid evidence of learning.

As is evident from the findings reported in Part 2, the embedded type of implementation of AfL (Chapter 9) enables teachers to collect evidence of learning in a continuous manner, alongside the teaching. Notably, in that type, teachers tended to implement AfL techniques with medium to high intra-lesson frequency. This demonstrates that within each lesson, there could be on average three opportunities for collecting evidence of what learners can already do and comparing it to the LO. Additionally, high inter-lesson frequency indicates that this was the case in 89%–91% of lessons taught by the teachers in this category. Arguably, these findings indicate that by embedding AfL in their practice, teachers can create conditions which allow for an ongoing collection of evidence of learning. This interpretation is reflected in a comment made by T1 who said that 'students have the assessment like AfL built into what they do in the lessons so they know that it's a part of the lesson and it's also important (1) I also think that it's continuous and it's more meaningful because they know it's about the things we learnt to do that lesson' (T1/INT).

In the quote cited, T1 indicates that by integrating AfL into lesson activities, (s)he was able to make assessment more meaningful and relevant to the learners because they received immediate feedback on the ongoing learning. Arguably, it also helped to contextualise assessment through the teaching tasks. The findings discussed in Chapters 6 and 7 provide plenty of evidence that AfL techniques were implemented by integrating them into the teaching activities. In the words of T6, AfL is 'just a part of what you're doing anyway with them just teaching them in a slightly different way and it is helpful' (T6/INT). T6 suggests that incorporating AfL into lessons may affect how teachers deliver lessons. The findings discussed in Part 2 indicate that this is achieved by incorporating the classroom processes discussed in the previous section. Reassuringly, T6's opinion that such a change is 'helpful' seems to corroborate research findings which suggest that such processes are beneficial for learning.

The findings summarised here indicate that by embedding AfL in their practice, teachers could create conditions in which assessment is contextualised through age-appropriate teaching activities. Consequently, teachers could create conditions in which they can collect valid evidence of learning. Such evidence would help them make accurate judgements about learners' progress and support the children on their individual pathways towards meeting their LOs.

Interactions

In addition to the classroom and assessment processes discussed in the previous sections, language learning has been shown to benefit from collaborative and expert-novice types of interactions (Chapter 10). Admittedly, each of the processes involved in the assessment spiral, as discussed in the two previous sections, could provide conditions which facilitate different interaction types. Therefore, it is worth considering whether the findings of the core study which informs much of the discussion in this volume provide any evidence of the role of interactions in creating the assessment spiral in primary language lessons.

Collaborative and expert–novice-type interactions (Storch, 2002) require that interlocutors demonstrate a medium to high level of mutuality through working towards the same conversational goal. The majority of extracts quoted in Chapter 10 illustrate that while AfL was being used, medium to high levels of mutuality were observed. This can be explained by the observation that AfL techniques aim to facilitate meeting the LOs. Consequently, the interlocutors shared the same conversational goal of moving the learner towards meeting the LO.

As discussed in Chapter 6, another factor which has been shown to facilitate language learning through interaction is the learners' familiarity with the task structure (Pinter, 2007). As recalled in the previous section, Chapters 6 and 7 provide empirical evidence that suggests that AfL techniques become an integral part of teaching tasks. Therefore, it would seem logical to propose that by familiarising learners with the structure of AfL techniques through embedded implementation, teachers could provide a degree of familiarity with the structure of teaching tasks. This could be true even for tasks types which learners have never previously attempted.

Attainment

The definition of the assessment spiral requires that the next steps in learning be continuously identified as learners' progression towards the attainment targets is evaluated. In primary language teaching, attainment targets are often predefined. They may take the form of adapted Common European Framework of Reference (CEFR) descriptors (e.g. Goodier, 2018a; Hasselgreen, 2005) or be provided by governments (Butler, 2009). Regardless of where they are sourced from, it has been suggested that attainment targets for primary-aged language learners should be expressed in small, incremental steps that can demonstrate children's relatively slow progress (Nikolov & Mihaljević Djigunović, 2011) because a list of end of year targets or adapted CEFR statements may not capture children's progress adequately (Enever, 2011). In primary language education, small steps which are identified through the assessment spiral could help to guide learners through their individual paths to meeting the predefined attainment targets. In this section, I examine the evidence that AfL may support teachers in identifying the next steps in learning, therefore contributing to creating the assessment spiral in primary language classes.

The main body of empirical evidence to address this focus was presented in Chapter 7. Eleven AfL techniques for providing feedback were identified. Notably, those techniques included components which explicitly aimed to indicate what students should focus their efforts on next in order to advance their learning towards meeting the LO.

The interpretation that AfL allowed for providing ongoing guidance about the next steps for the learner to take on the learning journey was verified through teacher interviews and the focus group. For example, T8 explained that AfL is 'like setting up goals and then kind of being accountable for those goals all the time with them (1) and they [the students] know what they should achieve' (T8/INT). Moreover, T5 noticed that when using AfL techniques a teacher pays regular attention 'to the students' progress and their needs (1) what they need actually (1) and you keep putting this in your teaching' (T5/INT). The latter quote indicates that regular reflection and adaptation of teaching to suit the learning needs of children can also be observed when AfL is embedded in the practice. Furthermore, it was highlighted that children do not have to rely on their teachers but instead, they can play an active role in the process of identifying the next steps in learning. For example, T6 explained that 'you're not just handing them a mark and telling them you're poor at this or good at this but you're getting them to try and think about the aim and whether they've achieved it and if not then help them work out exactly how to achieve this' (T6/INT). T4 even suggested that 'the main aim of this [AfL] is to get them thinking about how to get better' (T4/FG), indicating that learners could provide their own next steps with their teacher's guidance.

The evidence recalled in this section strongly suggests that AfL could offer opportunities for identifying next steps in learning. It also points out the potential for developing learners' skills in doing so independently.

Assessment Spiral in Primary Language Education

In this chapter, I have discussed empirical evidence which strongly suggests that embedding AfL into primary language teaching and learning could facilitate the occurrence of the assessment spiral. The discussion has indicated that AfL:

- Incorporates classroom processes which are beneficial to learning, such as setting clear goals, monitoring progress, providing opportunities for learning, evaluating and providing feedback.

- Helps to ensure that during the assessment process, teachers collect valid evidence of learning as they contextualise assessment though lesson activities.
- Can be implemented in a continuous manner.
- Enables teachers and their learners to set next steps in learning to move towards the attainment targets.
- Provides conditions for such interaction types which can support learning.

These findings illustrate how the assessment spiral could be enacted in primary language classes. Specifically, AfL techniques could be used to evaluate the current level of knowledge and skills; to provide feedback; and to set next steps which aim to help learners modify their performance; and then to evaluate that modified performance; and so on. This sequence of performance–evaluation–feedback–(modified) performance–evaluation–feedback and so on is what constitutes the core of the assessment spiral. The evidence from the study classrooms indicates that within the embedded type of implementation, there are on average three instances of using AfL in almost every lesson. This constitutes evidence which indicates that it is possible to build in multiple opportunities for evaluation and feedback provision within lessons. Importantly, activities which aim to encourage learners to take next steps in order to further develop their learning have been shown to be an integral part of many of those AfL techniques which were used for the purpose of providing feedback on learning in the study classrooms (Chapter 7). These findings confirm that the assessment spiral can be enacted in primary language classes by implementing AfL techniques. Specifically, embedding AfL into their classroom practice enables teachers to design lessons in such a way that allows learners to receive feedback on their learning several times, while they are still working towards meeting their LO.

This outcome is especially interesting for three reasons. First, by definition, the assessment spiral aims for 'ever-increasing improvement of the quality of student learning' (Wehlburg, 2007: 1). Therefore, it could be hypothesised that by facilitating the assessment spiral in primary language education, AfL could benefit learning. In the face of the virtual absence of published empirical evidence on how AfL could contribute to improving learning outcomes, this research focus gains currency and would constitute a valuable focus for future studies. Second, as discussed in Chapter 2, teachers confirm that AfL is relatively easy to implement in primary language classes. For example, they reported that 'this is all seamless and normal and very informative to show what they have learnt' (T2/INT) or that AfL 'is the means to an end just a part of what you're doing anyway with them just teaching them in slightly different way and it is helpful' (T6/INT). Therefore, an implementation of an assessment spiral in primary language education is evidently not only possible, but more importantly, through AfL it may be easy to introduce in primary language education. Third, if the assessment spiral can be implemented in primary language contexts to improve learning, then it becomes especially interesting to explore the nature of the next steps activities and the AfL techniques which aim to provide feedback. This links the research on AfL to the vast body of research on modifications of output (Chapter 5). This not only provides a useful indication of the direction for further research into the impact of AfL on learning (see Chapter 12) but importantly, also helps to situate studies on AfL with relation to other research in the field – a need recognised, for example, by Black and Wiliam (2009).

A visual representation of the assessment spiral as discussed in this chapter is proposed in Figure 11.1. The central part of the figure is occupied by the repeated 'performance–evaluation–feedback–(modified) performance–evaluation' sequence, which creates the assessment spiral. Importantly, there is no end to the assessment spiral, as indicated by the dashed line on the model. This means, that as learners progress and their

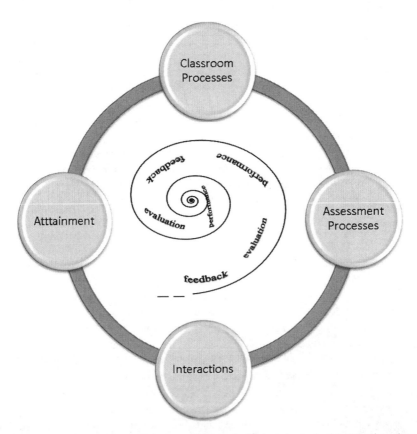

Figure 11.1 Assessment Spiral enacted through AfL in primary language education

language skills develop, they can continue to improve their performance 'minute-to-minute and day-by-day' (Thompson & Wiliam, 2007: 6), and presumably further than that; week by week and year by year.

The assessment spiral can be implemented under favourable conditions. The four areas identified through the empirical findings reported in this volume include classroom processes, assessment processes, attainment and interactions. As demonstrated throughout the current chapter, when AfL is embedded in a teacher's practice, the types of classroom processes and the types of interactions which occur can benefit learning (Butler & Zeng, 2014; Edelenbos & Vinje, 2000; Pinter, 2007). With direct reference to assessment, the discussion has demonstrated that AfL can support teachers in collecting valid evidence of learning when assessment tasks are contextualised through the ongoing teaching activities (Hasselgreen, 2000). Importantly, when the assessment spiral is enacted in the classroom through AfL, it helps to create opportunities for teachers and learners to set next steps to guide learners on their individual learning paths. This is an important finding which provides a useful indication of the way in which AfL could help to facilitate learning.

The concept of the assessment spiral could be helpful in designing future studies, especially those which hope to explore the relationship between AfL and achievement. The core sequence of evaluation–feedback–performance–evaluation–etc. is what promises to create classroom conditions which are conducive to learning. By exploring the impact that different feedback practices can have on performance, future studies could provide evidence which demonstrates if/how AfL could be empirically linked to improved achievement. By exploring each of the components of this sequence, future studies could provide much-needed guidance for effective implementation of the assessment spiral.

Summary of the Chapter

In this chapter, I have explored the assessment spiral – a conceptualisation of assessment as a repeated process of evaluating and providing feedback on performance in order to aid learning. The discussion has highlighted the ways in which using AfL can contribute to enacting the assessment spiral in primary language classes. Most importantly, the sequence of evaluation–feedback–(modified) performance has been identified as a key feature of the assessment spiral in primary language education. Ample empirical evidence reported in Part 2 confirms that this sequence can occur in primary language lessons and, importantly, also suggests that it can be repeated up to three times within a 60-minute lesson. As discussed in the present chapter, the evaluation–feedback–(modified) performance sequence does not happen in isolation but is closely linked with classroom and assessment processes, attainment and types of interactions which occur during lessons.

The concept of an assessment spiral could be used to design future studies which would provide empirical evidence of how AfL contributes to language learning in childhood. It would address frequent calls for studies in this area. Finally, the discussion has linked research on AfL to that on modifications of input and output. This is an important outcome of the discussion not only because it could facilitate future studies but importantly because it helps to place AfL in relation to other pedagogical concepts.

12 Looking into the Future

Introduction

Throughout this volume, I have focused on the use and possible impact of assessment for learning (AfL) on primary language teaching and learning. By drawing on the findings from a significant data set, collected through lesson observations ($n = 28$), teacher interviews ($n = 8$), a focus group ($n = 1$), a delayed teacher questionnaire ($n = 8$) and from the school records of 448 lessons, I have provided a detailed account of the ways in which teachers ($n = 8$) implemented AfL when teaching learners aged 7–11 ($n = 148$). As stated in the introductory chapter, the purpose of this volume was threefold: to provide much needed insights into the practical use of AfL in primary language classes, by reporting in detail on the ways in which eight experienced primary language teachers implemented this type of assessment into their practice; to discuss the relationship between AfL and language learning in childhood; and finally, to highlight paths for future action with the focus on implementing and/or researching AfL in primary language contexts. To satisfy the third aim of this volume, in this chapter, I focus on highlighting possible future action. In order to contextualise the discussion, I first provide a brief overview of the relevant points discussed in previous chapters. This is followed by reflections on the implications of the discussion presented throughout this volume for implementing AfL in primary language contexts. Finally, I outline some possible paths for future inquiry into AfL and its impact on learning.

Throughout the volume, it is emphasised that when assessing primary-aged language learners, we should carefully consider not only the assessment methods used but also children's individual characteristics, including those connected to their age. As discussed in Part 1, many factors can have an impact on the usefulness and appropriateness of an assessment method in primary language education. First and foremost, in any context, an assessment method should be selected to accurately serve the intended purpose of assessment. Consequently, fitness for purpose should drive assessment decisions. However, in contexts where children are assessed, there are plenty of other factors to consider. These include: children's cognitive and metacognitive development; their affective profiles; their first language (L1) literacy levels; and contextual factors such as experience of schooling.

Throughout Parts 2 and 3, I reflect on the learning environments that learners encounter in a language classroom when AfL is used. Most significantly, the discussion points to the potential of AfL techniques to help teachers: (1) scaffold activities focused on language production; (2) provide a degree of familiarity with the structure of lesson activities; and (3) develop children's positive affective profiles. These findings link insights into the use of AfL with research which has investigated the impact on learning that could be expected from modifications of output (Oliver, 2000, 2002; Oliver & Mackey, 2003; Swain, 2000) and familiarity with the task structure (Pinter, 2007; Skehan & Foster, 1999). Additionally, the report on the practical implementation of AfL provides ample evidence of a relationship between this type of assessment and the development of children's affective dispositions, linking my study to the growing body of research in this area (Aydin, 2013; Mihaljević Djigunović, 2012, 2015; Mihaljević Djigunović & Lopriore, 2011).

Considerations for Implementing AfL in Primary Language Teaching

Throughout Part 2, I explore the practical implementation of AfL in primary language teaching. In this section, I build on the findings and discussions presented throughout Part 2 and review the considerations that are important when introducing and/or promoting the use of AfL in various educational contexts. First, I review the type of implementation that is most appropriate for primary-aged language learners. This is followed by a summary of the factors that may facilitate or inhibit the implementation of AfL. The aim of this section is to present, in a concise form, those outcomes of the discussion from Part 2 that can offer advice for the practical implementation of AfL.

Types of implementation

Four types of AfL implementation were identified in primary language classrooms: embedded, developing, experimental and tokenistic. In Chapter 9, I discuss the characteristics of each of these, together with the changes that occurred in teachers' practice over 16 months. The discussion demonstrates that the embedded type is stable over time, indicating that the teachers who implement AfL in that way, do not tend to make significant changes to the frequency and diversity of their use of AfL over time. Importantly, this way of implementing AfL seems to promote classroom processes that are not only appropriate for primary-aged language learners but also, and even more significantly, may offer benefits to learning. Therefore, those who aim to implement AfL in primary language classrooms should not only aim to facilitate the implementation of the embedded type but should also consider what factors affect the type of implementation. I discuss these below.

Factors affecting implementation

The factors that may influence the way in which teachers implement AfL include: the compatibility of the assessment methods with the teaching methods used in each context and with the existing assessment culture; teacher knowledge of using AfL gained through training and/or experience; the appropriateness of the assessment methods to individual learner characteristics, especially their age.

Compatibility with teaching methods and the existing assessment culture

As part of the decision-making about how best to incorporate AfL into the teaching methods used in a given context, teachers and leaders should carefully consider the purposes for which they use assessment. As discussed in Parts 1 and 2 of this volume, the overarching purpose of AfL is to support learning. This firmly situates this type of assessment within the pedagogical paradigm. Unlike psychometric testing, AfL is not focused on measurement. Therefore, first and foremost, it is vital to consider *the compatibility of such an approach with the educational culture* of the contexts in which AfL is being implemented. If there is an assessment culture dominated by summative testing (e.g. Lee & Coniam, 2013), measurement and/or competitiveness and norm-referenced reporting, then a cultural shift will be needed to effectively implement AfL. Such change would need to be sensitively navigated by leaders, who should aim to educate all stakeholders in the teaching and learning process, especially the teachers, learners and parents/carers. Importantly, they would also need support and guidance at policy level. Rixon (2017) discusses the introduction of AfL into mainstream schools in England as an example of successful educational innovation. She explains that the main reason for its success was the 'great responsibility that senior school staff there currently have taken on for observation and coaching of colleagues' (Rixon, 2017: 90). As a result, 'major changes in practice such as Assessment for Learning (Black & Wiliam, 1998) seem to have become successfully embedded in many schools over the last ten years' (Rixon, 2017: 90–91).

Three specific *purposes of AfL* were identified in my research of classroom practice: setting expectations; monitoring progress; and evaluating achievement. They help to enact assessment in a way that ensures that the overarching purpose of supporting learning is fulfilled. These three purposes illustrate that AfL can and should be incorporated into teaching and learning activities from their early stages, when tasks and learning objectives are introduced to learners. Importantly, this demonstrates that assessment such as AfL is an integral part of the teaching and learning process (Prošić-Santovac & Rixon, 2019). This is an important consideration that has implications for the planning of the pedagogical process. Most specifically, it means that teachers should have clearly defined learning objectives and criteria for success before they start teaching a new lesson or unit of work. Additionally, this approach to assessment requires that learners are active participants of the teaching, learning and assessment processes from the beginning when such objectives and criteria are shared with them. This impacts on the roles of teachers and learners in the learning process, as well as the level of responsibility that they take for achievement.

Appropriateness for learners of various ages

Assessment methods used in primary language education should be aligned with teaching methods. Importantly, the teaching activities should be appropriate for *learners' age*; they should account for age-related characteristics such as levels of cognitive, metacognitive and socioemotional development. This is an important consideration which has implications for the validity of the assessment data. This is primarily because by designing assessment tasks in a way that enables learners to best demonstrate what they have achieved, teachers can collect evidence which accurately represents their students' language ability and those gaps in knowledge, skills and understanding that should be addressed by future teaching. In order to ensure that this criterion is met, teachers should ensure that:

(1) Tasks used for assessment are aligned to the tasks which are routinely used for teaching in primary language classes.
(2) Learners are made familiar with the structure of the tasks used for collecting evidence of learning, for example, by frequent use of AfL techniques within tasks.
(3) Assessment is integrated into the teaching and learning activities, for instance, by incorporating AfL techniques into the structure of tasks.
(4) Evidence of learning is collected over a period of time to build up a coherent picture of achievement, rather than through a one-off assessment opportunity.
(5) Assessment methods promote learners' noticing the gap between target production and their own interlanguages.
(6) Assessment methods activate learners as assessors and sources of their own learning, for example, through formative peer or self-assessment.
(7) The form in which assessment and feedback are presented is accessible (understandable) to learners, for example, a greater reliance on

visual representations should be the aim in lower age groups where children have not yet mastered L1 literacy skills.

(8) Assessment methods promote positive affective profiles, for example, by highlighting achievement and success through feedback.

The techniques discussed in Chapters 6 and 7 illustrate that AfL can fulfil the above requirements and is therefore appropriate for use with primary-aged language learners. Importantly, the discussion in Chapter 8 highlights the age-related characteristics of AfL, demonstrating how techniques can be adapted according to the age-related characteristics of learners, such as their L1 literacy levels (see Tables 8.4 and 8.5). This highlights the flexibility of AfL techniques, emphasising that actual class-room implementation can be adapted to best suit the context in which it is used, as long as the purposes for assessment are fulfilled.

Teacher knowledge

Teachers and leaders play an important role in ensuring the success of pedagogical innovations (Rixon, 2017). The outcomes of my own research confirm that teachers play a key role in determining the way in which AfL can be implemented in primary language classrooms. This was especially evident in the findings about the reasons for changes in teachers' practice over time. Teacher cognition appears to be closely linked to the way in which they implement AfL. The findings indicate that formal and informal training in AfL and observing how colleagues use this form of assessment could contribute to developing their own practice in ways that resemble the desired embedded type of implemen-tation. Furthermore, teachers' own experience of experimenting with various technique types in the lessons can help them develop professional knowledge and gain experience, which informs their decisions about the way in which they implement AfL in their lessons. On the contrary, train-ing in other ways of assessing learners and/or lack of experience of using AfL through observing colleagues and their own practice were linked to less desirable types of implementation, resembling or moving towards the tokenistic type over time.

Developing teacher knowledge is an important consideration for those readers who might be interested in implementing AfL in various contexts. As convincingly argued by Rixon (2017), teachers are key stakeholders in the process of introducing a pedagogical innovation and should be sup-ported through training, coaching and opportunities to experiment with the approach in their own classrooms and without judgement from school administrators. As reported earlier in this chapter, this approach has been successful in England. It seems to offer opportunities to develop ways for practical implementation of AfL that are sensitive and appropriate for the educational context in which it is to be used, while simultaneously upskill-ing teachers and embedding the pedagogical paradigm for assessment.

Paths for Future Inquiry

I hope that by reporting a detailed account of the use of AfL, complete with a description of the four types of implementation and the concept of the assessment spiral in primary language education, alongside clarification of the theoretical framework of AfL, this volume will facilitate, or perhaps even inspire, further research into AfL. Future studies should focus on exploring the practical use of AfL in teaching languages at the primary level across various educational traditions globally. Moreover, there is also a clear need for gathering and reporting on empirical evidence pertaining to the impact that AfL may have on language learning in childhood. Such insights would play an important role in informing pedagogical practice and assessment policy in the future. In this section, I outline possible paths for future inquiry within the two broad areas specified above.

Further research into the impact of AfL on learning

In Chapter 9, I describe four types of AfL implementation. Future studies which aim to evaluate the impact of AfL on learning should account for those various types of implementation, as they may determine the quality of AfL's impact on learning. Furthermore, in Chapter 11, I discuss the assessment spiral and consider how implementing AfL could facilitate this improvement-focused process in primary language education. Therefore, it would seem useful for future studies to explore the impact of the assessment spiral on language learning in childhood. Specific paths for future enquiry could aim to explore: the impact of using AfL on developing positive affective dispositions in young learners; the impact of interactions that occur during AfL on language learning in childhood; the impact of next step activities on learning; the impact of scaffolding delivered through AfL on performance; the impact of AfL on familiarity with the task structure and its relationship to learning; the impact of using non-literacy-dependent AfL techniques with children who have not yet developed L1 literacy to assess language learning in childhood.

Further research into practical implementation of AfL

Throughout this volume, I report on findings from my own research into classroom use of AfL with primary-aged learners. This offers unique insights based on a large data set, which were not accessible in published research at the time of writing this book. However, one obvious limitation of these findings is that they are based in just one educational context. It would be valuable to gain insights into classroom practice across a variety of contexts globally. Therefore, another focus for future research could be the specific nature of AfL in primary language education, including the roles of teachers and learners, and learner agency in the assessment process.

It would also be useful to have reports of the types of implementation that can be observed in various contexts. This would help to verify and further develop the model of AfL implementation in primary language teaching discussed in Chapter 9.

The proposed paths for future enquiry highlight some of the possible avenues for taking the research on AfL primary language education forward but are by no means an exhaustive list. Researching AfL specifically in primary language contexts is important because understanding the processes that occur in lessons during the use of AfL and their impact on performance promises to have numerous pedagogical implications. Not only would such studies help to inform the effective use of age- and context-appropriate assessment techniques, but more importantly, they could also provide much needed insights into the ways in which we can support early language learning through assessment.

References

Ahlquist, S. (2019) Opportunities for formative assessment in the storyline approach. In D. Prošić-Santovac and S. Rixon (eds) *Integrating Assessment into Early Language Learning and Teaching* (pp. 140–154). Bristol: Multilingual Matters.

Alcón, E. (2007) Incidental focus on form, noticing and vocabulary learning in the EFL classroom. *International Journal of English Studies* 7 (2), 41–60.

Anderson, P. (2005) *Cognitive Psychology and Its Implication*. London: Macmillan.

ARG (Assessment Reform Group, 2002) Assessment for learning: 10 principles. Research-based principles of assessment for learning to guide classroom practice. See http://web archive.nationalarchives.gov.uk/20101021152907/ http://www.ttrb.ac.uk/ViewArti cle2.aspx?ContentId=15313 (accessed 3 March 2012).

Aydin, S. (2013) Factors affecting the level of test anxiety among EFL learners at elementary schools. *E-International Journal of Educational Research* 4 (1), 63–81.

Bachman, L. (2007) What is the construct? The dialectic of abilities and contexts in defining constructs in language assessment. In J. Fox, M. Wesche, D. Bayliss, L. Cheng, C. Turner, and C. Doe (eds) *Language Testing Reconsidered* (pp. 41–71). Ottawa: University of Ottawa Press.

Bacsa, É. and Csíkos, C. (2016) The role of individual differences in the development of listening comprehension in the early stages of language learning. In M. Nikolov (ed.) *Assessing Young Learners of English: Global and Local Perspectives* (pp. 263–289). New York: Springer.

Bailey, A.L. (2005) Cambridge young learners English (YLE) tests. *Language Testing* 22 (2), 242–252.

Baumert, J., Fleckenstein, J., Leucht, M., Köller, O. and Möller, J. (2020) The long-term proficiency of early, middle, and late starters learning English as a foreign language at school: A narrative review and empirical study. *Language Learning* 70 (4), 1091–1135.

Benigno, V. and de Jong, J. (2016) The 'Global Scale of English Learning Objectives for Young Learners': A CEFR-based inventory of descriptors. In M. Nikolov (ed.) *Assessing Young Learners of English: Global and Local Perspectives* (pp. 43–64). New York: Springer.

Bennett, R.E. (2011) Formative assessment: A critical review. *Assessment in Education: Principles, Policy & Practice* 18 (1), 5–25.

Bialystok, E. (2001) *Bilingualism in Development: Language, Literacy, and Cognition*. New York: Cambridge University Press.

Bialystok, E. and Hakuta, K. (1999) Confounded age: Linguistic and cognitive factors in age differences for second language acquisition. In D. Birdsong (ed.) *Second Language Acquisition and the Critical Period Hypothesis* (pp. 161–181). New York: Routledge.

Birjandi, P. and Hadidi Tamjid, N. (2012) The role of self-, peer and teacher assessment in promoting Iranian EFL learners' writing performance. *Assessment & Evaluation in Higher Education* 37 (5), 513–533.

Black, T.R. (2005) *Doing Qualitative Research in the Social Sciences: An Integrated Approach to Research Design, Measurement and Statistics.* London: Sage.

Black, P.J. and Wiliam, D. (1998) Assessment and classroom learning. *Assessment in Education: Principles Policy and Practice* 5 (1), 7–73.

Black, P. and Wiliam, D. (2009) Developing the theory of formative assessment. *Educational Assessment, Evaluation and Accountability* 21 (1), 5–31.

Black, P., McCormick, R., James, M. and Pedder, D. (2006) Learning how to learn and assessment for learning: A theoretical inquiry. *Research Papers in Education* 21 (2), 119–132.

Bloom, B.S. (1984) The search for methods of instruction as effective as one-to-one tutoring. *Educational Leadership* 41 (8), 4–17.

Boekaerts, M. and Cascallar, E. (2006) How far have we moved toward the integration of theory and practice in self-regulation? *Educational Psychology Review* 18 (3), 199–210.

Borg, S. (2003) Teacher cognition in language teaching: A review of research on what language teachers think, know, believe, and do. *Language Teaching* 36 (2), 81–109.

Borkowski, J.G. (1985) Signs of intelligence: Strategy generalization and metacognition. In S.R. Yussen (ed.) *The Growth of Reflection in Children* (pp. 105–144). Orlando, FL: Academic Press.

Britton, A.M. (2015) Assessment for Learning in Teaching English to Young Learners: Teachers' Understanding, Classroom Practice and Impact on Interactions. PhD thesis, University of Reading.

Burstall, C., Jamieson, M., Cohen, S. and Hargreaves, M. (1974) *Primary French in the Balance.* Slough: National Foundation for Educational Research.

Butler, R. (1988) Enhancing and undermining intrinsic motivation: The effects of task-involving and ego-involving evaluation on interest and performance. *British Journal of Educational Psychology* 58 (1), 1–14.

Butler, Y.G. (2009) Issues in the assessment and evaluation of English language education at the elementary school level: Implications for policies in South Korea, Taiwan, and Japan. *Journal of Asia TEFL* 6 (2), 1–31.

Butler, Y.G. and Lee, J. (2006) On-task versus off-task self-assessments among Korean elementary school students studying English. *The Modern Language Journal* 90 (4), 506–518.

Butler, Y.G. and Lee, J. (2010) The effects of self-assessment among young learners of English. *Language Testing* 27 (1), 5–31.

Butler, Y.G. and Zeng, W. (2014) Young foreign language learners' interactions during task-based paired assessments. *Language Assessment Quarterly* 11 (1), 45–75.

Bygate, M. (1996) Effects of task repetition: Appraising the developing language of learners. In J. Willis and D. Willis (eds) *Challenge and Change in Language Teaching* (pp. 136–146). Oxford: Macmillan Education.

Cable, C., Driscoll, P., Mitchell, R., Sing, S., Cremin, T., Earl, J., Eyres, I., Holmes, B., Martin, C. and Heins, B. (2010) *Languages Learning at Key Stage 2: A Longitudinal Study.* United Kingdom of Great Britain and Northern Ireland, GB, Department for Children, Schools and Families (DCSF Research Reports DCSF-RR198). See http://epr ints.soton.ac.uk/143157/1/DCSF-RR198.pdf (accessed 26 March 2018).

Cameron, L. (2003) Challenges for ELT from the expansion in teaching children. *ELT Journal* 57 (2), 105–112.

Carless, D. (2005) Prospects for the implementation of assessment for learning. *Assessment in Education: Principles, Policy & Practice* 12 (1), 39–54.

Carless, D., Joughin, G. and Liu, N.F. (2006) *How Assessment Supports Learning: Learning-Oriented Assessment in Action.* Hong Kong: Hong Kong University Press.

Case, R., Kurland, D.M. and Goldberg, J. (1982) Operational efficiency and the growth of short-term memory span. *Journal of Experimental Child Psychology* 33 (3), 386–404.

Cenoz, J. (2003) The influence of age on the acquisition of English: General proficiency, attitudes and code mixing. In M. García Mayo and M. García Lecumberri (eds) *Age and the Acquisition of English as a FL* (pp. 77–93). Clevedon: Multilingual Matters.

Chamot, A. and El-Dinary, P.B. (1999) Children's learning strategies in language immersion classrooms. *The Modern Language Journal* 83 (3), 319–338.

Chan, D.Y.C. and Wu, G.C. (2004) A study of foreign language anxiety of EFL elementary school students in Taipei County. *Journal of National Taipei Teachers College* 17 (2), 287–320.

Chappuis, S., Stiggins, R.J., Arter, J. and Chappuis, J. (2004) *Assessment for Learning: An Action Guide for School Leaders*. Portland, OR: Assessment Training Institute.

Cheng, L., Rogers, T. and Hu, H. (2004) ESL/EFL instructors' classroom assessment practices: Purposes, methods, and procedures. *Language Testing* 21 (3), 360–389.

Csizér, K. and Kormos, J. (2009) Learning experiences, selves and motivated learning behaviour: A comparative analysis of structural models for Hungarian secondary and university learners of English. In Z. Dörnyei and E. Ushioda (eds) *Motivation, Language Identity and the L2 Self* (pp. 98–119). Bristol: Multilingual Matters.

Clarke, S. (2005) *Formative Assessment in Action: Weaving the Elements Together*. London: Hodder Murray.

Clarke, S. (2014) *Outstanding Formative Assessment: Culture and Practice*. London: Hachette.

Cohen, L., Manion, L. and Morrison, K. (2007) *Research Methods in Education* (6th edn). London: Routledge.

Colby-Kelly, C. and Turner, C.E. (2007) AFL research in the L2 classroom and evidence of usefulness: Taking formative assessment to the next level. *Canadian Modern Language Review/La Revue Canadienne des Langues Vivantes* 64 (1), 9–37.

Cojocnean, D. (2012) Perspectives on assessing young learners' English language competence in Romania. *Academica Science Journal, Psychologica Series* 1 (1), 55–66.

Council of Europe (2001) *Common European Framework for Languages: Learning, Teaching, Assessment*. Strasbourg: Council of Europe. See www.coe.int/lang-cefr (accessed 3 July 2020).

Council of Europe (2020) *Common European Framework of Reference for Languages: Learning, Teaching, Assessment – Companion Volume*. Strasbourg: Council of Europe. See www.coe.int/lang-cefr (accessed 12 September 2014).

Cowie, B. and Bell, B. (1999) A model of formative assessment in science education, *Assessment in Education* 6 (1), 101–116.

Daneman, M. and Carpenter, P.A. (1980) Individual differences in working memory and reading. *Journal of Verbal Learning and Verbal Behavior* 19 (4), 450–466.

Daneman, M. and Merikle, P.M. (1996) Working memory and language comprehension: A meta-analysis. *Psychonomic Bulletin & Review* 3 (4), 422–433.

Dann, R. (2002) *Promoting Assessment as Learning: Improving the Learning Process*. London: Routledge.

Debyser, D. and Tagliante, C. (2001) *Mon premier portfolio*. Paris: Didier.

DeKeyser, R.M. (2000) The robustness of critical period effects in second language acquisition. *Studies in Second Language Acquisition* 22 (4), 499–533.

Dimroth, C. (2008) Age effects on the process of L2 acquisition? Evidence from the acquisition of negation and finiteness in L2 German. *Language Learning* 58 (1), 117–150.

Dixon, H.R., Hawe, E. and Parr, J. (2011) Enacting assessment for learning: The beliefs practice nexus. *Assessment in Education: Principles, Policy & Practice* 18 (4), 365–379.

Donato, R., Tucker, G.R., Wudthayagorn, J. and Igaraschi, K. (2000) Converging evidence: Attitudes, achievements, and instruction in the later years of FLES. *Foreign Language Annals* 33 (4), 377–399.

Dörnyei, Z. (2005) *The Psychology of the Language Learner: Individual Differences in Second Language Acquisition*. Mahwah, NJ: Lawrence Erlbaum.

Dörnyei, Z. (2009a) *The Psychology of Second Language Acquisition*. New York: Oxford University Press.

Dörnyei, Z. (2009b) The L2 motivational self system. In Z. Dörnyei and E. Ushioda (eds) *Motivation, Language Identity and the L2 Self* (pp. 9–42). Bristol: Multilingual Matters.

Dörnyei, Z. (2019) Towards a better understanding of the L2 learning experience, the Cinderella of the L2 motivational self system. *Studies in Second Language Learning and Teaching* 9 (1), 19–30.

Doughty, C. and Varela, E. (1998) Communicative focus on form. In J. Wiliams (ed.) *Focus on Form in Classroom Second Language Acquisition* (pp. 114–138). Stuttgart: Ernst Klett Sprachen.

Drummond, M.J. (2003) *Assessing Children's Learning*. London: David Fulton.

Dunn, K.E. and Mulvenon, S.W. (2009) A critical review of research on formative assessment: The limited scientific evidence of the impact of formative assessment in education. *Practical Assessment, Research & Evaluation* 14 (7), 1–11.

Dweck, C.S. (2006) *Mindset: The New Psychology of Success*. New York: Random House.

Earl, L.M. (2012) *Assessment as Learning: Using Classroom Assessment to Maximize Student Learning*. Thousand Oaks, CA: Corwin Press.

Edelenbos, P. and Vinjé, M.P. (2000) The assessment of a foreign language at the end of primary (elementary) education. *Language Testing* 17 (2), 144–162.

Edelenbos, P. and Kubanek-German, A. (2004) Teacher assessment: The concept of 'diagnostic competence'. *Language Testing* 21 (3), 259–283.

Edelenbos, P. and Kubanek, A. (2009) Early foreign language learning: Published research, good practice and main principles. In M. Nikolov (ed.) *The Age Factor and Early Language Learning* (pp. 39–58). Berlin: Mouton de Gruyter.

Edelenbos, P., Johnstone, R. and Kubanek, A. (2006) *The main pedagogical principles underlying the teaching of languages to very young learners. Languages for the children of Europe: Published research, good practice and main principles*. European Commission Report. See http//ec.europa,eu/education/policies/lang/doc/youngsum_en. pdf (accessed 19 June 2011).

Ellis, G. (2014) 'Young learners': Clarifying our terms. *ELT Journal* 68 (1), 75–78.

Ellis, R. and Heimbach, R. (1997) Bugs and birds: Children's acquisition of second language vocabulary through interaction. *System* 25 (2), 247–259.

Ellis, G. and Rixon, S. (2019) Assessment for learning with younger learners: Is thinking about their learning a step too far? In D. Prošić-Santovac and S. Rixon (eds) *Integrating Assessment Into Early Language Learning and Teaching* (pp. 87–104). Bristol: Multilingual Matters.

Ellis, R., Tanaka, Y. and Yamazaki, A. (1994) Classroom interaction, comprehension, and the acquisition of L2 word meanings. *Language Learning* 44 (3), 449–491.

Enever, J. (2011) *ELLiE. Early Language Learning in Europe*. London: British Council.

Enever, J. and Driscoll, P. (2019) Introduction. Policy and practice in early language learning. *AILA Review* 32 (1), 1–9.

Flavell, J.H. (1992) Cognitive development: Past, present, and future. *Developmental Psychology* 28 (6), 998–1005.

Flavell, J.H., Miller, P.H. and Miller, S.A. (1993) *Cognitive Development* (3rd edn). Englewood Cliffs, NJ: Prentice Hall.

Flavell, J.H., Green, F.L. and Flavell, E.R. (2000) Development of children's awareness of their own thoughts. *Journal of Cognition and Development* 1 (1), 97–112.

Flege, J.E., Munro, M.J. and MacKay, I.R. (1995) Factors affecting strength of perceived foreign accent in a second language. *The Journal of the Acoustical Society of America* 97 (5), 3125–3134.

Flege, J.E., Yeni-Komshian, G.H. and Liu, S. (1999) Age constraints on second-language acquisition. *Journal of Memory and Language* 41 (1), 78–104.

Gan, Z. and Leung, C. (2020) Illustrating formative assessment in task-based language teaching. *ELT Journal* 74 (1), 10–19.

García-Mayo, M.D.P. and García-Lecumberri, M.L. (eds) (2003) *Age and the Acquisition of English as a Foreign Language*. Clevedon: Multilingual Matters.

Gardner, R.C. (2010) *Motivation and Second Language Acquisition: The Socio-Educational Model*. New York: Peter Lang.

Gardner, R.C. and MacIntyre, P.D. (1993) A student's contributions to second-language learning. Part II: Affective variables. *Language Teaching* 26 (1), 1–11.

Gass, S.M. (2013) *Input Interaction and the Second Language Learner*. New York: Routledge.

Gathercole, S.E. and Baddeley, A.D. (1993) Phonological working memory: A critical building block for reading development and vocabulary acquisition? *European Journal of Psychology of Education* 8 (3), 259–272.

Gattullo, F. (2000) Formative assessment in ELT primary (elementary) classrooms: An Italian case study. *Language Testing* 17 (2), 278–288.

Ghatala, E.S. (1986) Strategy-monitoring training enables young learners to select effective strategies. *Educational Psychologist* 21 (1–2), 43–54.

Gipps, C.V. (1994) *Beyond Testing: Towards a Theory of Educational Assessment*. London: Psychology Press.

Goh, C. and Taib, Y. (2006) Metacognitive instruction in listening for young learners. *ELT Journal* 60 (3), 222–232.

Goodier, T. (ed.) (2018a) *Collated Representative Samples of Descriptors of Language Competences Developed for Young Learners – Resource for Educators, Volume 1: Ages 7–10*. Brussels: Education Policy Division, Council of Europe. See https://rm.coe.int/16808b1688

Goodier, T. (ed.) (2018b) *Collated Representative Samples of Descriptors of Language Competences Developed for Young Learners – Resource for Educators, Volume II: Ages 11–15*. Brussels: Education Policy Division, Council of Europe. See https://rm.coe.int/16808b1689 (accessed 10 October 2020).

Gopher, D. (1993) The skill of attention control: Acquisition and execution of attention strategies. In D.E. Meyer and S. Kornblum (eds) *Attention and Performance XIV: Synergies in Experimental Psychology, Artificial Intelligence, and Cognitive Neuroscience* (pp. 299–322). Asco Trade.

Granena, G. and Long, M. (eds) (2013a) *Sensitive Periods, Language Aptitude, and Ultimate L2 Attainment*. Amsterdam: John Benjamins Publishing.

Granena, G. and Long, M.H. (2013b) Age of onset, length of residence, language aptitude, and ultimate L2 attainment in three linguistic domains. *Second Language Research* 29 (3), 311–343.

Griffiths, C. (2003) Patterns of language learning strategy use. *System* 31 (3), 367–383.

Griva, E., Tsakiridou, H., Nihoritou, I. and Nikolov, M. (2009) A study of FL composing process and writing strategies employed by young learners. In M. Nikolov (ed.) *Early Learning of Modern Foreign Languages* (pp. 132–148). Bristol: Multilingual Matters.

Gu, P.Y., Hu, G. and Zhang, L.J. (2005) Investigating language learner strategies among lower primary school pupils in Singapore. *Language and Education* 19 (4), 281–303.

Harlen, W. (2005) Teachers' summative practices and assessment for learning: Tensions and synergies. *The Curriculum Journal* 16 (2), 207–223.

Harlen, W. and James, M. (1997) Assessment and learning: Differences and relationships between formative and summative assessment. *Assessment in Education* 4 (3), 365–379.

Hasselgreen*, A. (2000) The assessment of the English ability of young learners in Norwegian schools: An innovative approach. *Language Testing* 17 (2), 261–277.

Hasselgreen, A. (2005) Assessing the language of young learners. *Language Testing* 22 (3), 337–354.

Hasselgreen, A. and Caudwell, G. (2016) *Assessing the Language of Young Learners.* Sheffield: Equinox Publishers.

Hattie, J. (2012) *Visible Learning for Teachers: Maximizing Impact on Learning.* Abingdon: Routledge.

Hawe, E.M. and Dixon, H.R. (2014) Building students' evaluative and productive expertise in the writing classroom. *Assessing Writing* 19, 66–79.

Hild, G. and Nikolov, M. (2010) Teachers' views on tasks that work with primary school EFL learners. In M. Lehmann, R. Lugossy and J. Horvath (eds) *UPRT 2010: Empirical Studies in English Applied Linguistics* (pp. 47–62). Pecs: Lingua Franca Csoport.

Hill, K. and McNamara, T. (2012) Developing a comprehensive, empirically based research framework for classroom-based assessment. *Language Testing* 29 (3), 395–420.

Huhta, A., Alanen, R., Tarnanen, M., Martin, M. and Hirvelä, T. (2014) Assessing learners' writing skills in a SLA study: Validating the rating process across tasks, scales and languages. *Language Testing* 31 (3), 307–328.

Inbar-Lourie, O. and Shohamy, E. (2009) Assessing young language learners: What is the construct? In M. Nikolov (ed.) *The Age Factor and Early Language Learning* (pp. 83–96). Berlin: Mouton de Gruyter.

James, M.E. (2013) *Educational Assessment, Evaluation and Research: The Selected Works of Mary E. James.* London: Routledge.

Jia, G. and Fuse, A. (2007) Acquisition of English grammatical morphology by native Mandarin-speaking children and adolescents: Age-related differences. *Journal of Speech, Language, and Hearing Research* 50 (5), 1280–1299.

Johnstone, R. (2000) Context-sensitive assessment of modern languages in primary (elementary) and early secondary education: Scotland and the European experience. *Language Testing* 17 (2), 123–143.

Jones, J. (2014) Developments in formative assessment: A retrograde step for teaching and learning? In P. Driscoll, A. Swarbrick and E. Macaro (eds) *Debates in Modern Languages Education* (pp. 150–162). London: Routledge.

Jones, J. and Wiliam, D. (2008) *Modern Foreign Languages Inside the Black Box: Assessment for Learning in the Modern Foreign Languages Classroom.* London: GL Assessment.

Kennedy, T.J., Nelson, J.K., Odell, M.R.L. and Austin, L.K. (2000) The FLES attitudinal inventory. *Foreign Language Annals* 33 (3), 278–289.

Kim, Y. and McDonough, K. (2008) The effect of interlocutor proficiency on the collaborative dialogue between Korean as a second language learners. *Language Teaching Research* 12 (2), 211–234.

Klenowski, V. (2009) Assessment for learning revisited: An Asia-Pacific perspective. *Assessment in Education: Principles, Policy and Practice* 16 (3), 263–268.

Klenowski, V. (2011) Assessment for learning in the accountability era: Queensland, Australia. *Studies in Educational Evaluation* 37 (1), 78–83.

---

* Please note that when this article was published, the author's name was misspelled. Although the author's name is Hasselgreen, her name in the published article is spelled: Hasselgren. The correct spelling of the author's name is used in this reference list but it is acknowledged that the article can best be identified using the following reference: Hasselgren, A. (2000) The assessment of the English ability of young learners in Norwegian schools: An innovative approach. *Language Testing* 17 (2), 261–277.

Knell, E., Haiyan, Q., Miao, P., Yanping, C., Siegel, L.S., Lin, Z. and Wei, Z. (2007) Early English immersion and literacy in Xi'an, China. *The Modern Language Journal* 91 (3), 395–417.

Kormos, J. and Csizér, K. (2008) Age-related differences in the motivation of learning English as a foreign language: Attitudes, selves, and motivated learning behavior. *Language Learning* 58 (2), 327–355.

Krashen, S.D. (1985) *The Input Hypothesis: Issues and Implications*. New York: Longman.

Laine, E.J. (1988) The Affective Filter in Foreign Language Learning and Teaching. Report 2: A Validation Study of Filtering Factors with a Focus on the Learner's FL Self-Concept. *Jyvaskyla Cross-Language Studies, No. 15*. See http://files.eric.ed.gov/fullt ext/ED303992.pdf (accessed 11 May 2015).

Lamb, M. (2012) A self system perspective on young adolescents' motivation to learn English in urban and rural settings. *Language Learning* 62 (4), 997–1023.

Lee, I. (2007) Assessment for learning: Integrating assessment, teaching, and learning in the ESL/EFL writing classroom. *Canadian Modern Language Review/La Revue canadienne des langues vivantes* 64 (1), 199–213.

Lee, I. and Coniam, D. (2013) Introducing assessment for learning for EFL writing in an assessment of learning examination-driven system in Hong Kong. *Journal of Second Language Writing* 22 (1), 34–50.

Lefever, S. (2019) Assessment policy and practices of early language learning in Iceland. In D. Prošić-Santovac and S. Rixon (eds) *Integrating Assessment into Early Language Learning and Teaching* (pp. 236–250). Bristol: Multilingual Matters.

Leow, R.P. (2000) A study of the role of awareness in foreign language behavior. *Studies in Second Language Acquisition* 22 (4), 557–584.

Leung, C. and Mohan, B. (2004) Teacher formative assessment and talk in classroom contexts: Assessment as discourse and assessment of discourse. *Language Testing* 21 (3), 335–359.

Lightbown, P.M. and Spada, N. (2008) *How Languages are Learned* (2nd edn). Oxford: Oxford University Press.

Little, D. (2005) The Common European Framework and the European language portfolio: Involving learners and their judgements in the assessment process. *Language Testing* 22 (3), 321–336.

Little, D. (2009) *The European Language Portfolio: Where Pedagogy and Assessment Meet*. Eighth International Seminar on the European Language Portfolio, Graz, 29 September–1 October 2009. Council of Europe: Language Policy Division.

Little, D., Dam, L. and Legenhausen, L. (2017) *Language Learner Autonomy: Theory, Practice and Research*. Bristol: Multilingual Matters.

Long, M.H. (1981) Input, interaction, and second-language acquisition. *Annals of the New York Academy of Sciences* 379 (1), 259–278.

Long, M.H. (1990) Maturational constraints on language development. *Studies in Second Language Acquisition* 12 (3), 251–285.

Long, M.H. (2005) Problems with supposed counter-evidence to the Critical Period Hypothesis. *International Review of Applied Linguistics in Language Teaching* 43 (4), 287–317.

Long, M. (2013) Maturational constraints on child and adult SLA. In G. Granena and M. Long (eds) *Sensitive Periods, Language Aptitude, and Ultimate L2 Attainment* (pp. 3–41). Amsterdam: John Benjamins.

Lyster, R. and Ranta, L. (1997) Corrective feedback and learner uptake. *Studies in Second Language Acquisition* 19 (1), 37–66.

MacIntyre, P. and Gregersen, T. (2012) Emotions that facilitate language learning: The positive-broadening power of the imagination. *Studies in Second Language and Teaching* 2 (2), 193–213.

Mackey, A. (1999) Input, interaction, and second language development. *Studies in Second Language Acquisition* 21 (4), 557–587.

Mackey, A. (2006) Feedback, noticing and instructed second language learning. *Applied Linguistics* 27 (3), 405–430.

Mackey, A., Oliver, R. and Leeman, J. (2003) Interactional input and the incorporation of feedback: An exploration of NS–NNS and NNS–NNS adult and child dyads. *Language Learning* 53 (1), 35–66.

Marschollek, A. (2002) *Kognitive und affektive Flexibilität durch frmde Schprachen. Eine empirische untersuchung in der primarstufe. [Cognitive and affective flexibility in foreign languages. Empirical study of first grade].* Lit.

Masgoret, A.M., Bernaus, M. and Gardner, R.C. (2001) Examining the role of attitudes and motivation outside the formal classroom: A test of the mini-AMTB for children. In Z. Dörnyei and R. Schmidt (eds) *Motivation and Second Language Acquisition* (pp. 281–296). Honolulu, HI: University of Hawaii Press.

Matsuzaki Carreira, J.M. (2006) Motivation for learning English as a foreign language in Japanese elementary schools. *JALT Journal* 28 (2), 135–158.

McKay, P. (2006) *Assessing Young Language Learners.* New York: Cambridge University Press.

Mihaljević Djigunović, J. (2006) Role of affective factors in the development of productive skills. In M. Nikolov and J. Horvath (eds) *UPRT 2006: Empirical Studies in English Applied Linguistics* (pp. 9–24). Pecs: Lingua Franca Csoport.

Mihaljević Djigunović, J. (2007) Croatian EFL learners' affective profile, aspirations and attitudes to English classes. *Metodika* 8 (14), 115–126.

Mihaljević Djigunović, J. (2010) Starting age and L1 and L2 interaction. *International Journal of Bilingualism* 14 (3), 303–314.

Mihaljević Djigunović, J. (2012) Dynamics of learner affective development in early FLL. *Studies in Second Language Learning and Teaching* 2 (2), 159–178.

Mihaljević Djigunović, J. (2015) Individual differences among young EFL learners: Age- or proficiency-related? A look from the affective learner factors perspective. In J. Mihaljević Djigunović and M. Medved Krajnovic (eds) *Early Learning and Teaching of English: New Dynamics of Primary English* (pp. 10–36). Bristol: Multilingual Matters.

Mihaljević Djigunović, J. (2016) Individual learner differences and young learners' performance on L2 speaking tests. In M. Nikolov (ed.) *Assessing Young Learners of English: Global and Local Perspectives* (pp. 243–261). New York: Springer.

Mihaljević Djigunović, J. (2019) Affect and assessment in teaching L2 to young learners. In D. Prošić-Santovac and S. Rixon (eds) *Integrating Assessment Into Early Language Learning and Teaching* (pp. 19–33). Bristol: Multilingual Matters.

Mihaljević Djigunović, J. and Legac, V. (2009) Foreign language anxiety and listening comprehension of monolingual and bilingual EFL learners. *Studia Romanica et Anglica Zagrabiensia* 53, 327–347.

Mihaljević Djigunović, J. and Lopriore, L. (2011) The learner: Do individual differences matter? In J. Enever (ed.) *ELLiE: Early Language Learning in Europe* (pp. 29–45). London: British Council.

Mihaljević Djigunović, J., Nikolov, M. and Ottó, I. (2008) A comparative study of Croatian and Hungarian EFL students. *Language Teaching Research* 12 (3), 433–452.

Morgan, D.L. (1988) *Focus Groups as Qualitative Research.* Thousand Oaks, CA: Sage.

Moyer, A. (2004) *Age, Accent, and Experience in Second Language Acquisition: An Integrated Approach to Critical Period Inquiry.* Clevedon: Multilingual Matters.

Munnich, E. and Landau, B. (2010) Developmental decline in the acquisition of spatial language. *Language Learning and Development* 6 (1), 32–59.

Muñoz, C. (ed.) (2006) *Age and the Rate of Foreign Language Learning.* Clevedon: Multilingual Matters.

Murphy, V. (2014) *Second Language Learning in the Early School Years: Trends and Contexts: An Overview of Current Themes and Research on Second Language Learning in the Early School Years.* Oxford: Oxford University Press.

Nicol, D.J. and Macfarlane-Dick, D. (2006) Formative assessment and self-regulated learning: A model and seven principles of good feedback practice. *Studies in Higher Education* 31 (2), 199–218.

Nikolov, M. (1999) 'Why do you learn English?' 'Because the teacher is short.' A study of Hungarian children's foreign language learning motivation. *Language Teaching Research* 3 (1), 33–56.

Nikolov, M. (ed.) (2016) *Assessing Young Learners of English: Global and Local Perspectives*. New York: Springer.

Nikolov, M. and Mihaljević Djigunović, J. (2011) All shades of every color: An overview of early teaching and learning of foreign languages. *Annual Review of Applied Linguistics* 31, 95–119.

Nisbet, J. and Shucksmith, J. (1986) *Learning Strategies*. London: Routledge and Kegan Paul.

Ohta, A. (1995) Applying sociocultural theory to an analysis of learner discourse: Learner–learner collaborative interaction in the zone of proximal development. *Issues in Applied Linguistics* 6 (2), 93–121.

Oliver, R. (1998) Negotiation of meaning in child interactions. *The Modern Language Journal* 82 (3), 372–386.

Oliver, R. (2000) Age differences in negotiation and feedback in classroom and pairwork. *Language Learning* 50 (1), 119–151.

Oliver, R. (2002) The patterns of negotiation for meaning in child interactions. *The Modern Language Journal* 86 (1), 97–111.

Oliver, R. and Mackey, A. (2003) Interactional context and feedback in child ESL classrooms. *The Modern Language Journal* 87 (4), 519–533.

O'Malley, J.M. and Chamot, A.U. (1990) *Learning Strategies in Second Language Acquisition*. New York: Cambridge University Press.

O'Sullivan, B. and Green, A. (2011) Test taker characteristics. In L. Taylor (ed.) *Examining Speaking: Research and Practice in Assessing Second Language Speaking* (pp. 36–64). Cambridge: Cambridge University Press.

Oxford, R.L. (1999) Anxiety and the language learner: New insights. In J. Arnold (ed.) *Affect in Language Learning* (pp. 58–67). Stuttgart: Ernst Klett Sprachen.

Öz, H. (2014) Turkish teachers' practices of assessment for learning in the English as a foreign language classroom. *Journal of Language Teaching & Research* 5 (4), 775–785.

Pfenninger, S.E. and Singleton, D. (2017) *Beyond Age Effects in Instructional L2 Learning: Revisiting the Age Factor*. Bristol: Multilingual Matters.

Pfenninger, S.E. and Singleton, D. (2019) Making the most of an early start to L2 instruction. *Language Teaching for Young Learners* 1 (2), 111–138.

Pica, T. (1994) Research on negotiation: What does it reveal about second language learning conditions, processes, and outcomes? *Language Learning* 44 (3), 493–527.

Pinter, A. (2007) Some benefits of peer–peer interaction: 10-year-old children practising with a communication task. *Language Teaching Research* 11 (2), 189–207.

Pinter, A. (2011) *Children Learning Second Languages*. Basingstoke: Palgrave Macmillan.

Popham, W.J. (2008) *Transformative Assessment*. Alexandria: Association for Supervision and Curriculum Development.

Porter, A. (2019) Exploring roles for formative assessment in primary FL classrooms: Looking through a primary FL classroom window. In D. Prošić-Santovac and S. Rixon (eds) *Integrating Assessment into Early Language Learning and Teaching* (pp. 105–121). Bristol: Multilingual Matters

Prošić-Santovac, D. and Rixon, S. (eds) (2019) *Integrating Assessment into Early Language Learning and Teaching*. Bristol: Multilingual Matters.

Prošić-Santovac, D., Savić, V. and Rixon, S. (2019) Assessing young language learners in Serbia: Teachers' attitudes and practices. In D. Prošić-Santovac and S. Rixon (eds) *Integrating Assessment into Early Language Learning and Teaching* (pp. 251–266). Multilingual Matters.

Plutsky, S. and Wilson, B.A. (2004) Comparison of the three methods for teaching and evaluating writing: A quasi-experimental study. *The Delta Pi Epsilon Journal* 46 (1), 50–61.

Ramaprasad, A. (1983) On the definition of feedback. *Behavioural Science* 28 (1), 4–13.

Rea-Dickins, P. (2001) Mirror, mirror on the wall: Identifying processes of classroom assessment. *Language Testing* 18 (4), 429–462.

Rea-Dickins, P. (2006) Currents and eddies in the discourse of assessment: A learning-focused interpretation. *International Journal of Applied Linguistics* 16 (2), 163–188.

Rea-Dickins, P. and Gardner, S. (2000) Snares and silver bullets: Disentangling the construct of formative assessment. *Language Testing* 17 (2), 215–243.

Rea-Dickins, P. and Rixon, S. (1999) Assessment of young learners' English: Reasons and means. In S. Rixon (ed.) *Young Learners of English: Some Research Perspectives* (pp. 89–101). Harlow: Longman.

Ridderinkhof, K.R. and van der Molen, M.W. (1997) Mental resources, processing speed, and inhibitory control: A developmental perspective. *Biological Psychology* 45 (1), 241–261.

Rixon, S. (2013) British Council survey of policy and practice in primary English language teaching worldwide. British Council. See https://www.teachingenglish.org.uk/article/british-council-survey-policy-practice-primary-english-language-teaching-worldwide (accessed 1 July 2020).

Rixon, S. (2017) The role of early language learning teacher education in turning policy into practice. In E. Wilden and R. Porsch (eds) *The Professional Development of Primary EFL Teachers: National and International Research* (pp. 79–93). Münster: Waxmann.

Robinson, P. (1995) Attention, memory, and the 'noticing' hypothesis. *Language Learning* 45 (2), 283–331.

Rosa, E. and O'Neill, M.D. (1999) Explicitness, intake, and the issue of awareness. *Studies in Second Language Acquisition* 21 (4), 511–556.

Ruiz-Primo, M.A. and Furtak, E.M. (2006) Informal formative assessment and scientific inquiry: Exploring teachers' practices and student learning. *Educational Assessment* 11 (3–4), 237–263.

Sarason, I.G. (1984) Stress, anxiety, and cognitive interference: Reactions to tests. *Journal of Personality and Social Psychology* 46 (4), 929–938.

Sardareh, S.A. and Saad, M.R.M. (2012) A sociocultural perspective on assessment for learning: The case of a Malaysian primary school ESL context. *Procedia-Social and Behavioral Sciences* 66, 343–353.

Schmidt, R. (1992) Awareness and second language acquisition. *Annual Review of Applied Linguistics* 13, 206–226.

Schmidt, R. (2010) Attention, awareness, and individual differences in language learning. In W.M. Chan, S. Chi, K.N. Cin, J. Istanto, M. Nagami, J.W. Sew, T. Suthiwan and I. Walker (eds) *Proceedings of CLaSIC 2010*, Singapore, 2–4 December (pp. 721–737). Singapore: National University of Singapore, Centre for Language Studies.

Schmidt, R. and Frota, S.N. (1986) Developing basic conversational ability in a second language: A case study of an adult learner of Portuguese. In R.R. Day (ed.) *Talking to Learn: Conversation in Second Language Acquisition* (pp. 237–326). Rowley, MA: Newbury House.

Schneider, W. and Pressley, M. (2013) *Memory Development between Two and Twenty*. New York: Psychology Press.

Schumann, J. (2001) Learning as foraging. In Z. Dörnyei and R. Schmidt (eds) *Motivation and Second Language Acquisition* (pp. 21–28). Honolulu, HI: University of Hawaii Press.

Scriven, M. (1967) The methodology of evaluation. In R.W. Tyler, R.M. Gagne and M. Scriven (eds) *Perspectives of Curriculum Evaluation* (pp. 39–83). Chicago, IL: Rand McNally.

Shaaban, K. (2001) Assessment of young learners. *English Teaching Forum* 39 (4), 16–24.

Shepard, L.A. (2005) Linking formative assessment to scaffolding. *Educational Leadership* 63 (3), 66–70.

Shepard, L.A. (2008) Formative assessment: Caveat emptor. In C.A. Dwyer (ed.) *The Future of Assessment: Shaping Teaching and Learning* (pp. 279–303). New York: Routledge.

Shepard, L.A., Hammerness, K., Darling-Hammond, L., Rust, F., Snowden, J.B., Gordon, E., Gutierrez, C. and Pacheco, A. (2005) Assessment. In L. Darling Hammond and J. Bransford (eds) *Preparing Teachers for a Changing World: What Teachers Should Learn and be Able to Do* (pp. 275–326). San Francisco, CA: Jossey-Bass.

Shin, J.K. and Crandall, J. (2019) Developing assessment practices for young learner English teachers: A professional development model in Peru. In D. Prošić-Santovac and S. Rixon (eds) *Integrating Assessment into Early Language Learning and Teaching* (pp. 223–235). Bristol: Multilingual Matters.

Sidhu, G.K., Chan, Y.F. and Sidhu, S.K. (2011) Students' reactions to school-based oral assessment: Bridging the gap in Malaysia. *Asian EFL Journal* 13 (4), 300–327.

Siegler, R.S. (1994) Cognitive variability: A key to understanding cognitive development. *Current Directions in Psychological Science* 2 (1), 1–5.

Skehan, P. (1996) Second language acquisition research and task-based instruction. In J. Willis and D. Willis (eds) *Challenge and Change in Language Teaching* (pp. 17–30). Oxford: Heinemann.

Skehan, P. (1998) *A Cognitive Approach to Language Learning*. Oxford: Oxford University Press.

Skehan, P. and Foster, P. (1999) The influence of task structure and processing conditions on narrative retellings. *Language Learning* 49 (1), 93–120.

Sly, L. (1999) Practice tests as formative assessment improve student performance on computer-managed learning assessments. *Assessment & Evaluation in Higher Education* 24 (3), 339–343.

Somekh, B. and Lewin, C. (2005) *Research Methods in Social Sciences*. Los Angeles, CA: Sage.

Spadaro, K. (2013) Maturational constraints on lexical acquisition in a second language. In G. Granena and M. Long (eds) *Sensitive Periods, Language Aptitude, and Ultimate L2 Attainment* (pp. 43–68). Amsterdam: John Benjamins.

Storch, N. (2002) Patterns of interaction in ESL pair work. *Language Learning* 52 (1), 119–158.

Stoynoff, S. (2012) Looking backward and forward at classroom-based language assessment. *ELT Journal* 66 (4), 523–532.

Sun, Z., Lin, C.H., You, J., Shen, H.J., Qi, S. and Luo, L. (2017) Improving the English-speaking skills of young learners through mobile social networking. *Computer Assisted Language Learning* 30 (3–4), 304–324.

Swaffield, S. (2011) Getting to the heart of authentic assessment for learning. *Assessment in Education: Principles, Policy & Practice* 18 (4), 433–449.

Swain, M. (2000) The output hypothesis and beyond: Mediating acquisition through collaborative dialogue. In J.P. Lantof (ed.) *Socio-Cultural Theory and Second Language Learning* (pp. 97–114). New York: Oxford University Press.

Swain, M. and Lapkin, S. (1998) Interaction and second language learning: Two adolescent French immersion students working together. *The Modern Language Journal* 82 (3), 320–337.

Szpotowicz, M. and Szulc-Kurpaska, M. (2009) *Teaching English to Young Learners*. Warsaw: Wydawnictwo Naukowe PWN.

Szpotowicz, M., Mihaljevic Djigunovic, J. and Enever, J. (2009) Early language learning in Europe: A multinational, longitudinal study. In J. Enever, J. Moon and U. Raman (eds) *Young Learner English Language Policy and Implementation: International Perspectives* (pp. 141–147). Reading: Garnet Publishing.

Taguchi, T., Magid, M. and Papi, M. (2009) The L2 motivational self system amongst Chinese, Japanese, and Iranian Learners of English: A comparatives study. In Z. Dörnyei and E. Ushioda (eds) *Motivation, Language Identity and the L2 Self* (pp. 66–97). Bristol: Multilingual Matters.

Teasdale, A. and Leung, C. (2000) Teacher assessment and psychometric theory: A case of paradigm crossing? *Language Testing* 17 (2), 163–184.

Thompson, M. and Wiliam, D. (2007) Tight But Loose: A Conceptual Framework for Scaling Up School Reforms. Paper presented at a symposium titled 'Tight But Loose: Scaling Up Teacher Professional Development in Diverse Contexts' at the annual conference of the American Educational Research Association, 9–11 April, in Chicago, IL. See https://www.ets.org/Media/Research/pdf/RR-08-29.pdf (accessed 24 May 2014).

Torrance, H. (1995) Teacher involvement in new approaches to assessment. In H. Torrance (ed.) *Evaluating Authentic Assessment* (pp. 44–56). Buckingham: Open University Press.

Tsagari, D. (2016) Assessment orientations of state primary EFL teachers in two Mediterranean countries. *CEPS Journal* 6 (1), 9–30.

Tsagari, D. and Meletiadou, E. (2015) Peer assessment of adolescent learners' writing performance. *Writing & Pedagogy* 7 (2/3), 305–328.

Tsang, W.K. (2004) Feedback and uptake in teacher-student interaction: An analysis of 18 English lessons in Hong Kong secondary classrooms. *RELC Journal* 35 (2), 187–209.

UNESCO (2011) International Standard Classification of Education. See http://uis.unesco.org/sites/default/files/documents/international-standard-classification-of-education-isced-2011-en.pdf (accessed 29 November 2018).

Upshur, J.A. and Turner, C.E. (1995) Constructing rating scales for second language tests. *ELT Journal* 49 (1), 3–12.

van Lier, L. (2014) *Interaction in the Language Curriculum: Awareness, Autonomy and Authenticity*. New York: Routledge.

Vandergrift, L. (2002) 'It was nice to see that our predictions were right': Developing metacognition in L2 listening comprehension. *Canadian Modern Language Review/La revue canadienne des langues vivantes* 58 (4), 555–575.

Vann, R.J. and Abraham, R.G. (1990) Strategies of unsuccessful language learners. *TESOL Quarterly* 24 (2), 177–198.

Vilke, M. and Vrhovac, Y. (1995) *Children and Foreign Languages II*. Zagreb: Faculty of Philosophy, University of Zagreb.

Vurpillot, E. (1968) The development of scanning strategies and their relation to visual differentiation. *Journal of Experimental Child Psychology* 6 (4), 632–650.

Vygotsky, L.S. (1987) *Mind in Society: The Development of Higher Psychological Processes*. London: Harvard University Press.

Walsh, S. (2006) *Investigating Classroom Discourse*. London: Routledge.

Watanabe, Y. and Swain, M. (2007) Effects of proficiency differences and patterns of pair interaction on second language learning: Collaborative dialogue between adult ESL learners. *Language Teaching Research* 11 (2), 121–142.

Wehlburg, C.M. (2007) Closing the feedback loop is not enough: The assessment spiral. *Assessment Update* 19 (2), 1–2.

Wen, Z. (2012) Working memory and second language learning. *International Journal of Applied Linguistics* 22 (1), 1–22.

Wen, Z. and Skehan, P. (2011) A new perspective on foreign language aptitude research: Building and supporting a case for 'working memory as language aptitude'. *Journal of English Language, Literatures in English and Cultural Studies* 60, 15–44.

Wilden, E. and Porsch, R. (2014) Children's receptive EFL competences at the end of primary education: Evidence from the German 'Ganz In'. In J. Enever, E. Lindgren and S. Ivanov (eds) *Conference Proceedings from Early Language Learning: Theory and Practice 2014* (p. 59). Umea: University of Umea.

Wiliam, D. (2009) Assessment for Learning: Why, What and How? An Inaugural Professorial Lecture by Dylan Wiliam. London: Institute of Education, University of London.

Wiliam, D. (2011) What is assessment for learning? *Studies in Educational Evaluation* 37 (1), 3–14.

Wiliam, D. and Thompson, M. (2007) Integrating assessment with instruction: What will it take to make it work? In C.A. Dwyer (ed.) *The Future of Assessment: Shaping Teaching and Learning* (pp. 53–82). Mahwah, NJ: Lawrence Erlbaum Associates.

Williams, J. (2001) The effectiveness of spontaneous attention to form. *System* 29 (3), 325–340.

Wilson, J.T., Scott, J.H. and Power, K.G. (1987) Developmental differences in the span of visual memory for pattern. *British Journal of Developmental Psychology* 5 (3), 249–255.

Winer, G.A., Craig, R.K. and Weinbaum, E. (1992) Adults' failure on misleading weight-conservation tests: A developmental analysis. *Developmental Psychology* 28 (1), 109–120.

Wood, D. (1998) *How Children Think and Learn: The Social Contexts of Cognitive Development*. Oxford: Blackwell Publishing.

Yim, S.Y. (2014) An anxiety model for EFL young learners: A path analysis. *System* 42, 344–354.

Appendices

Appendix 1: The Transcribing Convention.

The transcribing convention was adapted from Walsh (2006). In order to represent the conversations that occurred and limit the impact of the process of transcribing the spoken conversations, two main considerations that guided the transcriptions are

(1) No corrections were made to the language.
(2) Standard conventions of punctuation were not used.
(3) If the transcriber was unable to understand what was being said, that fragment of the conversation is marked *unintelligible*.

Codes used in transcribing:

T – teacher
L – learner (not identified)
L1: L2: etc., identified learner
LL – several learners at once or the whole class
/ok/ok/ok/ – overlapping or simultaneous utterances by more than one learner
[do you understand?] } overlap between teacher and learner
[I see] }
= turn continues, or one turn follows another without any pause
(1) pause of one second or less marked by number 1 in brackets
(4) silence; length given in seconds
? rising intonation – question or other
CORrect emphatic speech: falling intonation
((4)) unintelligible four seconds: a stretch of unintelligible speech with the length given in seconds
Anna, Tomek – capitals are only used for proper nouns
T organises groups – transcriber's comments (in bold type)
(...) in extracts quoted in this volume, the ellipsis in brackets is used to signify that a fragment of the original transcript is excluded from the quotation

Appendix 2: Inventory of Empirical Studies on Assessment for Learning (AfL) in primary English as an Additional Language (EAL) or Modern Foreign Languages (MFL) Teaching (EAL) and Teaching English as a Foreign Language (TEFL)

	References	Focus of the study	Participants	Context
AfL in Primary EAL or MFL	Rea-Dickins and Gardner (2000)	Nature of classroom assessment	9 inner-city schools	Primary schools, England
	Rea-Dickins (2001)	Assessment cycle	Inner city schools with 98% EAL learners	Primary schools, England
	Rea-Dickins (2006)	Teacher–learner interactions	2 language support teachers, 1 mainstream teacher and their learners aged 6–7	Primary schools, England
	Leung and Mohan (2004)	Interactions during classroom-based formative assessment	2 Year 4 classes (8 to 9-year-olds)	Primary school, England
	Dann (2002)	Implementation of self-assessment	Children aged 7–11	Primary schools, England
	Hawe and Dixon (2014)	Students' evaluative competence	3 teachers of students aged 9, 11 and 12	New Zealand
AfL in TEFL	Lee and Coniam (2013)	AfL in writing	2 teachers 12-year-old students	Secondary school in Hong Kong
	Lee (2007)	Feedback in writing, including AfL	26 teachers 174 pieces of feedback, students aged 12–16	Secondary school in Hong Kong
	Sidhu et al. (2011)	Students opinions about AfL	2684 students	Malaysian secondary schools
	Colby-Kelly and Turner (2007)	AfL in English for academic purposes (EAP) speaking	9 teachers, 42 students: adults	Pre-university course in Canada
	Cheng et al. (2004)	Classroom-based assessment methods and procedures	267 teachers	Canada, China and Hong Kong tertiary education

Appendix 3: An Example of School Documents called *Records of Work* (ROWs)

These are T1's ROWs from six lessons. The bold black-edged rectangles have been superimposed digitally to cover the teacher's name.

Appendix 4: Applying the Storch (2002) Model to Interactions which Occurred during the Use of AfL

Extract No.	Turn	Transcript
E6 T-1L 7 to 9-year-olds	[1] [2] [3] [4] [5] [6] [7]	T1: what else makes it good (1) L14: the text A is bigger= T1: = yes it's bigger (1) what do you mean by bigger (1) there are lots of (1) L14: words= T1: =there are longer (1) L14: sentences T1: sentences (1) T underlines a sentence on the board

Equality – low to medium (T1 initiated and led the conversation)
Mutuality – medium to high (student's suggestions were acknowledged by the teacher, e.g. in Turn 3, L14 reacted appropriately to T1's requests for clarification, providing alternative answer when in Turn 6, the answer from Turn 4 did not seem satisfactory to the teacher)
Outcome: Q4, expert-novice

Extract No.	Turn	Transcript
E7 T-1L 7 to 9-year-olds	[1] [2] [3] [4] [5] [6] [7] [8] [9]	T5: ok (1) which one are you going to give yourself? L13: what? T5: you think you're green (1) yellow or red? L13: looking at the teacher for 2s T5: do you know eight words? (1) do you know eights words [NAME]? L13: what? T5: do you know eight of these expressions? do you know EIGHT? yes? L13: yes T5: ok then (1) do green light (1) that's good

Equality – low (T5 initiated and controlled this interaction)
Mutuality – medium to low (T5 offered guiding questions but seemed to fail to allow time for L13 to reflect on them, L13 did not contribute a suggestion, a question or an independent answer)
Outcome: Q3, dominant/passive

Extract No.	Turn	Transcript
E8 T-1L 10 to 11-year-olds	[1] [2] [3] [4]	L11: how is throwing? T7: give me the correct question (2) L11: how (1) do we spell (1) the word throwing T7: excellent stuff T writes 'throwing' on the whiteboard

Equality – medium to low (T7 controlled the conversation by requesting a correct question before answering the initial question, T7 knew and finally provided the correct answer)
Mutuality – medium to high (L11 initiated conversation, responded to the teacher's request, T7 and L11 both had their requests met by the interlocutor)
Outcome: Q4, expert-novice

Extract No.	Turn	Transcript
E9 T-1L 10 to 11-year-olds	[1] [2] [3] [4] [5] [6] [7] [8]	L12: too MUCH fans? T6: yes (1) too many fans? (1) yes (1) L12: too many (1) of much? T6: because 1 fan (1) 2? L12: fans T6: so that means that much or many? L12: many T6: many fans (1) so 1 fan (1) 2 fans (1) many fans

Equality – medium to low (T6 controlled the conversation by guiding the student towards revising a grammar rule)
Mutuality – medium to high (L12 initiated the conversation and asked for confirmation in Turn 2, T6 and L12 both had their requests met by the interlocutor)
Outcome: Q4, expert-novice

Extract No.	Turn	Transcript
E10 L–L 7 to 9-year-olds	[1] [2] [3] [4] [5] [6] [7]	L9: cinema L10: let's go to see Harry Potter at half past eight am L9: am?(1) or pm?(1) L10: evening? L9: yeah pm L10: and we will meet at half past eight pm= L9: =pm

Equality – medium to high (both learners participated actively)
Mutuality – medium to high (L9's initial suggestion was accepted and developed [time proposed] by L10. L9 and L10 engaged in some negotiation of meaning of phrases am and pm to finally reach an agreement)
Outcome: Q1, collaborative

| E11
L–L
7 to 9-year-olds | [1]
[2]
[3]
[4] | L7: can we put on it a black?
L8: it's green for christmas tree (1)
L7: hmm (2)
L8: I think you know it green Both Ls reach for green colouring pencils |

Equality – medium to high (both learners participated actively)
Mutuality – medium to high (L8 responds to the suggestion made by L7 with a counter suggestion, L7 acknowledged the counter suggestion somewhat hesitantly, to which L8 responded by reinforcing it)
Outcome: Q1, collaborative

| E12
L–L
10 to 11-year-olds | [1]
[2]
[3]
[4]
[5]
[6]
[7]
[8]
[9] | L1: has (1) he (1) tidied the kitchen yet?
L2: yes he has L2 draws a tick on the corresponding picture (2) have he taken the rubbish out yet? (1)
L1: has he (1)
L2: ok (1) he (2) has (2) L2 draws a tick on the corresponding picture
L1: no (1) but has he taken the rubbish yet (1)
L2: no (1) this now (1) L2 points to a different picture
L1: but this one is has he taken the rubbish yet
L2: yes he has (1) now you |

Storch's (2002) model:
Equality – medium to high (both learners participated actively)
Mutuality – medium to low (corrections by L1 not understood by L2, L1 did not change correction giving strategy to indicate lack of understanding but continued to provide implicit corrections)
Outcome: Q2, cooperative

| E13
T-1L
7 to 9-year-olds | [1]
[2]
[3]
[4]
[5]
[6]
[7]
[8]
[9]
[10]
[11]
[12]
[13]
[14]
[15]
[16]
[17] | T3: This is Stas34 (1) can he do it (1) can you talk about beach activities using like/love and ing words T points to the board which has WALT written on it (2) the same statement (1) T points to a speech bubble in the activity
L15 (reads from the speech bubble): I like to sleeping
T3: What do you think (1) is that a happy face (1) medium face (1) or a frown (1)
L15: medium=
T3: = medium=
L15: =medium
T3: yeah (1) this is not so good (1) to sleeping (1) do people sleep on the beach (1)
L15: shakes head
T3: sometimes (1) but what's better (1)
L15: sleeping
T3: what can he do to get a happy face (3) can he cross something here (1)
L15: I like sleeping
T3: yes (1) this is better |

Extract No.	Turn	Transcript

Equality – low to medium (the conversation was initiated and controlled by the teacher; especially evident in Turns 10–11 when T3 does not discuss the student's suggestion that people never sleep on the beach but moves the conversation towards the grammatical focus)
Mutuality – medium to high (overall T3 and L15 agreed the judgement of correctness of Stas' sentence and the improvement needed; both interlocutors offered suggestions and responded to one another)
Outcome: Q4, expert-novice

E14	[1]	L3: what time (2)
L-L	[2]	L4: when (2)
10 to 11-year-	[3]	L3: did you (2)
olds	[4]	L4: what time when did you (2)
	[5]	L3: nie dobrze (1) [Eng. *not good*]
	[6]	L4: nie no co ty? (1) może być [Eng. *no what are you*
	[7]	*saying? (1)it's ok*]
	[8]	L3: kiedy ty rano wstałeś? (1) [Eng. *when did you get up*
	[9]	*in the morning?*] when did you get up in the morning
	[10]	L4: chyba o której rano wstałes? (1) [Eng. m*aybe what*
	[11]	*time did you get up in the morning?*]
	[12]	L3: what time (2) what time did you get up in the
	[13]	morning=
	[14]	L4: =what time (1) did you co? [Pol. co = Eng. *what*] L4
		writes on TSAW template.
		L3: get up in the morning

Equality – medium to high (both learners participated actively)
Mutuality – medium to high (L3 and L4 made suggestions and responded to their interlocutor's suggestion, finally agreement was reached)
Outcome: Q1, collaborative

Index